Herman Noordegraaf
Rainer Volz
(Eds.)

European Churches Confronting Poverty

Social Action Against Social Exclusion

With forewords by
Jean-Arnold de Clermont
and Jürgen Gohde

© 2004 SWI Verlag, Bochum
Selbstverlag des Sozialwissenschaftlichen Instituts
der Evangelischen Kirche in Deutschland
Postfach 25 05 63, 44743 Bochum
Cover design: Ulf Claußen (SWI)
Setting, Layout: Manuela vom Brocke
Herstellung: Books on Demand GmbH, Norderstedt
All rights reserved
Printed in Germany
ISBN 3-925895-90-6

Content

I. Prefaces

Jean-Arnold de Clermont
Foreword 9

Jürgen Gohde
Foreword 11

Herman Noordegraaf; Rainer Volz
Introduction 13

II. European level

Benjamin Benz
Poverty policy at the European level in the process of European
integration 19

Doris Scheer
Poverty questions in Europe – what are the churches and diaconia
doing? 56

Jürgen Boeckh
Poverty in Middle and Eastern Europe, or:
Can the Eastward enlargement of the European Union be organized
on an economic *and* social basis? 73

Peter Pavlovic
The churches and the poverty in Central and Eastern Europe 98

III. Country reports

Martin Schenk
Austria 117

Herwig Hermans
Belgium 131

Hans Raun Iversen
Denmark 148

Mikko Malkavaara
Finland 160

Peter Bartmann; Saskia Jung
Germany 176

Niall Cooper
Great Britain 192

Herman Noordegraaf
The Netherlands 210

Ninni Smedberg
Sweden 226

IV. Contrast

Justin Beaumont
Workfare, associationism and the "underclass" in the United States: contrasting faith-based action on urban poverty in a liberal welfare regime 249

V. Epilogue

Herman Noordegraaf; Rainer Volz
Concluding remarks 281

Personalia 295

I. Prefaces

Jean-Arnold de Clermont

Foreword

Following the enlargement of the European Union, Europeans can measure the distance covered since the Second World War by the disappearance of totalitarian regimes, the absence of conflicts, the free movement of people, the development of solidarity between regions, industrial, scientific and technical cooperation and the taking into consideration of environmental needs. However, we know that this enlargement requires of governments, political leaders of all kinds, as well as public opinion, a renewed commitment in service of the project started by the founders of the European Union. This is a commitment in favour of reconciliation and peace, a commitment to social justice and the fight against poverty and all forms of exclusion, as a priority, not only on the European scene but on the international scene as well.

The Conference of European Churches (CEC) calls on and commits Churches and their specialised associations in Europe to share their inspiration and their skills in the service of this project. For the Churches, "it is unacceptable that human beings would not have enough to eat, nor a safe place to lay their head, nor be considered as full participants in society" (extract from the Charter of the Protestant Federation for Mutual Aid, France). Solidarity with the poor and excluded is part and parcel of the social justice and hope to which the Gospel of Jesus Christ calls us.

The European Union was built on the ideal of reconciliation and peace, rooted in the heart of those who, yesterday, were confronting each other on the battle field. One of the instruments of this reconciliation has been the institution of the single market. However, the Europe of today will only maintain this ideal if social justice and the fight against poverty can be placed at the heart of their project. The Churches in Europe and their specialized agencies can and have to play in this effort a substantial role.

15 May 2004 *Jean-Arnold de Clermont, President of CEC*

Jürgen Gohde

Foreword

Being poor bears a lot of risks. Globalisation, with all its opportunities and consequences has reached Europe. Diaconia will continue to support the poor. Whoever takes a risk has to commit himself to helping those he encounters. Whoever takes a risk enters a sphere of freedom. He has to be aware of the limits set by the freedom and the dignity of others. He, who takes a risk must be willing to introduce reforms which are not at the expense of the weak.

"You have been told, o man, what is good; and what does the LORD require of you: but to do justice, and love kindness, and to walk humbly with your God" (Micah 6,8)

You have been told that humans need the solid foundation of God's word; love needs space to live. The abandonment of the aim to be more than a human being helps life. Without knowing the true circumstances of people this is not possible.

We are told that everything depends on work. Happy are those who are able to work and to realise plans. Are all those who do not have work, or are not able to work, unhappy, or even worse, condemned to unhappiness?

We are told that work depends on markets. I do not know if the forces of the market are sufficient to create enough chances. We have a long way to go before the resources of the economy and the society are assessed carefully enough and are measured according to solidarity and justice.

Everything depends on humankind, on how I understand them: whether I see God's creation in them, different, unique, capable of happiness, capable of exploiting the state, hard-working or idle, ready to be human, capable of suffering, rich and poor.

Our discussion about the social state is not only deficient because it does not sufficiently take into account the framework conditions of economy and society, but because it does not reach the horizons of the meaning of human life. Without the knowledge of humankind, without respect for life, every reform is in vain.

It is our task to avoid the unproductive confrontation of advocatory and entrepreneurial diaconia. We have to look for a balance and to create and sustain a diaconal framework that ensures participation and rights of access.

It is possible for diaconia to take risks because God himself has taken his place in risk and has identified himself with the risky circumstances of human beings.

God is the eye and the ear for people suffering oppression, he knows their misery and their lamentations, their feeling of being dispensable. "Today those become easily dispensable who do not work, who do not buy, who do not experience. In the maelstrom of becoming dispensable there are the old people, those in need of help, the dying, the disabled, those without employment, children who disturb, young people who do not find their place in life, the poor and those who have been made poor." (Passauer Pastoralplan – Being near to God and to people).

15 May 2004   *Rev. Dr. hc. Jürgen Gohde, President of Eurodiaconia*

Herman Noordegraaf and Rainer Volz

Introduction

The last quarter of the twentieth century was characterised by sweeping changes across the whole of Europe.

In Western and Northern Europe, the welfare state has come under pressure, because of transformations in the world-economy and cultural changes which are characterised by terms such as "individualization" and "globalization". These were mirrored in socio-economic policies that were directed at expanding markets and strengthening the competitive power of the economy. This meant lowering the budgets for social security and social welfare. This, in turn, meant that those people in particular who were dependent on welfare, faced more and more difficulties in participating in society.

Although poverty had also been present in the "heyday" of the welfare state, it now came to the fore again, paradoxically, in very rich societies. There is no country in Western and Northern Europe in which this is not the case.

Another development had to do with the European Union (EU): On the basis of the European Single Act (1987), the EU became one single market in 1992 with free traffic for capital, goods, services and people. Since then, this process of integration has continued. Within the EU, the problem of social exclusion has proven to be very difficult and the question is, how the process of economic integration is related to the less well-developed social dimensions of the EU.

Another point concerning the EU is of course its enlargement to include new members in Central and Eastern Europe. This highlights the questions about the relationship between economic developments and social policies.

This leads us to the developments in Central and Eastern Europe: the developments there have been even more dramatic than in other parts of

Europe. The collapse of the wall, that is to say of communist regimes, led to enthusiasm, but after that, to disenchantment. The big problems associated with the transition from a state led economy to a market economy, phenomena such as disintegration of state and society, corruption and even civil wars, all this led to very deep problems, and, in a lot of countries, to a level of economic production below that at the end of the communist period.

What can and should be the commitment of churches regarding the problems of poverty and social exclusion in Europe in the context of an economy which is under pressure from globalization and competition? What do biblical words such as mercy and justice mean in this context?

This publication has its origins in the European Diaconal Forum at Järvenpää (Finland) held in September 2001. On this occasion, we, the editors, became acquainted with each other, and we established several contacts that allowed us to find the contributors of articles for this book. By looking back at this very open and stimulating conference, we developed the idea of bringing together the widespread ecclesiastical competences and experiences in the field of social exclusion. When we realized that no publication existed at the European level, we could not abandon the idea to fill this need.

In this book, we deal with the questions of social inequality in the context of the Christian churches and diaconal institutions by offering articles about the activities of churches and diaconia at the European level and in several European countries, both in the field of combating poverty and social exclusion.

The first part of the book deals with the developments and policies in the EU in general. The first contribution (Benjamin Benz) in this field focuses, after a short comparison of different member countries, on the content, difficulties and possibilities of poverty policies on the level of the EU. The second article contains an overview of the activities of churches and diaconia on the EU level (Doris Scheer). The third article (Jürgen Boeckh) deals with the transformation processes of communist and state controlled economies to a free market society and with the question of which perspectives the EU offers for these countries of Central- and Eastern Europe that have entered the EU. The last article (Peter Pavlovic) in this section presents an overview of church and diaconal activities in a number of Central and Eastern European countries.

In the second part of the book, in the country reports, the reader can find facts and descriptions (a) of the situation of social inequality, poverty (and, in less detail, if data are available: of wealth) and social exclusion in each country, and (b) the dominant social policies realized in this field. Furthermore, each article analyses (c) the views and activities of churches and diaconal institutions. There are contributions for the following countries (in alphabetical order): Austria (Martin Schenk), Belgium (Herwig Hermans), Denmark (Hans Raun Iversen), Germany (Peter Bartmann, Saskia Jung), Finland (Milko Malkavaara), Great Britain (Niall Cooper), The Netherlands (Herman Noordegraaf) and Sweden (Ninni Smedberg).

We very much regret that we couldn't include articles about countries in Southern Europe. The persons we had asked to contribute were not able to send in their articles for a variety of reasons and unforeseen circumstances. After several delays it was not possible for us to find other authors at short notice.

As a contrasting viewpoint, we have included an article about church action against poverty in the United States (Justin Beaumont). In our opinion, this can sharpen a comparative perspective on the role of churches, because, among western societies, the United States have an under-developed welfare state: What is the role of churches in this context? Which questions are they confronted with?

The publication closes with a short reflection by the editors about church action against poverty while taking a look at the contributions.

We hope the book will serve to spread information, to enhance the mutual exchange of ideas and will provide a basis for further action in solidarity on a European level.

We thank our authors for preparing their contributions in spite of the many professional duties they had to fulfill in the meantime.

We thank the foundations that supported this publication: the Foundation "Hans Böckler" at Düsseldorf (Germany), the Foundation "Stichting Niet voor jezelf" (The Netherlands) and another Dutch foundation that has expressed the wish not to be mentioned by name.

We express our sincerest thanks to Mrs. Manuela vom Brocke (Bochum, Germany) who completed the whole layout work accurately and with dedication. We also thank the Director of the Sozialwissenschaftliches Institut der EKD (Institute for Social Research and Social Ethics of the Protestant Church of Germany), Hartmut Przybylski, who encouraged and supported the publication and has been a distinguished colleague of Rainer Volz for more than thirteen years.

Herman Noordegraaf (Leiden, The Netherlands)
Rainer Volz (Bochum and Düsseldorf, Germany)

II. European level

Benjamin Benz

Poverty policy at the European level in the process of European integration

The jurisdiction for approving the type and extent of social-policy to deal with poverty and distribution (for example through public welfare and social insurance systems, child and housing benefits, non-cash social benefits and services such as temporary accommodation, care and counselling services) in the Europe of the Union actually lies exclusively with the member states and their regions and communes. So why should and how can there be talk of a poverty policy at European level?

Firstly, the lack of political jurisdiction does not mean the absence of scientific and political controversies concerning its possibility and necessity, its chances and limits. The creation of a single market for goods, capital and services, communalisation of monetary policy and thus the coordination of the economic and budget policies of the participating member states, whilst retaining national fiscal and socio-political jurisdiction in such an integrated common economic, political and social zone, are all having a growing influence on poverty and distribution in the member states, and their policies for tackling this. Since its foundation as the "European Economic Community" through the "Treaties of Rome" of 1957/58, the creation and development of a common zone and a political level between nation state and global international level have led to argumentation figures and endeavours in favour of, but also to objections and resistance to, both assigning more responsibility to this zone and this political level for problems of poverty and distribution policy, and for looking for solutions these problems.

Secondly, on closer inspection, it becomes clear that the contours and first signs of an EU-European policy against poverty and exclusion actually date back to the 1970s. However, this policy has faced resistance, obviously to a greater extent than in other political fields, to brush with obstructing interests and structures, to give its attention to misgivings and fears, to accept setbacks and work towards breakthroughs.

This paper begins with an attempt to collect brief, essentially extracted and simplified, empirical material regarding some parameters at national level[1] outlining the background on which Brussels politics move in this field and which is indispensable in explaining its peculiarities in the "choice" of means and the ways of its politics. In a second step, this material will be put into relation with explanations and systemizations with differing socio-political models in the member states. Against this background then, the history and form of the poverty policy at European level can be explained in detail, and finally, challenges and perspectives of the poverty policy of the European Union can be outlined.

The empirical picture of social polarization and income poverty in a comparison of Western Europe[2]

A consolidated account and discussion of prosperity in the member states is not possible here. What the member states have achieved to a limited extent in the case of its antithesis, i.e. poverty, in other words coming closer after more than thirty years to agreeing on definition, dimensions, measurement, interpretation and conclusions, this is still lacking for wealth of income and assets. Without having to determine/choose a wealth ceiling (for operationalization reasons), the S80/S20 ratio, for example, can be applied at least to outline and compare the degree of unequal income distribution in a society. This method compares the income of the poorest 20 per cent of the population as a share of the total income with that of the richest 20 per cent.

Table 1: S80/S20 Ratios in the EU member states[3] 1998

EU	DK	FIN	S	A	NL	L	F	D	IRL	UK	B	I	EL	E	P
5,4	2,7	3,0	3,4	3,8	4,4	4,6	4,7	4,8	5,3	5,7	5,8	5,9	6,5	6,8	7,2

Luxembourg = 1996

Source: Eurostat, ECHP, from: Eurostat/European Commission 2002: 23

Applied to the whole EU, the table 1 shows that the richest 20 per cent of the EU population in 1998 had a share of the total income which was 5.4 times that of the poorest 20 per cent, with considerable differences between the member states. In comparison to other world regions, however, the West European states not only belong to the richest economic regions along with the North American and Southeast Asian states; when compared with the unequally poor successor states of the Soviet Union and the Latin American states, they also show an altogether moderate disparity of income (cf. Huster 1996: 137 following). In this way the inwardly heterogeneous picture of a "European social model" clearly dissociates itself outwardly from the situations of mass poverty and/or social polarization in other world regions. Since the political and economic upheaval around 1989, the Central and East European states which have acceded to the EU on 1 May 2004 have developed from formerly more "Scandinavian values" toward West European diversification, admittedly from an entirely different absolute level of economic wealth, which suffered a massive collapse at the beginning. Today, the gross domestic product of these states amounts to roughly a quarter of the EU average in Bulgaria and Romania and up to roughly three quarters in Cyprus (CY) and Slovenia (SI). With the accession of at first eight Central and East European states, plus Cyprus and Malta, the heterogeneity of economic strength between the member states will therefore increase enormously. But within the former Union of the 15 member states, the prosperity as defined by "quality" of poverty and wealth is already considerable.

Ever since the first poverty programme of the EEC (1975-80; cf. Commission 1981), the relative poverty line, defined as 60 per cent half of the respective national median income weighted according to household size, has become an important aspect in the discussion about poverty policies. This poverty rate describes (to a limited degree) the share of the population that can be considered as excluded from the average living standard of a society. Whilst the S80/S20 ratio measures the size of the gap between poor and rich, the poverty rate reflects how many citizens are affected by income poverty.

Table 2: Economic strength (gross domestic product per capita in purchasing power standards) of the EU states 1995/2000, EU 15 = 100

State	1995	2000	State	1995	2000	State	1995	2000
EU 15	100	100	I	103	102	M	52	55
L	171	195	F	104	101	HU	46	50
DK	118	119	UK	96	100	SK	46	48
IRL	93	115	E	78	82	EE	34	40
A	110	114	P	70	68	PL	34	39
NL	109	111	EL	66	68	LT	32	36
B	113	107	12 new members	38	38	LV	25	31
S	106	107	CY	83	76	BG	33	26
D	110	106	SI	63	67	RO	28	23
FIN	97	104	CZ	62	56	EU 27	86	87

Source, from: Commission 2003: Table 12

Table 3: Relative income poverty, in per cent of the population, defined as income below 60% of the national equivalent median income 1993/1998

	EU	FIN	DK	S	L	NL	A	D	B	IRL	F	E	I	P	UK	EL
'98	18[1]	8[2]	9	10	12	12	13	16	16	17	18	19	20	20	21	22
'93	19[3]	:	9	:	16	9	:	18	19	20	17	20	21	22	22	23

[1] Estimated value excluding L and FIN; [2] FIN: Figures for 1997 instead of 1998; [3] excluding FIN, S, A

Source: for both years ECHP; 1993, from: EAPN 2000: 8; 1998 from: Eurostat/European Commission 2002: 24

First of all, the table 3 shows the broad extent to which income poverty ranges in the member states. In the South European countries and the United Kingdom, it is almost three times higher than in the Scandinavian countries. Secondly, when observed EU-wide, the poverty rate remained relatively constant around the mid-1990s. Finally, from a comparison of Tables 1 to 3, it becomes evident that greater economic efficiency alone is not accompanied by a reduction in poverty and inequality (see Ireland and United Kingdom).

Income from dependent employment, participation of non-wage earning household members in the household income, and the drawing of benefits from the funds of the social security system in the case of lacking or insufficient earned occupational/household income represent the major sources of livelihood for the overwhelming majority of EU citizens. Thus the intention here is to report and provide a comparison – also only possible in outline – of unemployment trends and of the total financial volume of social protection in the member states, as well as taking a look at the growing importance of the so-called "last net" within these expenditures, the systems of minimum safeguards applied by the member states[5], which crucially serve as a deficiency guarantor for problematic developments in the cohesion of families, on the job market and the social security systems.

Table 4: Unemployment Rates in the Years 1991, 1994, 1999, 2000

	EU	L	NL	A	P	IRL	DK	UK	S	B	D	F	FIN	I	EL	E
'00	8,2	2,4	3,0	3,7	4,1	4,2	4,7	5,5	5,9	7,0	7,9	9,5	9,8	10,5	11,1	14,1
'99	9,1	2,4	3,4	4,0	4,5	5,6	5,2	6,1	7,2	8,8	8,6	11,2	10,2	11,3	11,6	15,9
'94	11,1	3,2	7,1	3,8	6,9	14,3	8,2	9,6	9,4	10,0	8,4	12,3	16,6	11,1	8,9	24,2
'91	8,3	1,5	7,3	3,5	3,9	15,8	9,1	8,6	2,9	7,0	5,3	9,2	7,6	10,1	7,7	15,9

Source: for 1991: Eurostat 1996: 304; for 1994, 1999 and 2000: Eurostat/European Commission 2002: 21 (Comparative Estimates of the EU Labour Survey)

The level and the development of unemployment in the member states largely explains both the spread of poverty and the development of expenditure for social security systems. Nevertheless, this parameter also shows in two respects that work alone does not determine poverty. For example, we can see that comparatively low unemployment accompanies a very high degree of social polarization and poverty (working poor) in Portugal, whilst the opposite applies for Finland. In an EU-wide comparison of time, the entire 1990s must be considered as a lost decade in the battle against unemployment. Not until the year 2000 did the unemployment rate return to the values of the early 1990s. On the other hand, the developments between the member states differ considerably.

As a rule, there is a significantly negative correlation between high total expenditure for social protection and low relative poverty rates. After the social security benefits rose throughout the Union at the start of the last decade from 25.4 (1990) to 28.8 (1993) in the wake of Europe-wide weak economic development and rising unemployment, this trend reversed after 1993. It can be seen here that the most extensive falls took place in two Scandinavian states (Finland and Sweden), followed by The Netherlands, Ireland and Spain. Only in Greece, Portugal and Germany did the expenditure for social protection rise.

Table 5: Expenditure for social protection in per cent of the gross domestic product 1990-1999

	EU	S	F	D	DK	A	B	NL	UK	FIN	EL	I	P	L	E	IRL
1999	27,6	32,9	30,3	29,6	29,4	28,6	28,2	28,1	26,9	26,7	25,5	25,3	22,9	21,9	20,0	14,7
1993-99	-1,2	-5,7	-0,4	+1,2	-2,5	-0,3	-1,3	-5,5	-2,2	-7,9	+3,5	-1,1	+2,2	-2,0	-4,0	-5,5
1990-99	+2,1	-0,2	+2,4	+4,2	+0,7	+1,9	+1,8	-4,4	+3,9	+1,6	+2,6	+0,6	+7,5	-0,2	+0,1	-3,7

Source: (from) Eurostat/European Commission 2002: 22

As a rule, the expenditure level of the benefit systems of the minimum protection which replace or supplement lacking income lies below the relative poverty threshold (50% of the arithmetical or 60% of the median average income) and thus allows an insight into the developments of the circumstances within the segment of people affected by relative poverty. These benefit systems have been (and some are still being) developed

Figure 1: Relationship between relative poverty and social expenditure per capita (in purchasing power standards), 1997

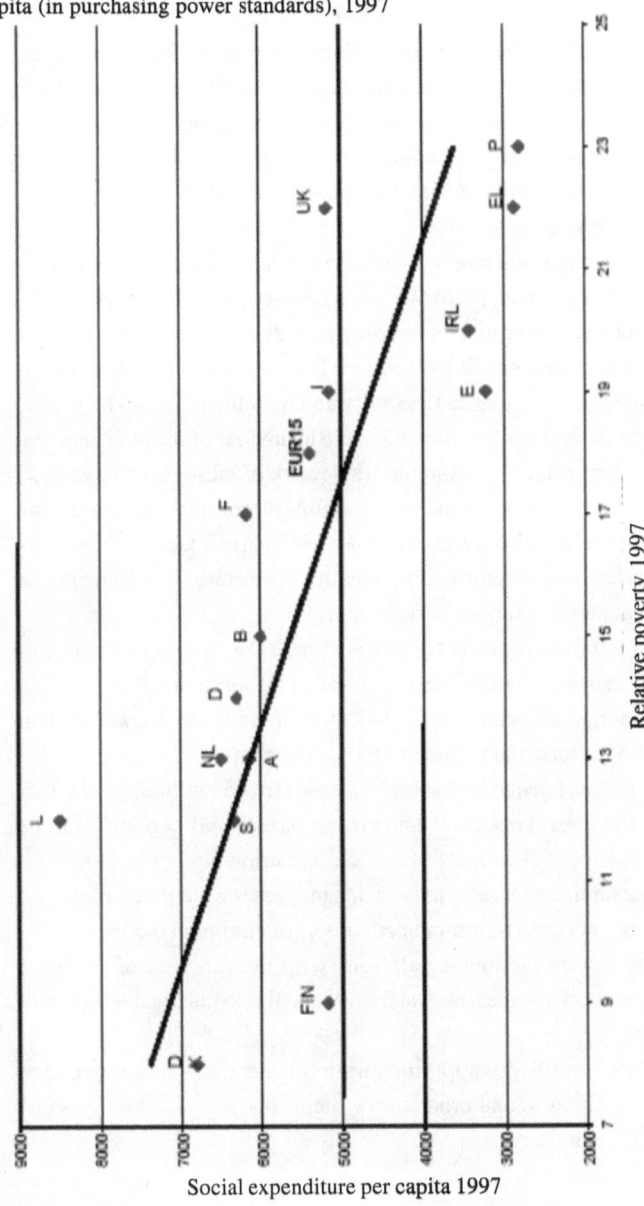

Source: European Commission 2002:229

since the start of industrialization as protection against at least total poverty, and since the second third of the 20th century have increasingly taken on the form of a (also regarding amount) guaranteed individual right (not only) in Europe. Besides this protective function, a number of further motives for establishing or demanding it are listed below. They tie up with a variety of political persuasions and strategies and also (contradictorily) characterize the grounds for a European-level policy against poverty and social exclusion:

- the recognition that poverty not only has individual, but also societal (economic, political, social) causes (impoverishment following war and/or mass unemployment due to growing individualization and the eroding protective function of the family as a consequence of increased flexibility and mobility demands);
- the control and monitoring of the behaviour of the poor segment of the population within the framework of these benefit systems;
- the recognition of the indivisibility of political, economic and social basic rights (protecting the basic right to a decent life by guaranteeing a minimum income, creating the material requirements for implementing further basic rights);
- the stimulating effect of the guarantee of a minimum income for the increased willingness and ability of the individual to adopt economic and spatial flexibility, mobility and risks despite the danger of failure (the argument of risk aversion);
- the dependence of a society, characterized not least on the part of European policy as "knowledge-based" and "ageing", on the protection and support of its "human resources";
- the implications of immiserizing processes which encourage violence yet could be diminished through a minimum income;
- minimum income regulations with the function of setting a framework for the low-wage level and the social disintegration of society;
- the possibility of applying minimum income systems to relieve the strain on social protection systems under pressure of revenue and expenditure.

Since the mid 1970s, structural unemployment, declining growth rates, rising social risks (decreasing family solidarity, the ageing of society, growing demands on spatial and professional mobility) and, to a varying degree, cutbacks in social insurance services and extension of public welfare benefits have been accumulating and becoming established in most of the member states. In the wake of these processes, there have been and still are at times considerable increases in the numbers of welfare recipients in the minimum protection systems (for the period from the mid-1970s until the mid-1980s, see Commission 1992: 55):

Table 6: Welfare recipient figures of minimum protection benefits (social welfare benefits) in the first half of the 1990s

State	Year	Recipients	Year	Recipients
Belgium	1990	49.479	1997	ca. 126.000
Denmark	1991	131.100	1995	152.400
Germany (total)	1991	2.129.426	1996	2.723.580
East Germany	1991	254.042	1996	313.932
West Germany	1991	1.875.384	1996	2.409.648
Spain	1992	104.721	1995	186.568
Finland	1990	314.029	1994	584.100
France	1990	510.146	1995	946.010
Luxembourg	1990	6.079	1994	6.804
Netherlands	1990	530.000	1995	493.000
Great Britain	1990	4.200.000	1995	5.700.000

Source: own compilation, from: Guibentif / Bouget 1997: 148; Commission 1999: Table 3; Federal Statistical Office 2002: 130

Above all in the southern member states, this can at least partly be put down to the creation and expansion of minimum income systems. Internationally, however, these trends indicate a significant erosion of the protective entities of paid employment and family solidarity.

All in all, the reported empirical data[6], provides clear indications to characteristic differences in poverty and distribution in the member states, as well as to their respective disparate development trends community-wide, despite the many problems involved in the definition and measurement of poverty and inequality and the interpretation of correlations.

Socio-political models

Comparative welfare state research assigns the various poverty and distribution-political problems to different "social state philosophies", to socio-political intrinsic views and models which dominate in the member states. For when stating socio-political needs, when determining the duty or limits of the state to ensure provision of the resources required to influence or satisfy these needs, value judgements are unavoidable. A scientifically neutral ascertainment of socio-political needs and the entity responsible for meeting them (family, market, state) is not possible. "These value judgements are accounted for in socio-political intrinsic views which can only be revealed, but not proven." (Hauser 1994: 24) This situation sets limits on every EU-European attempt to identify and recommend the quasi non-political "best practice" by comparing the social systems of the nation state, the funds needed for it, the poverty rates which are largely determined by them or other parameters. On the one hand, the dominating models in the member states are (more or less) subject to dynamic changes in the interest structures, and the example of other solutions certainly provides a basis for learning. Yet comparative research of the welfare state also explains normative and system-related "path dependencies" of the national reforms which stand in the way of a quick, conflict-minimizing and far-reaching convergence or harmonization of the nation state policies.

The most influential classification to this day, from Gøsta Esping-Andersen (1990) identifies three welfare state models. They represent conservative, liberal and social democratic orientations, characterized by specific intrinsic views and priorities regarding social policy and economic policy, even if they do not each represent closed schools of thought. Besides the degree of universality of the system of social protection, it looks at their degree of redistribution of income and characteristics of the labour market.

Figure 2: Welfare state types according to Gøsta Esping-Andersen

Type of welfare state	Liberal	Conservative	Social democrat
Classic representatives:	UK	D	S
Decommodification: protection from market forces and losses of income - income replacement quota - share of individual financing contributions	weak	medium	strong
Residualism - share of welfare benefits to total social expenditure	strong	strong	weak
Privatisation - share of private expenditure for old age to total expenditure	high	low	low
Corporatism/budgetism - share of protective systems differentiated according to occupational groups	weak	strong	weak
Redistribution capacity - Degree of progression of the fiscal system - Equality of benefits	weak	weak	strong
Guarantee of full employment - Expenditure for active labour market policy - Unemployment rates, weighted with labour force participation - State as employer	weak	medium	strong

Source: Heinze / Schmid / Strünck 1999: 103, shortened

For Esping-Andersen, what is all-important is the shaping of the connection between welfare state redistribution and employment policy, as well as the political strength of the organized labour movement. His matrix forms the so-called "(de-)commodification" as a degree of protection for the citizens against market forces and losses of income. Esping-Andersen thus arrives at the three types of welfare state: "social democratic" (e.g. Sweden, Norway), "conservative" (e.g. Germany, Austria, France, Italy) and "liberal" (e.g. United States, Switzerland, United Kingdom). He does not look at the Southwest European states in closer detail. But in these states, too, the above-mentioned "ideal types" are more or less established; the regulations in these welfare states can also be assigned to the three models.

Poverty Policy in the "Liberal Base State"

The model of liberalism, which is closely linked with the Enlightenment, is based on the concept of the rational free individual. The (property owning) middle class should free itself from the barriers of crown, church and guild, all barriers and borders affecting the individual and his possibilities to lead a fulfilled life should be rationally legitimised or fall, be comprehensible and enforceable. A fundamental scepticism to collective compositions is typical of liberal thinking, after all it is all about maximum individual freedom. Yet the concept of freedom and the concept of equality which, equally typical to liberalism (equality of all citizens before the law), are complexly ambivalent. It is obviously cynical to forbid all citizens to sleep under bridges. Can one do justice to the concept of equality without the concept of equal opportunities? Citizens are not born with the same starting conditions. The liberal interpretation of the welfare state confronts this tense relationship of desired maximum freedom from the intervention of third parties (not least in private property) and the obvious negation of freedom through "absolute" poverty, with the formulation of minimum conditions which are to be guaranteed to every citizen as a civil right to life. These are realized ideally in a universal social insurance system with uniform low contributions and benefits which, if necessary, can be supplemented through the social welfare benefit systems for those who have a legal claim to needs-tested minimum protection benefits, which – quite intentionally – are frequently wanting: "Since its introduction at the end of the 1940s, for example, the basic pension has always remained below the level of social welfare. In this way, the state attempts to persuade the individual to take private measures against the risk of poverty associated with old age, unemployment or invalidity. The relatively low social benefits in the British welfare state are supposed to be supplemented by services purchased on the private market." (Scharf 2001: 53) This is therefore a protection model in which social policy acquires not a shaping function but a strictly secondary function. "The welfare state describes the necessary minimum opportunities for all citizens of a civilized society, no more, but also no less" (Dahrendorf 1992: 267).

(Above all the Anglo-Saxon) Countries which mainly orientate themselves toward this liberal definition of the duties and limits of the welfare state display a high degree of social polarization and a high level of needs-tested minimum protection benefits for large segments of the population, through the combination of this both universal and minimalist protection model with a weakly regulated labour market (autonomy of contracts, disempowerment of the trade unions, high wage gaps). As the empirical study outlined above clearly shows, the parameters of their policies on poverty frequently resemble those of the South European type of European welfare states.

Poverty Policy in the "Conservative Welfare State"

The legitimacy and protection of handed down hierarchical social communities and orders (family, status, nation) is the focal point of the conservative orientation of the welfare state. In the question of secondary distribution of the societal wealth to prevent or cure income poverty, this concept of welfare state professes not to back intersocial redistribution, but to emphasize the maintenance obligation of family-members, and the precautionary duty of employees to pay into social welfare funds in the equivalent form of the contribution-benefits relationship. In contrast to the liberal ideal, for the conservative welfare state it is not a question of "just" a state guarantee to protect subsistence, rather it centres on the adjustment of status and living standard outside the world of work. If these adjustments of the living standard into the secondary income distribution lead to benefits below the subsistence minimum, then they must be topped up with social welfare benefits. The conservative or Continental-European welfare state, therefore, imposes an adjustment of the status hierarchy in working life into parastate social protection, which moreover is realized in the form of protection systems divided according to occupational groups (for civil servants, white-collar workers, blue-collar workers, farmers; to some extent also for the self-employed). The relationship and occupational model of this type which serves as a reference point depicts the "normal family" with a male, fully employed breadwinner in permanent dependent work on a medium income. Households of this type are protected to a high degree by such a developed welfare state against the main risks of impoverishment (through ageing, illness, accident, invalidity, loss of work). However, on the periphery of this type is an increasing number of people in households with broken or low-income work and relationship biographies confronted with growing expectations of modern societies concerning spatial, social, professional mobility and flexibility. Their benefit claims upon entering one of the insured poverty risk groups frequently do not suffice for subsistence, due to insufficient contribution payments. If the contribution-benefits logic is not broken by contribution-dependent elements (e.g. minimum pensions), the people affected become clients of social welfare benefits.

Compared with the rest of Europe, states which traditionally orientate themselves towards this model are usually to be found midfield as regards expenditure for social protection, the poverty rate and social inequality.

Poverty Policy in the "Social Democratic Full Employment State"
The core of classic social democratic economic policy is the fundamental retention of capitalist economic systems, although these are to be democratised and politically organized, and do not in the sense of Adam Smith's "invisible hand" inevitably satisfy the interests of all without crisis through the pursuit of personal interests. Rather, state intervention is necessary – even in the distribution of the fruits of budgeting. Whilst the classic national economy and neoliberal concepts deny the state the right and ability to *actively* pursue a permanently successful policy of full employment, Keynesianism – followed by classically social democratic orientation – considers this to be not only possible but necessary. In addition to and in dissociation from the central vocabulary of liberalism (freedom) and conservatism (community in hierarchical order), the democratic socialism orientation focuses on "equality" (as a right). The right to equality is set against the *de facto* inequality of the citizens (particularly due to their efficiency, property, disadvantages and advantages resulting from their social origins and their changing circumstances), which is substantiated in material and non-material rights to have a share in the welfare state and the employment system that level out social inequality. However, the determination of the justifiable extent on the one hand, and the extent of intersocial redistribution to be called for on the other, is controversial. Typical of welfare states characterized by the orientations of social democratic values are efforts for an active policy of full employment which levels out income inequalities to integrate its resident population by means of paid work. Besides market-determined labour demand, this type also advocates a high degree of public employment, not

least in the field of social services. A public guarantee of teaching, daycare and nursing care is intended to make access to the job market easier for women, but at the same time raise the demand for workers. This model thus characterizes a comparably high employment rate, due to the low numbers of social welfare recipients and poverty rates as a result of its services and the social insurance which embraces the entire resident population.

It can be seen that the "star state" of this model, Sweden, under the pressure of massively increasing unemployment and in view of the implications of its accession to the EU (1995), in the 1990s drastically reduced its social security benefits. Nevertheless, the Scandinavian states, traditionally strongly oriented towards this model, still show the lowest levels of poverty and social inequality.

Poverty Policy in the "Mediterranean Familial State"

This (on the other hand conceptionally exaggerated) model which can be assigned to Spain, Greece and Portugal, characterizes an altogether incomplete mixture of system elements of the three systems described above. The family as a protection entity plays a particularly important role compared to the other models, although this role is also eroding in these states in the course of social "modernization". In countries of this model, comparatively limited economic strength, widespread insecure employment and underground economy, high unemployment and lacking or incomplete social protection accumulate to cause a high unemployment rate and a high risk of poverty for broad segments of the population. At the same time, there are certainly signs to the contrary, indicating an alignment of the social protection systems of this type to the average of the EU. On the one hand, social benefit rates have fallen significantly in Spain in recent years, whilst the Italian welfare state was massively "restructured" in the 1990s not least due to pressure to comply with the Maastricht convergence criteria for monetary union (cf. Gohr 2001: 152ff), and there is still no sign that a minimum protection will be introduced in Greece. On the other hand, such systems were established in Spain (regional) and Portugal (central) in the 1990s and introduced at least on a trial basis in Italy (selectively communal), but discontinued at the end of 2002. Portugal and Greece also increased their expenditure for social protection in contrast to the European trend between 1993 and 1999.

The Social Dimension of the European Integration Process

This national empirical study and the socio-political value judgements and priorities behind it form the background of EU social policy. The „social dimension", the „social Europe", the „European social zone"; these terms attempt to embrace the socio-political arena of Brussels, a political level „*sui generis*", which is neither state nor international system of sovereign states such as the United Nations or the World Trade Organization. The peculiarity of this level is reflected in its objects and instruments, the way and degree of social policy of the European Union.

The start of European integration with the "European Community for Coal and Steel" (ECCS, 1952-2002) and then the foundation of the European Economic Community already showed several of its characteristics still effective today:

- (At first) This was a sectoral integration of political fields, beginning with the industrial policies for coal and steel which were important for war, to ensure peace through cooperation and mutual control on a continent ravaged by two world wars.
- The process of integration (consolidation) is a result of the economic dimension, which also represents the primary motive for the accession of further states (enlargement). Besides the peace motive, the creation of a common economic zone – not least with a view to the economies of scale of the US American economic zones – played a second very significant role. There was and still is, however, no consensus between the protagonists of European integration as to the type and extent of the "increasingly closer merging" beyond the creation of an economic zone without internal borders.
- Only the first (ECCS) treaty includes an "expiry date" (50 years after coming into effect). The treaties of the "European Atomic

Community", the "European Economic Community", since the treaty reform of the "Single European Act" of 1986, "European Community" (EC), and the treaty for the foundation of the "European Union" (EU or Maastricht Treaty, 1992) have been laid down permanently and as a process "(...) endeavoured to create the foundations for creating in increasingly closer merging of the European nations (...)" (Preamble EU Treaty). This refers to both an "increasingly closer merging" (consolidation) and the openness of this process for all "European nations" (enlargement[7]).

At the negotiations for the Treaty of Rome, no consensus could be reached on the possibility and necessity of socio-political convergence or harmonization of the member states following the step-by-step creation of a single market and the realization of the inner-community "four freedoms" anchored as basic provisions of the EEC in the treaties: free mobility of capital, goods and service transactions and free mobility of workers. The postulate therefore of the necessity of harmonizing the social systems is based on the assumption of French experts that the cost burdens of the highly developed French social benefits system could prove to be a competitive disadvantage in the Common Market. The majority of experts from the other countries did not agree with this argument and saw harmonization of social conditions as a result and consequence, but not as a condition of the effective functioning of the Common Market. This view could catch on." (Kowalsky 1999: 62) Both sides appear to have been right. A common market functions without socio-political harmonization; however it evidently creates pressure toward cost shifting, away from employer contributions to social protection systems (cf. Benz 2000: 86) and to tax cuts in their favour (ibidem.: from 90) in the sense of socio-political "competition states". Interests and protagonists with varying degrees of power (which cannot simply be separated dichotomically and antagonistically into the interests of the economy on the one hand and the employee and/or welfare recipient on the other) work for and against the generation and transformation of this pressure into socio-political *realpolitik* in the member states; (cf. Winter 1997: 18). As in the case of the interests of national governments, of the European Commission, etc., this is not about homogeneous monoliths of constantly clear and rigid interest (cf. Eichener 2000).

Of the four freedoms, the creation of free mobility for workers and the regulation of their socio-political implications presents one of the most important and oldest topics of EU social policy. Free mobility was put into fact at the end of the 1960s, thus socio-politically guaranteeing that, firstly the social insurance biographies of different countries be linked for entitled citizens (so that, for example, Spanish "migrant workers" working in the Netherlands would not lose their entitlement to the pension fund from the time when they were employed in Spain), and secondly a ban on discrimination was established, obliging the immigration country to grant the same welfare state benefits to migrant workers as to all its nationals. A second classic area of EU-European social policy, to an increased extent since the 1980s, is occupational safety and health protection for workers. The minimum standards achieved were not simply the "smallest common denominator", but harmonisations of standards beyond the protection level of the most developed national provisions (cf. Eichener 2000). Finally, (thirdly), also to an increased extent since the 1980s, the policy of gender equality has become a prominent area of EU-European social policy. Here the French government was able to push through its ambitious socio-political demands as early as the Treaties of Rome. In four EC Treaty sections, the community and the member states undertake to promote the equality of men and women and to remove inequality (Article 3), where necessary to adopt precautions against discrimination on the grounds of gender (Article 13), to guarantee equal opportunities on the job market and equal treatment in the workplace, if applicable through minimum regulations (Article 137), and to push through equal pay and allow "positive discrimination" measures (Article 141).

However, the member states concede virtually no jurisdiction to "Brussels" in the core areas of social policy, i.e. benefit laws: the general systems of social insurance (for illness, invalidity, old age, accident, care), the benefit allowance systems (child benefit, family allowance, housing benefit, etc.) and welfare systems (social welfare benefit). The ban on discrimination and the aggregation of claims for migrant workers are the only provisions which work in reality. The social protocol of the 11 member states (excluding the United Kingdom) of the Maastricht Treaty also provided for the possibility to pass minimum regulations unanimously at Union level for the systems of social protection; yet since the adoption of this regulation in the EC Treaty of Amsterdam (thus binding for all 15 members), this possibility has not been made use of to this day. As for example with the subjects of employment and education, attempts are made to a varying degree rather with resources of "soft control" within the framework of an "Open Method of Coordination" to stimulate the exchange of information and cooperation between member states:

- through the agreement of guidelines and targets (such as: to direct socio-political measures so as to reach the neediest members of society and to significantly reduce the number of people affected by poverty and social exclusion);
- through the agreement of indicators and benchmarks (such as: to reduce the number of school drop-outs to the level of the three most successful member states);
- through reports, mutual information and studies ("National Action Plans" in which the governments of the member states describe their measures for achieving the common targets; a "Joint Report" in which the European Commission summarizes and evaluates the National Action Plans; scientific studies which are carried out within the framework of an accompanying action programme of the community);
- and through the identification of tried-and-tested procedures (best practice) and innovative approaches within the framework of the Joint Report (such as: reference to exemplary established counselling services for insolvent citizens in a member state or the introduction of a new promising package of measures for this in a member state).

The socio-political distribution of jurisdiction can thus be summarized roughly using a systematisation devised by Franz-Xaver Kaufmann: Instead of one uniform trend applying to all socio-political subjects, a differentiation of socio-political jurisdiction can be seen at the European and nation state level "(...) which follows a distinct pattern: Regulations of occupational and health protection and regulations which strive for a standardization of the conditions of production are developed at European level dynamically and beyond the national locations, whilst the redistribution of income and the service systems are left to the national level" (Kaufmann 1997: 133). Only mobility-relevant (interaction of the national social protection systems for migrant workers (cohesion) and competition-relevant yet redistribution-neutral fields (health protection and occupational safety) are dealt with at European level, whilst the social policy based on the poverty- and distribution-political entitlement to benefits (minimum protection and social insurance) have so far remained entirely the responsibility of the nation state. This *de facto* deferment of social policy for dealing with redistribution and fighting poverty becomes comprehensible, despite pressure building up from a socio-political dumping competition through the Common Market and Economic and Monetary Union, only when we look at the different socio-political models referred to, historically substantiated in varying proportions in the national welfare states.

Fields of Action of EU-European Policy Against Poverty and Social Exclusion

The final report of the first joint programme for poverty (Poverty I, 1975-80) refers to the definition of poverty as declared by the Council in 1975. This comprised: "Impoverished persons: individuals or families whose income is so low that they live below the minimum level considered to be an acceptable living standard in the member state in which they live. Income: goods, cash benefits, additional services from public and private sources." (quote from Commission 1981: 16) This is already reminiscent of three milestones of the definition of poverty in the context of the European debates on poverty which end up appearing in all later variations:

- Poverty is relative, dependent on place and time: the term must be defined against the background of the general living standards in the respective society of each member state.
- Poverty is multidimensional, depending on resources and exclusion issues: income plays a central role, but even including assets

(goods) such a definition of poverty would not cover the multidimensionality of potential circumstances of poverty. Further factors include a lack of public and private services (social services, daycare and nursing) etc.

- Poverty can be determined neither purely subjectively[8], nor purely objectively: poverty is defined here as exclusion from the living standard "considered to be acceptable". On the one hand a self definition of (putatively) poor people does not suffice, on the other hand it is defined by an entity/community not determined here. The "minimum level" is not already given "objectively".

The final report on the second programme for poverty (Poverty II, 1986-89) emphasizes more clearly the multidimensionality of poverty: "An objective, complete definition of poverty relates to individual or family circumstances characterized by deficiencies and insufficiencies in various areas: insufficient income, above all diverse weaknesses and gaps in non-financial areas, such as education, ability to work, health, housing, social integration: Poverty has numerous dimensions, in varying combinations for each individual affected. (...) Insufficient income is just one of many aspects of poverty. However, it is the common denominator of the different situations of poverty and can therefore represent a useful indicator for the spread of poverty." (Commission 1991: 4)

However, an "objective, complete definition" was not generally recognized scientifically or politically even upon the completion of Poverty II, which becomes clear when one considers, firstly the values bound to the term, and secondly the politically controversial nature of the efforts at European level to establish reporting and analyses of the development trends and their causes for the national governments (to a varying degree), and finally also for the European level itself. Besides a broadening of the term, doubtless with scientific justification, toward "multidimensionality", this also seems politically welcome. After all, by including different subject fields, it opens up the possibility to avoid the necessity to stick the European thumb in the national wounds of distribution and poverty and replace the hitherto politically rather unattractive term "poverty" with "social exclusion" or – as in the recent case of the poverty-political National Action Plans – with the effort for improved "social inclusion" (cf. Kronauer 2002). A "Report by the Commission on Poverty in the EU Member States" is thus transformed – not just formally – to the "Joint Report on Social Integration". At least politically, this appears to make sense, perhaps even a precondition that in 2001 now " (...) for the first time, the European Union has approved a political document on poverty and social exclusion" (European Commission 2002: 7).

The first activities dealing with poverty policies at EU-European level were set in motion over 30 years ago on the initiative (not least of the social democratic German head of government, Willy Brandt) for the First Socio-Political Action Programme of the Community for 1974-76, the first large-scale socio-political advance at EC level (cf. Commission 1981: 5; Kowalsky 1999: 70ff). Within the framework of this action programme, the first of three Poverty Programmes "Programme of model projects and model studies for tackling poverty", in short Poverty I) was set up for the period 1975-80. The others followed in 1985-1989 (Poverty II) and 1989-94 (Poverty III). Poverty IV (1994-99) were finally prevented at the European Court of Justice by Germany and the United Kingdom on the grounds of lacking contractual basis (cf. Huster 1997: 202 following). With funds of between 20 million European units of account (Poverty I) and 55 million ECU (Poverty III) the programmes comprised model projects and studies in which expert opinions and action research projects scientifically investigated, and practice projects which effectively prevented, overcame or relieved the extent, causes, trends and solutions for poverty and exclusion. Three central principles originate from this: multidimensional definition of poverty and exclusion, the accentuation of participation/involvement of those affected and "partnership of all agents", as well as important pillars of the European poverty policy (development of poverty indicators, transnational networking of scientists and non-governmental organizations).

Looked at systematically, the poverty programmes emphasized, above all, the aspect of obtaining and spreading information for the definition and empirical study of poverty and for "best practice" methods and "innovative measures". This matter of concern can be described as the first of four fields of action of EU-European poverty policy. The poverty programmes and the interest in obtaining and spreading information in general serve the European level strategically to identify and discuss the significance of and challenges facing local, regional, national and not least EU-European poverty policy. Information, therefore, always has political functions: it prepares the basis for the three other (potential) fields of action of EU-European poverty policy: law, money and agreement on targets.

After first attempts failed, unlike in the areas of migrant workers and gender equality, to adopt political jurisdiction for a framework legislation on social benefit at Community level in the founding treaties, which through interaction between the Commission and (the majority) of the national governments, had enabled steps towards a conforming (minimum standards) or standardization of wage or socio-political standards against poverty and exclusion, questions increasingly began to arise once more about the "social dimension" of the integration process, since the negotiations on the Single European Act of 1986 with which the Single European Market was introduced by 1992. The willingness and efforts of individual national governments, as well as the interest of the trade unions and social NGOs in combining further economic steps toward integration with socio-political minimum standards increased again following the agreement of the Economic and Monetary Union in the Maastricht Treaty and the adoption of the Stability and Growth Pact of 1997.

In particular due to the neoliberal structure of the combination of common economic zone and a monetary union equipped with the convergence criteria of Maastricht and the Stability and Growth Pact, with continued decentralized fiscal and social policy, the countries with high standards are threatened by dumping competition for wage structure and social legislation, whilst states with low standards risk the absence of an "upward" adjustment. Critics fear that wage and social legislation will become the last remaining corrective instrument between competing states. Despite continuously growing socio-political needs (care, health, old age, education, daycare), declining resources (social benefit quotas) since 1993, the decreasing contribution by employers to the financing of social protection, the persistently high poverty rates observed EU-wide despite an overall rise in economic prosperity, and the more or less visible exclusion of "fringe groups" (e.g. as a result of immigrant and asylum legislation, partly including the creation of inferior special rules related to the minimum protection for these groups), among other things, point in this direction.

In view of the economically liberal diagnoses of labour market and socio-political causes of problems (lacking adaptability of the poor and unemployed population, encouragement of inactivity through high social benefit levels, reduction of the international competitiveness of European companies due to comparably high social protection levels) and possibly target-oriented action strategies (restructuring of a "provider" to an "active" welfare state, "strengthening of individual responsibility", etc.) which are dominant in the majority of the national governments and Commission agencies, there is nevertheless interest in reserving legal instruments still (*de facto*) exclusively in the jurisdiction of national politics, particularly in social policy for dealing with poverty and redistribution and based on entitlement to benefits, and thus to strategically use and maintain pressure towards a social policy between competing states. Despite numerous advances, the legislative field of action in European poverty policy is therefore *bis dato* understandably weakly developed. Particularly in the field of redistributive policy, different interests and agents have been successfully working against an "adjustment on the way to progress" (Article 137 EU Treaty).

Since the Treaty of Amsterdam (1999) came into force, it has been possible in principle, according to Article 137 of the EU Treaty, to conceive EU-wide resolutions in the Council on minimum regulations for systems of social protection[9], which represents enormous progress. Nevertheless, in view of the traditionally rejective attitude of certain national governments (United Kingdom), such resolutions remain unlikely, at least for the time being. Nor does the Treaty, reformed again in Nice (2000), provide for this possibility for tackling social exclusion – despite the formidable obstacle of the unanimity rule. There are three examples for potential links and initial starting points of a poverty-political primary and secondary framework legislation at EU level.

In 1992 the Council passed a "recommendation for common criteria for adequate allowances and benefits within the framework of the systems of social protection" (recommendation 92/441/EEC from 24.06.1992), in which the member states are advised in detail on quite ambitious development features for the national minimum protection legislation: guarantee of no time limit on entitlement to benefits, regular adjustment of the level of benefits, right to lodge objections and information about entitlement to benefits, etc. As in the second example, the Charter of Fundamental Rights, this recommendation has not yet been made legally binding (directive).

The Charter of Fundamental Rights, announced with great celebration at the European Council in Nice (2000), pronounces in Article 34 Paragraph 3: "In order to tackle social exclusion and poverty, the Union recognises and respects the right to social and housing assistance so as to ensure a decent existence for all those lack sufficient resources, in accordance with the rules laid down by Community Law and national laws and practices." We can only wait and see whether the convention currently striving for a renewed treaty reform and constitutionalization for the Union will succeed in making the Charter legally binding as part of the reformed treaties and whether the European Court of Justice will lay down the Article (in its precedents certainly not for the first time) primarily in the interest of a high level of social protection for EU citizens. For so far there has been no definitive Community law, and in many Italian, Spanish and Greek areas, no definitive individual state legislation which would be able to guarantee every citizen a minimum income that would ensure a decent existence.

Thirdly (finally), this fundamental and constitutional approach of social protection against poverty and social exclusion was also pursued by the report of the "Committee of Wise Men" (1996) whose mandate from the Commission was to study the follow-up measures for the "Community Charter of Social Basic Rights for Workers" of 1989. Whilst the Committee proposes under the heading "Rights to be strived for" the issuing of minimum regulations for the realization of social basic rights only in a second phase of European framework legislation, it argues for the basic right to a minimum income to protect the existence and dignity of the individual: "In view of the extent of unemployment in the Community and bearing in mind the necessity to clearly underline the specifics of the European social model and fight against poverty and exclusion, the Committee saw itself induced to propose a minimum regulation in a single case.

In the opinion of the Committee, the principle should be formulated in the Treaty (i.e. at Union level) forthwith that every member state must introduce a minimum income for individuals who, despite all efforts, are unable to find employment and have no other sources of income. The level of this benefit would naturally depend on the development status of the state concerned, (…)" (ibidem: 55)

Money or, in the more general sense, material support represents the third systematic field of action of an EU poverty policy, which however – like the legal instruments – has so far been of little factual importance. These include measures dealing with certain points, such as the direct food aid provided by the EU, where agricultural products are distributed directly to needy EU citizens (cf. Venturini 1988: 50; Commission 2000: 12), or for example the support of practice projects within the framework of the European Poverty Programmes. Moreover, European funds were and are provided for the promotion of research projects in the field of poverty and social exclusion, for example within the framework of the Poverty Programmes and now the "Community Action Plan to Fight Social Exclusion (2002-2006)" as a component of the "Open Method of Coordination".

But this pillar would acquire another dimension if the creation or improvement of socio-political benefit rights for fighting poverty were supported systematically in the member states, in the form of supporting funds at "Brussels level". This (at present theoretical) option plays a role within the framework of legal considerations, which aim at a (primary) legal guarantee of the social basic right to an income that ensures dignity or the (secondary) legal understanding about minimum standards in poverty-political social benefit law. Financial assistance could facilitate an understanding about such legal instruments. At present distributive measures and measures to raise the budget of the EU are, however, being discussed and adopted more in the opposite direction under the dominance of neoliberal "locational state" argumentation models and with a view to the Stability and Growth Pact, besides the desire to keep the costs of eastward enlargement as low as possible in the way of a "cold integration". Nevertheless, such considerations have become effective many times in other areas of European *realpolitik* (such as in the creation and raising of structural and cohesion funds as compensation and political "lubricants" for agreement to European enlargement and consolidation projects, despite national political and/or social interests to the contrary), and have always played a significant role in debates about the promotion of progressive convergence in political multilevel systems (not only) of poverty policy (cf. Hauser 1987; Graser 2001).

With the efforts to set up networks within the framework of the three Poverty Programmes, the first conditions were finally created for the development of the fourth field of action, the *Agreement of Goals*. Behind the promotion of networks and support of "weak agents" of the poverty policy (especially through the institutional promotion of the European Anti Poverty Network – EAPN), as well as efforts towards consultations with different non-central state agents in this political field (for example with the churches in the consultation process in the mid-1990s; with sociopolitical forums held with NGOs, social partners, local and regional politicians – and/or administrative levels; through transnational scientific conferences, etc.) stands the realization that poverty policy is already a nationally "occupied" field. The communes, regions, churches, trade unions, affected organizations and not least the social NGOs/charities must inevitably be taken into view, if the EU does not wish to push politics and exchange past central "relevant agents" and thus act ineffectively. On the other hand, personal interests play a role here as political level and political protagonist, which have the Commission looking for reference partners and coalition partners beside the European Parliament and beyond the level of the national governments, in view of the power of the national governments in the European Council (of heads of government) and the Council (of Specialized Ministers). Target agreements can, must and will finally be passed only between the national governments, as the only political agents relevant in the end to decision-making in the construction of the European level, and the European Commission.

Whilst the first three poverty-political fields of action mentioned are discussed in the Venturini Report of 1998 on the social dimension of the Single Market[10], the formulation of explicit poverty-political targets represents a novelty of European policy, the concept of which dates from the European Employment Strategy (since 1997) and the resolutions of the European Councils of Lisbon (March 2000). At this summit, the EU-European national governments and the Commission formulated the following strategic target for the period 2000-2010: "(...) to make the Union the most competitive and dynamic knowledge-based economic zone in the world – an economic zone which is capable of achieving permanent economic growth with more and better jobs and a greater social cohesion. To attain this target, a global strategy is needed within framework of which (...) social exclusion is to be tackled (...)". And further: "The implementation of this strategy will be achieved by improving the existing processes, whereby a new open method of coordination will be introduced at all levels (...) which should ensure an (...) effective monitoring of the progress." (Conclusions of the Presidency of the European Council of Lisbon, 23/24 March 2000)

In the field of policy on poverty and social exclusion, this Open Method is operationalized through five elements:

- through the agreement of common goals (Nice, December 2000: 1. Promotion of employment and access to resources, rights, goods and services; 2. Prevention of the risks of exclusion; 3. Help for the most needy; 4. Mobilization of all relevant agents);
- through the agreement of common indicators for measuring progress and identifying best practice procedures and innovative approaches (such as: 40, 50, 60 and 70% poverty level, according to duration, gender, age, employment status, household type, home ownership, long-term unemployment; life expectancy; S80/S20 ratio);
- through the creation of two-year National Action Plans (NAPincl) (beginning with June 2001 for the period 2001-2003);
- through the working out of a Joint Report on the social integration by the European Commission which summarizes the 15 National Action Plans, and analyses and evaluates them separately according to member states;
- through a Community Action Programme to promote cooperation between the member states in the three areas (1. Analysis of the features, processes, causes and trends of social exclusion; 2. Conceptional cooperation and exchange of information and best practice procedures; 3. Participation of interest groups and pro-

motion of networks at EU level (period of validity: 2002-2006; financial volume: 75 million euros in total).

It is too early for an assessment of this new approach of European poverty policy. Yet first reactions to the establishment of the Open Method of Coordination in the EU-European poverty policy and systematic considerations about the pressure of problems and the conditions and problem-solving capacity of the different fields of action of European poverty policy at least provide first indications of their chances, difficulties and limits: "The effects of favourable economic and employment trends between 1995 and 2000 have helped to stabilize the situation which had worsened in many member states in the mid-1990s due to the economic recession." (European Commission 2002: 9) If the national policies and even favourable economic and employment trends only lead to a stabilization of the situation, the question arises whether the Open Method of Coordination promises sufficient additional poverty-political impetus.

"If the member states wish to achieve their target and create societies without exclusion, considerable improvements in the distribution of social resources and opportunities are necessary to ensure the social integration and participation of all people and their access to their basic rights." (ibidem: 14f) It is doubtful whether the instruments mentioned can bring about sufficient changes in the dynamics of the political business of the member states in favour of poverty policy. "Even the process of Open Coordination which has now begun will have an effect on national politics only in the very long term. To me, the repercussions of the Economic and Monetary Union on national social policy and social welfare benefit policy in particular which are not openly discussed appear much more important." (Bäcker 2001: 50) For the race to cut taxes induced by it eventually undermines the financial strength of the states (and communes) and thus threatens to lead to a sinking of social standards.

On the other hand, the Open Method certainly provides an important contribution to poverty-political agenda-setting at Union level, and offers the national NGOs, the communal and regional political levels, the scientific community and specialists amongst the public important arguments and information to use the targets, indicators, reports and studies in their national contexts in the same way. The Open Coordination can also perspectively encourage the preconditions for consensus necessary for the community-wide recognition of the basic right to a minimum income to ensure a decent standard of living and for secondary legal minimum standards in social legislation.

For some of the "relevant agents", however, the Open Method already touches pain thresholds and provokes defence reactions. Although the governments of Italy and the United Kingdom endorse so-called performance indicators which are supposed to describe the social circumstances (poverty rate, number of school drop-outs, etc.), as opposed to so-called political indicators which provide information about political efforts (e.g. expenditure for social welfare benefit, number of homeless supported), they have "expressly stated" that they will "not be considered" (European Commission 2002: 90). The German Federal Council – representing the states, the third most important level in German social policy besides the communes and the Federal Government – is concerned about possible intervention in the national autonomy within this area of policy, guaranteed by treaty in Article 137 of the EU Treaty. "In the view of the Federal Council, the coordination activities of the European Union agreed in the Method of Open Coordination (...) must be thoroughly examined as to what extent they limit the scope for action of the member states and the German federal states. They must therefore be bound to the scope of jurisdiction of the EU. (...) It emphasizes in particular its concern that the newly created Method of Open Coordination paves the way for a procedure which can overlook the jurisdiction arrangement set out in the treaty and give the European Union the possibility to lay down concrete specifications to be implemented by the member states and in Germany by the federal states. (...)The Federal Council has emphasized repeatedly (...)competition for the most successful (...) social policy, rather than the central fixing of the targets to be pursued by the Community, member states and regions, is the right model in order to be able to successfully meet the challenges of globalisation. Increased cooperation at EU level can certainly be productive here. But it must be limited to an improved exchange of experience and information." On the other hand, it rejects common targets/guidelines, evaluations based on agreed indicators, and (already) legally non-binding recommendations from Brussels to the nation states, their regions and communes. (Federal Council 2001:3f)

Challenges and Perspectives

With this, the binding of values and interests of poverty policy comes back into view, for no competition for the objectively "best" social policy takes place in the process of European integration and "globalisation". Secondly the competition takes place in a socio-political "dynamic multilevel system", structured differently depending on the nation (Jachtenfuchs / Kohler-Koch 1996), in which the personal interests of the Commission, the national governments, the regions, communes and finally economic and social interest groups come to fruition. Fears of a European "superstate" (through the backdoor) conflict with fears of a decentralized social policy which does without a "helping presence" of competing states which are *de facto* no longer sovereign and empowered to act. The search for perspectives to effectively fight poverty and social exclusion in Europe, even with a policy at European level, appears urgently needed and must be looked for potentially politically conflict-ridden between the poles of a "cold" European integration through (*de facto*) non-social policy and the (neither desirable nor realistic) general supranationalization of poverty and social policy, in a combination of the four poverty-political fields of action.

Since the end of the 1990s, a second qualitative leap in this direction was achieved with the "soft" politicisation and the poverty-political agenda-setting by means of the Open Method of Coordination, after just a few years earlier, the first involving the implementation of poverty programmes had been stopped and legislative measures (provisions on basic rights and minimum standards) have not been achieved to this day. The Open Method of Coordination can, in my view, be helpful in a minimum protection policy mix (for its other parts there are historical links in EU policy: Poverty I-III, Recommendation 92/441/EEC; Report of the Committee of Wise Men) (inclusion of all agents, target agreements, agenda-setting, etc.) as well as possibly even a necessary precondition for further steps toward European social legislative minimum standards. As it and its surroundings have so far shown themselves, however, its poverty-political effectiveness appears – at least in the short- and medium-term – questionable. The decisive factor will be if and when the Open Method is developed and expanded. If this development and expansion does not continue to be encouraged enthusiastically, it will cease, or if it is carried out only along the currently dominant neoliberal conflict views and reform proposals, the Open Method could prove to be useful for the continuation and forcing of a cold strategy of European integration that cuts out the social dimension of the European integration process, that at least tacitly accepts and acquiesces to a dismantling of the welfare state in the member states.

Annotations

1 At the same time, European figures frequently deviate from values of purely national surveys, probably due to varying sources of data or harmonized criteria and definitions. For this reason, even different European data records cannot always be compared with each other. So when comparing poverty rates, it should be noted that the definition of 50 per cent of the arithmetical average income changes to 60 per cent of the median average income. The switch from the old to the new OECD scale led to a change in the weighting of the needs of household members. The new OECD scale assumes higher economizing in joint budgeting and lower requirements of children. (cf. Hauser 2002)
2 For empirical evidence of poverty in Central and Eastern Europe see Huster 1996; Boeckh 2000
3 EU 15 = European Union of the 15 member states, DK = Denmark, FIN = Finland, S = Sweden, A = Austria, L = Luxembourg, NL = The Netherlands, D = Germany, F = France, I = Italy, IRL = Ireland, UK = United Kingdom, B = Belgium, EL = Greece, E = Spain, P = Portugal
4 Estonia (EE), Latvia (LV), Lithuania (LT), Poland (PL), the Czech (CZ) and Slovakian (SK) Republics, Slovenia (SI), Hungary (HU), Cyprus (CY) and Malta (M). Romania (RO) and Bulgaria (BG) are striving for accession in 2007.

5 Netherlands „Algemene Bijstand"; Belgium „Bestaansminimum / Minimum de Moyens d´Existence (Minimex)"; Denmark „Social Bistand"; France „Revenu Minimum d'Insertion (RMI)"; Ireland „Supplementary Welfare Allowance"; Luxembourg „Revenu Minimum Garanti"; United Kingdom „Income Support"; Austria and Germany „Sozialhilfe"; Finland „Toimeentulotuki"; Sweden „Socialbidrag"; Portugal „Rendimento minimo garantido". The regional Spanish systems "Ingreso minimo de insercion / Renta Minima" in the case of poor regional budgetary position and numerous household members do not guarantee adequate amounts, in Italy „Minimo Vitale / Reddito minimo" minimum income systems do not yet exist nationwide, in Greece there is no minimum protection system yet. (cf.: European Commission 2001: 516f)

6 Moreover, it is (not only) regarding social welfare recipient figures where a problem of data availability becomes evident, for which it appears there is only a political explanation. Until 1999 the information system of the Community provided figures concerning the social protective systems of the member states (MISSOC), some of which were completely out of date; since 2000 no figures whatsoever have been available. Even in publications of the European Commission concerning its efforts to fight poverty and social exclusion (for example European Commission 2002) or the Statistical Office of the Community (for example Eurostat 2000), one can search fruitlessly for relevant time series.

7 1958: EEC6 (France, Germany, Italy, Belgium, Netherlands, Luxembourg); 1973: EEC9 (accession of Denmark, the United Kingdom and Ireland); EC12 (after the accession of Greece in 1981 and Spain and Portugal in 1986); 1995: EU15 (accession of Austria, Sweden and Finland).

8 For the empirical evidence of subjective evaluations of poverty and social exclusion in the member states of the EU, see: Gallie / Paugam 2002.

9 The EU-European term „Social Protection" and the corresponding regulations of the Community do not traditionally include the social welfare systems of the member states. However, „Systems of social protection" and systems of social welfare are becoming increasingly difficult to separate (cf. Schulte 1991).

10 Law: „Convergence" and „Harmonization", Money: „Redistribution" and Information: „Supporting Measures" (Venturini 1988: 64).

References

Bäcker, Gerhard (2001): Das BSHG: Aktuelle Probleme in gesamteuropäischer Perspektive, Statement, in: Huster, Ernst-Ulrich, hrsg. im Namen des Rektorates der Evangelischen Fachhochschule Rheinland-Westfalen-Lippe: 40 Jahre Bundessozialhilfegesetz, Bochum [Current Problems of the German Social Assistance Scheme in European Perspective]

Benz, Benjamin/Boeckh, Jürgen/Huster, Ernst-Ulrich (2000): Sozialraum Europa – Ökonomische und politische Transformation in Ost und West, Opladen [European Social Area. Economical and Political Transformation in Western and Eastern Europe]

Benz, Benjamin (2004): Nationale Mindestsicherungssysteme und Europäische Integration – Von der Wahrnehmung der Armut und sozialen Ausgrenzung zur Offenen Methode der Koordination, Wiesbaden, zugleich: Dissertation, Universität Gießen 2003 [National Minimum Income Schemes and European Poverty Policy in the Process of European Integration]

Bundesrat (2001): Beschluss des Bundesrates zum deutschen Positionspapier für den Europäischen Rat in Stockholm am 23./24. März 2001: Für ein innovatives Europa – Wachstumspotenzial und sozialen Zusammenhalt stärken, Drucksache 86/01 (Beschluss) vom 09. März 2001 [Resolution of the German Bundesrat Concerning the German Position Paper for the European Council in Stockholm 2001]

Dahrendorf, Ralf (1992): Der moderne soziale Konflikt – Essay zur Politik der Freiheit, Stuttgart [The Modern Social Conflict]

EAPN - European Anti Poverty Network (2000): Armut in Europa, Brüssel [Poverty in Europe]

Eichener, Volker (2000): Das Entscheidungssystem der Europäischen Union – Institutionelle Analyse und demokratietheoretische Bewertung, Opladen [Decision-making in the European Union]

Esping-Andersen, Gøsta (1990): The Three Worlds of Welfare Capitalism, Cambridge

Europäische Kommission, Generaldirektion Beschäftigung und Soziales (2001): MISSOC 2001 – Soziale Sicherheit in den Mitgliedstaaten der EU und im Europäischen Wirtschaftsraum, Brüssel/Luxemburg [Mutual Information System on Social Protection in the EU-Member States 2001]

Europäische Kommission, Generaldirektion Beschäftigung und Soziales (2002): Gemeinsamer Bericht über die soziale Eingliederung, Brüssel/Luxemburg [Joint Report on Social Inclusion 2001-2003]

Eurostat (1996): Eurostat Jahrbuch '96 – Europe im Blick der Statistik 1985-1995, Luxemburg [Statistical Yearbook of the EU]

Eurostat (2000): European social statistics – Income, poverty and social exclusion, Luxembourg

Eurostat/Europäische Kommission (2002): Die Soziale Lage in der Europäischen Union 2002, Kurzfassung, Brüssel/Luxemburg [The Social Situation in the EU 2002]

Gallie, Duncan/Paugam, Serge (2002): Social Precarity and Social Integration, Report for the European Commission Directorate-General Employment, Eurobarometer 56.1, October 2002, Brussels

Gohr, Antonia (2001): Der italienische Wohlfahrtsstaat: Entwicklungen, Probleme und die europäische Herausforderung, in: Kraus, Katrin/Geisen, Thomas (Hg.): Sozialstaat in Europa – Geschichte, Entwicklung, Perspektiven, Wiesbaden, S. 143-169 [The Italian Welfare State. Developments, Problems and European Challenges]

Graser, Alexander (2001): Dezentrale Wohlfahrtsstaatlichkeit im föderalen Binnenmarkt? Eine verfassungs- und sozialrechtliche Untersuchung am Beispiel der Vereinigten Staaten von Amerika, Berlin, zugleich: Dissertation, Universität München [Decentral Welfare State in a Federal States? The Case of the United States of America]

Guibentif, Pierre/Bouget, Denis (1997): Mindesteinkommen in der Europäischen Union – Ein sozialpolitischer Vergleich, Lissabon [Minimum Income Policies in the EU]

Hauser, Richard (1987): Möglichkeiten und Probleme der Sicherung eines Mindesteinkommens in den Mitgliedstaaten der Europäischen Gemeinschaft, Arbeitspapier Nr. 246, Sonderforschungsbereich 3: Mikroanalytische Grundlagen der Gesellschaftspolitik, J.W. Goethe-Universität Frankfurt und Universität Mannheim, Frankfurt a. M. (Typoskript) [Possibilities and Problems of a Minimum Income Policy at European Level]

Hauser, Richard (1994): Perspektiven und Zukunftsaufgaben des Sozialstaates, in: Ministerium für Arbeit, Gesundheit und Soziales des Landes Nordrhein-Westfalen (Hg.): Zukunft des Sozialstaates – Leitideen und Perspektiven für eine Sozialpolitik der Zukunft, Düsseldorf, S. 23-64 [Perspectives and Future Tasks of the Welfare State]

Hauser, Richard (2002): Soziale Indikatoren als Element der offenen Methode der Koordinierung zur Bekämpfung von Armut und sozialer Ausgrenzung in der Europäischen Union, Vortrag am 19.02.2002 im Bundesministerium für Familie, Senioren, Frauen und Jugend, Typoskript [Social Indicators as an Element of the Open Method of Co-ordination in the Fight Against Poverty and Social Exclusion in the EU]

Heinze, Rolf G./Schmid, Josef/Strünck, Christoph (1999): Vom Wohlfahrtsstaat zum Wettbewerbsstaat – Arbeitsmarkt- und Sozialpolitik in den 90er Jahren, Opladen [From Welfare State to Competition State. Labour-market and Social Policy in the 1990s]

Huster, Ernst-Ulrich (1996): Armut in Europa, Opladen [Poverty in Western and Eastern Europe in a Multidimensional Perspective]

Huster, Ernst-Ulrich (1997): Armut in Europa – ausgewählte Ergebnisse des Armutsobservatoriums der Europäischen Union, in: Becker, Irene/ Hauser, Richard (Hg.): Einkommensverteilung und Armut – Deutschland auf dem Weg zur Vierfünftel-Gesellschaft?, Frankfurt a. M./New York, S. 199-230 [Results of the European Observatory on Poverty and Social Exclusion within the Framework of Poverty III]

Jachtenfuchs, Markus/Kohler-Koch, Beate (1996): Einleitung: Regieren im dynamischen Mehrebenensystem, in: Dies. (Hg.): Europäische Integration, Opladen, S. 15-44 [Governing in the European Dynamic Multilevel System]

Kaufmann, Franz-Xaver (1997): Herausforderungen des Sozialstaates, Frankfurt a.M. [Challenges of the Welfare State]

Komitee der Weisen (1996): Für ein Europa der politischen und sozialen Grundrechte – Bericht des Komitee der Weisen unter Vorsitz von Maria de Lourdes Pintasilgo, hrsg. von der Europäischen Kommission – Generaldirektion Beschäftigung, Arbeitsbeziehungen und soziale Angelegenheiten, Brüssel/Luxemburg [A Europe with Political and Social Basic Rights]

Kommission der Europäischen Gemeinschaften (1981): Schlußbericht von der Kommission an den Rat über das Erste Programm von Modellvorhaben und Modellstudien zur Bekämpfung der Armut, KOM(81) 769 endg., vom 15. Dezember 1981, Brüssel [Final Report of the First European Poverty Programme]

Kommission der Europäischen Gemeinschaften (1991): Schlußbericht des Zweiten Europäischen Programms zur Bekämpfung der Armut 1985 – 1989, KOM(91) 29 endg., vom 13. Februar 1991, Brüssel/Luxemburg [Final Report of the Second European Poverty Programme]

Kommission der Europäischen Gemeinschaften (1992): Auf dem Weg zur europäischen Solidargemeinschaft – Den Kampf gegen die Soziale Ausgrenzung intensivieren, die Eingliederung fördern, Mitteilung der Commission KOM(92)542 endg., vom 23. Dezember 1992, Brüssel/ Luxemburg [Commission Communication Intensify the Fight Against Social Exclusion on the Way to the European Unified Community]

Kommission der Europäischen Gemeinschaften (1999): Bericht der Kommission (...) über die Umsetzung der Empfehlung 92/441/EWG vom 24.

Juni 1992 über gemeinsame Kriterien für ausreichende Zuwendungen und Leistungen im Rahmen der Systeme der sozialen Sicherung, KOM(98)744 vom 25. Januar 1999, Internetversion: http://Europe.eu.int/comm/dg05/soc-prot/social/news/minimum_de.htm [Report on the Implementation of the Council Recommendation on Common Criteria Concerning Sufficient Resources and Social Assistance in Social Protection Systems]

Kommission der Europäischen Gemeinschaften (2000): Ein Europa schaffen, das alle einbezieht, Mitteilung der Commission KOM(2000) 79 endg., vom 01. März 2000, Brüssel [Commissions Communication Towards an Inclusive Europe]

Kommission der Europäischen Gemeinschaften (2003): Zweiter Zwischenbericht über den wirtschaftlichen und sozialen Zusammenhalt, Mitteilung der Kommission vom 30. Januar 2003, KOM(2003) 34 endgültig, Brüssel [Second Interim Report on Economic and Social Cohesion within the EU]

Kowalsky, Wolfgang (1999): Europäische Sozialpolitik – Ausgangsbedingungen, Antriebskräfte und Entwicklungspotentiale, Opladen [European Social Policy]

Kronauer, Martin (2002): Exklusion – Die Gefährdung des Sozialen im hochentwickelten Kapitalismus, Frankfurt am Main [Exclusion and Capitalism]

Scharf, Thomas (2001): Sozialpolitik in Großbritannien: Vom Armengesetz zum „Dritten Weg", in: Kraus, Katrin/Geisen, Thomas (Hg.): Sozialstaat in Europe – Geschichte, Entwicklung, Perspektiven, Wiesbaden, S. 43-61 [Social Policy in Great Britain]

Schulte, Bernd (1991): Das Recht auf ein Mindesteinkommen in der Europäischen Gemeinschaft – Nationaler Status quo und supranationale Initiativen, in: Sozialer Fortschritt, Heft 1/1991, S. 7-23 [Minimum Income Policy at National and European Level]

Statistisches Bundesamt (2002): Sozialleistungen, Fachserie 13, Reihe 2, Sozialhilfe, 2000, Wiesbaden [Empirical Material on Social Assistance in Germany]

Venturini, Patrick (1988): Ein Europäischer Sozialraum für 1992, Dokument hrsg. von der Kommission der Europäischen Gemeinschaften, Brüssel/Luxembourg

Winter, Thomas von (1997): Sozialpolitische Interessen – Konstituierung, politische Repräsentation und Beteiligung an Entscheidungsprozessen, Baden-Baden [Socio-political Interests]

Doris Scheer

Poverty questions in Europe – what are the churches and diaconia doing?

The churches and diaconia are involved in Europe in many ways. This is mirrored by their formal representation at the European institutions, the initiation of networks and their active support, the participation in European support programmes and even in their charitable operations in cases of emergency. As far as the churches' and diaconal activities are concerned, "Europe" has never been limited to the political and geographical borders of the European Union. For this reason, the following considerations will have to be looked at on different levels regarding the possibilities for participation within the institutional frameworks of the European Union and regarding the formulation of ethical questions and ecumenical amalgamation, that cannot be limited to this context.

Poverty in Europe today

Theoretical considerations attempt to find the right terms for poverty and bare figures in scientific discussions or debates, in poverty reports and European policy and strategy documents, outline the world as it is and show the everyday experiences of people who live in poverty and exclusion. Three examples of how people describe and interpret their own poverty and exclusion are shown below.

Mr. M.: "That was a bad time. Nothing went right. It was impossible to plan anything. When we got money, we had to look after the child first (...) I really got into debt. I borrowed money from my mother and from my brother. That was the way I got into debt in the first place. I was also in debt to credit institutes." (Tobias/Böttner, 1992, p. 64)

Mr. R. says: "It's o.k. to find a job up to the age of 35. After that it's difficult. Over 40 and you should be happy to get anything at all. I'm 46, so you can forget it, even though I'm healthy. The first time where I was told indirectly, that I was too old, I felt like a grandfather. What can you do? But it is odd when you hear that for the first time, because you don't feel old and you slowly but surely feel cast aside." (ibidem, p. 25)

Ms. S. reports that she can get by, but only because her life-partner gets unemployment benefit. They get meat once a week, beer with colleagues once a month, new clothes once a year and never go to restaurants or the cinema. The last time Ms S went on holiday was in 1988 – two weeks to a seaside resort on the Baltic. (Die ZEIT, Nr. 22, 22 of May 2003)

These voices express what Bourdieu call the "little needs". These "little needs", compared from the perspective of the macrocosmos with the great misery in the world, are indeed relative, but this doesn't make them any less depressing and demoralising for the person involved. Bourdieu points out that we must not let our view be diverted from seeing and understanding the suffering involved, "which is characteristic for a social order that has certainly abolished great need (but to a lesser extent than is normally stated), but has in its differentiation, increased social areas (specific fields and sub-fields) and thus enhanced the conditions for an unprecedented development of all forms of 'little needs'". (p.19)

Why does the society in which we live allow such developments? Why does it allow these little needs and this suffering? Why does it make it possible for this by the setting of its own framework conditions?

Human Dignity and the Market Economy

While looking for answers, the same keywords appear repeatedly: globalisation, neo-liberalism, more competition and growth, liberalisation and flexibility, crises in the social state, cuts in social services, cost-cutting, and slogans such as "more market, less state control" that point out that state intervention and regulations hinder free development and the self healing powers of the market.

The rules of the free market economy should also be applied to other areas of society. This sets the economy up as the most important protagonist, and all other areas are classified as less important and they are defined in terms of being dependent on economic necessity.

The question is no longer: what do we have to do to enable all people to live in dignity, but, under the dictatorship of economic pragmatism, human dignity becomes a commodity. The question becomes: how much dignity can we afford? Not what is just, but what pays, is what is asked for. Is it possible to judge human dignity in economic terms?

For Katterle (1989), the call for "less state" means cuts in social service safety nets for the purpose of market economy functionalism in all political areas and for the purpose of market oriented restructuring of public spending and income; in this context, this leads to the discrediting of the idea of the welfare state itself. (p. 180) In the end, this means individualisation and seeing life in terms of economics and a change of paradigm from the principle of a society based on solidarity to the principle of egocentricity.

By making free space and its formation available for a part of society, the question is raised as to what potential has to be available for the individual, in order to maximise and form them, and which new risks and dependencies are contained in this new structure of society. (Beck, 1986) The dream of the supposed independence of the modern person can quickly become a nightmare.

The question of fairness of distribution, which was denounced as antiquated and a hindrance to reform, but which is far from being replaced, follows close behind. The essence of justice in a social market economy also requires the imbalance of distribution to be corrected.

Ethical questions

The European reform debates, as witnessed by all member states at various times, make it clear that different economic and political directions are at issue. The conceptual divergence of the employment market reforms and social security system reforms are based on different economic, political and ethical assumptions. Too often, these basic assumptions, that accompany this subconsciously, and are assumed to be shared by all rational members of society, are not explained explicitly and so remain opaque. They are also emotional topics that define our conception of the world and are therefore part of our existence and determine our actions.

These preconceptions that determine our perception and interpretation of the world are part of our everyday life, of our orientation and actions. Thus it is clear that ethical questions and considerations are part of everyday life. Ethics cannot therefore be reduced to contemplative exercises, performed by the chosen few in total seclusion from the world. They can not be ghettoised, and they cannot be an exclusive area of work only for the church or church institutions which often have the authority and therefore the responsibility for ethical questions forced upon them – in the quiet hope that other areas such as politics and economy will be spared unpleasant questions and demands for justice, responsibility and participation.

But then, what are the tasks of the church and the diaconal institutions? What is the role that they can take on and want to take on within a European Union which has primarily economic aims?[1]

"Perception and description of crisis situations, that is the strength (of the diaconal institutions). How can you cope competently with plight if you do not know it, if you cannot look it in the eye, if you cannot speak with it?" writes Rev. Gohde, President of the Diaconal Institutions of the Protestant Church of Germany, in his presidential report 1999. (p. 15)

But is the perception and description of poverty enough? Why should we know about people's need and suffering? What shall we do with the knowledge that we have gained?

"The interior mission is now unfortunately involved in politics, and if the church does not work in this way, the church will go down with the state", declared Wichern in his speech at Wittenberg in 1848. (quote according to Gohde 1999 p. 15)

That means, that diaconal work should not take place behind the church walls, that the diaconia have always seen themselves as creative protagonists in the political arena. The diaconia have taken on a social mandate to take the perception and description of poverty into the public eye, to debate it politically and influence the changes and limitations of structures which cause exclusion, discrimination and marginalisation.

The diaconia has no patent recipe for solving all these special problems such as exclusion, unemployment and homelessness but it can make sure that the plight of these people does not become forgotten and, together with other protagonists, use its know-how to look for solutions.

A bible study of Isaiah 58 with the title "Shout out for Justice", the theologian Jürgen Ebach (1998) points out this awareness: "It is all about bearing witness and openly confessing. Even in the bible, a prophet is not primarily someone who prophesises but someone who makes open declarations. Prophecy in the bible is 'counter-public'; it is an open statement of that which is threatened with being shrouded in silence, of being forgotten and suppressed." (p.203)

Justice is not valued highly at the moment; courage and strength are needed to produce the necessary counter-public effect. In his contribution to the Diaconia Year Book 2000, the Professor Strohm points out the urgent necessity to speed up the structural changes: "under modern living conditions, responsibility should not be limited to direct and spontaneous actions towards sufferers of poverty or need, because the lives of people today are more than ever determined by political and social structures. Help for fellow-beings will therefore be realised to a great degree by the formation of human structures and in the removal and overcoming of destructive structures. One must understand that, today, love becomes effective within and by means of structures." (p. 91 f.) The EKD memorandum on *Grundlagen, Aufgaben und Zukunftsperspektiven der Diakonie* (1998) deduces a Christian duty in the last sentence, which is also in the memorandum "(...) that is why Christians have a duty to contribute to solidarity in society in the parish and community, in the spirit of a political diaconate." (S. 18)

The churches' social comment, *Für eine Zukunft in Solidarität und Gerechtigkeit* (1997) ("Towards a future in solidarity and justice"), refers to the fact that structures "must be embedded in a supporting structure that carries them, in order to ensure long term continuation. (...) To preserve a view for the suffering of others, is a condition for all cultures. Compassion as described in the Bible does not represent a coincidental, passing feeling (...) this compassion demands justice." (fig. 12 und 13)

This challenge is also contained in the following quotation from the French Bishops' Congress in 1996: "Reducing social inequalities is not just a matter of technical means but also a matter of intelligence and of the heart. Everybody who feels for humankind knows this is the first aim that people must have. Men and women in different fields of responsibility should not accept the gap in society as an unavoidable disaster." (quote Belitz, 1997, p. 29)

Church and Diaconal Commitment in Europe

As described in the French Bishops' Congress statement, the church and diaconal institutions together with their paid and voluntary workers and Christians in Europe are attempting to change the European economic and social structures in such a way that all people can live in dignity. The EKD Memorandum (Responsibility for a Social Europe), 1991) describes the requirements of a European social order and stresses that, when putting a new social policy into practice, basic socio-ethical and humanitarian orientations must have primary importance. The higher aim that must be striven for from the beginning is the protection of the dignity and welfare of people. This is a vision of a human Europe. (p. 32)

What possibilities of structuring and influence do the churches and diaconal institutions in the European Union have? How can they input their values, their experience, their knowledge and their creativity? How can they take part and influence the contents of public and political debate?

For many years, churches and diaconal institutions have been involved in European networks, co-operation and organisations acting at different institutional and hierarchical levels. Some of these forms of co-operation will be examined in the following pages; this short overview does not intend to belittle the large variety of church and diaconal activities. The selection is merely an indication of the continual persistent commitment of Christians who are devoted to creating human structures so that Europe is given a soul (Delors, speech to the Churches, Brussels, 14. April 1992).

The initiative "A Soul for Europe"

This amalgamation was formed in 1994 at the initiative of the former president of the European Commission Jacques Delors. Without a spiritual and ethical dimension, the European process of integration would be difficult to master – Delors was certain of this. Delors imagined a European Union that should be more than just a legal and economic system for its citizens. The initiative "A Soul for Europe" aims "to contribute to the building of a citizens' Europe." In combination with European organisations and institutions, it provides a discussion forum for all religions at different levels. Members of this association are representatives of various religious and political groups:

- Commission of the Bishops' Conferences of the European Union
- Church and Society Commission of the Conference of European Churches
- Orthodox Liaison Office
- Conference of European Rabbis
- European Humanist Federation
- The Muslim Council for Co-operation in Europe

http://europa.eu.int/comm/dgs/policy_advisers/activities/dialogue_religions_humanisms/issues/soul_for_europe/index_de.htm (Accessed 27. October 2003)

The Church and Society Commission of the Conference of European Churches

The formation of the Church and Society Commission took place in 1960 and was originally a Protestant / ecumenical association run by European civil servants of Protestant, Anglican and orthodox faiths. It was the civil servants' desire to sound out the meaning of the Christian message for the work of the European organisations. This organisation was later renamed "The European Ecumenical Commission for Church and Society". In January 1999, the work of the CEC (Conference of European Churches) for Church and Society and that of the European

Ecumenical Commission for Church and Society (EECCS) was combined in the Church and Society Commission.

The Church and Society Commission sees its task as being to offer help to the churches so that questions from church and society, especially those with a European content can be dealt with from a theological and socio-ethical viewpoint. A further task is to represent the member churches of the CEC in their relations with political institutions working in Europe. The work of the commission is mainly carried out in working groups:

- Working group for bioethics
- Working group for economic, environmental and social themes
- Working group for legislation in the European Community
- Working group for European integration
- Working group for human rights and religious freedom
- Working group for north-south topics
- Working group for peace and security.
- The European Churches and the Convention on the future of Europe

http://www.cec-kek.org
(Accessed 27. October 2003)

The Conference of European Churches (CEC)

The Conference of European Churches is the regional amalgamation of Orthodox, Anglican, Roman Catholic and Protestant churches in Europe. Their target is to promote the unification of Christians in serving the whole of the community. The Conference of European Churches works closely with the Ecumenical Council of Churches but it is an independent organisation. The CEC came into being in the 1950s during the Cold War, on a divided continent. After several years of preparation, the representatives of over 40 churches came to the first general assembly in Nyborg Strand in Denmark.

The CEC sees one main task as building bridges between Eastern and Western Europe. It has attempted to build such bridges between minority and majority churches and between Christians with different denominational traditions. Today the CEC has about 123 member churches in all European countries, about half of them in Central and Eastern Europe. All large denominational families are represented in the CEC, Orthodox Lutheran, Reformist, Anglican, Methodist, Baptist, Catholic and Pentecostal.

Church groups have been able to become associates of the CEC since 1992. 23 organisations have taken advantage of this possibility to date. The national church councils and associations of lay-persons, women and youth whose activities run parallel and often in co-operation with the CEC, number among these organisations.

http://www.cec-kek.org
(Accessed 27. October 2003)

Eurodiaconia

Eurodiaconia is an amalgamation of churches, welfare organisations and NGOs which are active on an international and national level. Eurodiaconia was born out of an amalgamation of international associations for interior missions and diaconal works, later known as the European Association of Diaconia and from the West European network of Eurodiaconia dating from 1992. This amalgamation took place in 1996. Eurodiaconia has an office in Brussels and has set itself the targets of improving the quality of life for all people in a socially structured Europe, to connect and strengthen co-operation between diaconal institutions, social initiatives and churches and to be a competence network and to help others in their work.

http://www.eurodiaconia.org
(Accessed on 27. October 2003)

The European Contact Group

The European Contact Group is an ecumenical network in 25 European countries. The aims of the network are the development and support of strategies against unemployment and social exclusion, against racism and

discrimination, to help in the setting up of community work and to show commitment to change in church and society. The starting point in the activities of the ECG is the people on the spot, their strengths, their concerns and problems. The contact group, together with their partners, organises seminars, workshops and educational events, supports studies in the fields of theology and spirituality, promotes socio-ethical criticism of social and economic policies and engages in the development of civil society and the renewal of the Ecumenical Church.
http://www.ecg.ecn.cz/
(Accessed 27. October 2003)

First Ecumenical General Assembly in Basel: "Peace in Justice" (1989)

The European Economical Meeting entitled "Peace in Justice" took place in Basel from 15 to 21 of May 1989. The decision to hold the meeting was taken at the CEC general assembly in 1986. About 700 delegates from the 120 member churches of the Conference of European Churches (CEC) and the 27 Bishops' Conferences of the Council of Europe Bishops' Conference (CCEE) came together and documented the great interest of the churches and peoples of Europe in an ecumenical dialogue. The ecumenical assembly in Basel has proven to be an important milestone in ecumenical co-operation. It was still subject to the reality of a geographically divided Europe and stood for reconciliation and the dialogue between the Eastern and Western blocks.

This painful division is also apparent in many parts of the closing document of the ecumenical assembly. The European unification process that was taking place was taken up willingly by the ecumenical assembly as a chance to secure peace and to stand up for reconciliation in spite of the political trenches and geographical borders.

The metaphor of the "common house of Europe" was chosen as a point of reference in chapter five of the closing document, in order to point out the common culture and basic values, but also to point out the bad state of affairs and the responsibilities that characterise living together in a "common house".

"Living in a shared house means shared responsibilities. The situation in some areas must not be permitted to deteriorate, while others enjoy luxury. (...) In this European house, the inhabitants must do something to fight the gap between the poor and the rich in Europe, against the tear between the North and South on this continent, against the discriminatory treatment of non-citizens, against the injustice of mass unemployment, against the neglect of youth and leaving the elderly to fend for themselves. Our daily bread should be shared out fairly amongst us all."
(ch. 5, fig. 66 + 68)
http://oikoumene.net/home/regional/basel/basel.1/
(Accessed 12. November 2003)

Second Ecumenical General Assembly in Graz: "Reconciliation – Gift from God and a Source of New Life" (1997)

700 delegates and church leaders from over 150 churches and more than 10.000 people from many different traditional backgrounds took part in the second ecumenical assembly from 23 to 29 of June 1997 in Graz. Men and women of all generations, from many European churches, from East and West, from North and South, representatives of other religions and guests from other parts of the world came together in Graz. Although the Cold War had already been overcome and political freedom and democracy had become a palpable reality in many regions of Europe, the new violent disagreements in Europe had badly shaken belief in the possibility of living together peacefully.

The closing document of the second ecumenical assembly pointed to the chasms that still exist between people and between sisters and brothers of Christian belief, in spite of the political convergence. The document recognises the differences in culture and traditions and confirms them as an expression of the wealth and liveliness of the European continent.

At the same time, the ecumenical assembly points out in its declaration *The Christian Witness for Reconciliation*, the contradictions and challenges that need to be overcome in a Europe that has been divided for several decades. Knowledge of and worry about this gap that seems to be a characteristic of European consciousness and a European reality, shapes the thoughts of reconciliation and is mirrored in the documents of the ecumenical assembly.

In addition to this, the second ecumenical assembly takes up a position on questions of exclusion and poverty in Europe in its closing message. Although chances might occur as part of the globalisation process, the text stresses that "people could become victims of economic interests and decisions, which are outside their control. The gap between rich and poor is widening, not only in other parts of the world, but also in many parts of Europe. Inconsiderate exploitation of non-renewable resources, environmental pollution and the destruction of ecosystems cause immeasurable damage and threaten the health of future generations and the whole of creation." (fig. 7)

The second ecumenical assembly sets out a whole list of concrete suggestions in its closing document, the redemption of which, six years later, has lost none of its urgency.

"We recommend that churches set up processes of consultation on economic and social questions. They should contribute to human rights having a part to play in economic life (...) we recommend that the churches stand up for just and human migration policies especially for war refugees and asylum seekers. The humanitarian standards based on human rights must be adhered to and further developed in national legislation and international agreements. (...) We recommend that the churches fight discrimination against women at all levels and with all means at their disposal and to look for ways to bring more justice to women, especially by overcoming sexist practices in economic and public life. (...) We recommend that the churches intensify measures for the protection and promotion of the family and address the special situation of the young and old. (...) We recommend that churches take part intensively in the debate on European political development processes to create tools for working together and to strengthen existing institutions."
(ch. 3, fig. 3.1-3.4, ch. 4, fig. 4.1)
http://oikoumene.net/home/regional/graz/graz.hand.3/index.html
(Accessed 12. November 2003)

The European Diaconal Forum in Järvenpää / Finnland, 26-29 September 2001

In October 1994, The Conference of European Churches agreed on the Bratislava Declaration, which mapped out a vision for a European diaconia, but certain steps were necessary to implement this vision. At the centre of the considerations stood a European forum, a round table to support and promote the exchange of experience, thorough analyses of spiritual dialogue and networking. These requirements formed the framework for the group preparing the forum in Järvenpää and was made up of members of the Conference of European Churches, Eurodiaconia, the European Contact Group for Municipal and Industrial Missions and the Commission on Migration (CCME).

More than 110 participants of diaconal organisations and churches from 26 European countries came together in Järvenpää from 26 to 29 of September 2001 for the European Diaconal Forum. The forum had set itself four targets: exchange of experience, analysis of the new challenges, intensification of theological reflection and the formulation of new strategies and visions. These targets were reflected by the following topics which were chosen to denote each day of the forum:

Analysis of the European challenges, theological reflection, new visions for diaconal strategies, diaconal institutions and political challenges. These topics were discussed in working groups which considered the value of work and employment, migration and mobility in the new Europe, the setting up of sustainable communities and the search for quality of life.

Three plenary assemblies dealt with horizontal questions which recurred in the work group discussions: Diaconal theology – diaconal institutions and civil society – diaconia and the political challenges. The follow-up process of the forum was not supposed to consist of a further declaration like the Bratislava one, nor was it supposed to consist of a follow-up conference, but rather of further concrete steps. Conclusions from these comprehensive and many-levelled discussions have resulted in the following; that the diaconia, the role of the diaconal office in the church and the theological socio-ethical basis of diaconal work were at the centre of many discussions; furthermore that the suggestions that a European

Diaconal Academy should be set up together with a network structure were widely accepted, as was the concept of "representative participation" (quote President Jürgen Gohde) that strives to encourage fruitful discussion between various social cultures and diaconal concepts. It remains to be seen which work steps are necessary to realise the Järvenpää forum results.
http://www.cec-kek.org/English/diaconalforum.htm
(Accessed 12. November 2003)

Future Prospects

The commitment of churches and diaconal institutions in the European context is manifold and heterogeneous, as this small selection shows. This picture of church and diaconal activities shows the independence and the great range of topics which church and diaconal commitment are involved in. But the result of this is that opinion forming processes often take a long time and are complicated. Coming to a consensus, representing positions that have been previously agreed on and common procedures create difficulties. The EKD Memorandum (1991) "Responsibility for a Social Europe" points out that "the work of the churches on a European level can be extended and is in need of extension; if there isn't a further strengthening of these initiatives and institutions, if there isn't intensive common opinion building of the churches, if there isn't a stronger presence of the churches in Brussels and Strasbourg, it will not be possible for the churches to fulfil their tasks of shared responsibility and formation in Europe at the necessary level. Their voice will hardly be heard, and their views will not be considered in important anthropological and socio-ethical questions on the formation of Europe. This would be a great loss for Europe. European politicians point this question out with justification and draw attention to important tasks for the churches." (p. 30)

This statement is as true today as it ever was. If churches and diaconia want to use some of the participation possibilities within the institutional European framework, for example the open methods of co-ordination as described in the different contributions to this compendium, then they must, as well as strengthening the already existing representations of church and diaconia, also focus on the inner church and inner diaconal communication and co-operation structures.

Our creativity, our potential for innovation and our will to start up processes of change are needed here, so that church and diaconia can present themselves as a "best practice model" for participation and co-operation.

"To give Europe a soul" in this area of conflict as illustrated here, means working inwards and outwards.

It is our task to make Europe continuously present in our daily work, to tie in our social services with European co-operation, to make legislative and financial bodies think about European developments, to include them in our work-planning and to support and promote networking with other services, institutions, initiatives and organisation of civil society, so that a European community with solidarity and justice can become reality.

Annotation

1 "The Union has today set itself a new strategic aim for the coming decade: the aim is to make the Union the most competitive and most dynamic knowledge based economic area in the world – an economic area that is capable of achieving sustainable economic growth with more and better workplaces and greater social solidarity." (conclusion of the chairman of the European Council. Lisbon 23 and 24 March 2000 – http://ue.eu.int/newsroom)

References

Beck, Ulrich (1986): Risikogesellschaft, Auf dem Weg in eine andere Moderne, [Risk Society: Towards a New Modernity] Frankfurt a. M.
Belitz, Wolfgang (1997): Armut und Reichtum, [Poverty and Wealth] in: Huhn, Martin / Segbers, Franz / Sohn, Walter (Hg.), Gerechtigkeit ist unteilbar – Beiträge zum Wirtschafts- und Sozialwort der Kirchen, [Justice cannot be divided – Contributions on the Churches' Comments on the Economic and Social Order in Germany] Bochum, S. 91-96.

Bourdieu, Pierre (Hg.) (1997): Das Elend der Welt, Zeugnisse und Diagnosen des alltäglichen Leidens an der Gesellschaft, [The Weight of the World, Social Suffering in Contemporary Society] Konstanz.

"Bratislava-Erklärung – Auf dem Weg zu einer Vision von Diakonie in Europa. Eine Einladung zur Teilnahme an dem Prozeß des Handelns und Nachdenkens" (1997), [Towards a Vision of Diakonie in Europe. An Invitation to participate in the Process of Action and Reflection] in: Strohm, Theodor (Hg.), Diakonie in Europa, Ein internationaler und ökumenischer Forschungsaustausch, [Diakonie in Europe, An International and Ecumenical Research Exchange] Heidelberg, S. 510-515.

Denkschrift der Kammer der Evangelischen Kirche für Soziale Ordnung (1991): Verantwortung für ein soziales Europa: Herausforderungen einer verantwortlichen sozialen Ordnung im Horizont des europäischen Einigungsprozesses, [Responsibility for a Social Europe: Challenges for a responsible social order as part of the European integration process] Gütersloh.

Ebach, Jürgen (1998): Lauthals für Gerechtigkeit, [For Justice on the the Top your Voice] in: Ebach, Jürgen, Weil das, was ist, nicht alles ist, [Because what there is, is not everything] Theologische Reden 4, [Theological Speeches 4] Bochum, S. 186-205.

Ebach, Jürgen (1998): Gott ist gerecht, und Gott macht gerecht, [God is righteous and God creates righteousness] in: Ebach, Jürgen, Weil das, was ist, nicht alles ist, [Because what there is, is not everything] Theologische Reden 4, [Theological Speeches 4] Bochum, S. 206-225.

Evangelische Denkschrift (^{3}1998): Herz und Mund und Tat und Leben: Grundlagen, Aufgaben und Zukunftsperspektiven der Diakonie, [Heart and Mouth and Action and Life: Foundations, Tasks and Perspectives of the Diakonie] Gütersloh.

Gohde, Jürgen (1999): Solidarität und Solidität, [Solidarity and Solidity] in: Gohde, Jürgen (Hg.), Diakonie Jahrbuch 1999 – Solidarität und Solidität, [Year Book of the Diakonie 1999 – Solidarity and Solidity] Reutlingen, S. 13-32.

Hanesch, Walter (2001): Armut und Armutspolitik, [Poverty and Politics on Poverty] in: Otto, Hans-Uwe / Thiersch, Hans (Hg.), Handbuch Sozialarbeit Sozialpädagogik, [Handbook on Social Work Social Education] Neuwied, S. 81-90.

Katterle, Siegfried (1989): Alternativen zur Neoliberalen Wende, Wirtschaftspolitik in der sozialstaatlichen Demokratie, [Alternatives to the Neo-Liberal Turn, Economic Policy in a Social Welfare Democracy] Bochum.

Kirchenamt der Evangelischen Kirche in Deutschland und Sekretariat der Deutschen Bischofskonferenz (Hg.) (1997): Für eine Zukunft in Solidarität und Gerechtigkeit, [For a Future in Solidarity and Justice] Wort des Rates der Evangelischen Kirche in Deutschland und der Deutschen Bischofskonferenz zur wirtschaftlichen und sozialen Lage in Deutschland.

Sachße, Christoph / Tennstedt, Florian (1980): Geschichte der Armenfürsorge in Deutschland, Vom Spätmittelalter bis zum ersten Weltkrieg, [A History of Care for the Poor from Late Medieval Times to the Great War] Stuttgart et al.

Strohm, Theodor (2000): Diakonie als Dienst der Versöhnung, [Diakonie as Reconciling Service] in: Gohde, Jürgen (Hg.), Diakonie Jahrbuch 2000 – Europa, [Yearbook of the Diakonie 2000 – Europe] Reutlingen, S. 87-95.

Tobias, Gertrud / Boettner, Johannes (Hg.) (1992): Von der Hand in den Mund. Armut und Armutsbewältigung in einer deutschen Großstadt, [To Live from Hand to Mouth. Poverty and Overcoming Poverty in a German City] Essen.

Jürgen Boeckh

Poverty in Middle and Eastern Europe, or: Can the Eastward enlargement of the European Union be organized on an economic *and* social basis?

For the European states, the start of the new millennium has been marked by far-reaching economic, political and social changes which began in the former USSR at the end of the 1980s, and in quick succession led to the collapse of the entire former Soviet Socialist Eastern Bloc.[1] At the same time, this collapse has been accompanied by (re-)integrations (cf. Menzel 1998). Particularly for some of the Central European states, there is a chance that, following the end of Soviet rule, a historical wheel will have turned full circle. For with its consent to the declarations of accession by the Central Europeans Estonia, Latvia, Lithuania, Poland, Slovenia, Slovakia, the Czech Republic, Hungary (as well as Malta and Cyprus) on 9 April 2003, the European Parliament paved the way for the largest enlargement round of the European Union. At the same time, it marked a "turning point in our history", as the Polish President Aleksander Kwasniewski expressed a few days later at a meeting of the heads of state and government of the European Union in Athens, even if this enlargement marks the close of a "very difficult and bloody chapter" of European history, as the Czech Prime Minister Vladimir Spidla put it (quoted from the Frankfurter Rundschau of 17/18.04.2003). Though the EU heads of state and the former accession candidates and now members emphasized the historical dimension of this decision *unisono* after the ratification of the accession treaties on 16 April 2003, the economic, political and social problems of the eastward enlargement will remain on the political agenda for a long time. Not only procedural issues concerning the effectiveness of the future political institutions of the EU, but above all social issues are likely to turn the EU enlargement into quite a fragile and strained process.

A definition of the positions, as analyzed and anticipated in (socio-)scientific research of these processes of state and social fragmentation along with a reorientation within the framework of Europeanization and globalization, is of more than academic interest in theoretical construction of post-socialist transformation processes. Then the fundamental awareness required for the shaping of the future political, economic and social conditions in the transformation countries becomes apparent, and consequently which repercussions are to be anticipated for the West European states. What then are the focal points of the studies; to what extent do the *scientific* and thus also the *political community* bring the economic and social processes into proportion in this historical phase of the reconstitution of Europe?

Some Transformation-Theoretical Explanation Attempts in the Post-Socialist Era

With the fall of the autocratic-dictatorial systems of South(East)ern Europe (Portugal, Spain and Greece) in the mid 1970s, a scientific and political debate concerning the development paths of formerly antidemocratic systems got going. This debate has risen from the academic shadows in the last ten years as a result of the dynamics and, above all, the scale of the system change in (Central) Eastern Europe (cf. Beyme²1996). In Germany, the observation of transformation processes first (re-)emerged spontaneously as mainly empirical accompanying research of the political and social change taking place in East Germany. Besides approaches which undertake to measure the speed and success, or rather the durability, of institutional, organisational and personal adjustment to mostly western role models, this research has generally consisted of investigations which perceive the transformations as largely open-ended processes. These descriptive analyses aim more directly at the naming of factors, participants and institutions which, as a link between controlled and autonomous processes, determine the development of political restructuring (cf. Reißig 1998). Since the end of the 1990s, discussion has been increasingly defined by concepts which combine empirical or historical explanations of how the change of system took place, with methods of measuring the durability and quality of achieved (democratic) changes, thus integrating the protagonist and institution level (*consolidation research*) (cf. Merkel 1999). To evaluate the fundamental issue, *what* is to be understood by *democracy*, this *mainstream* has come to an understanding based on a definition of democracy borrowed primarily from American tradition as a process of "checks and balances" (Joseph Schumpeter, Robert Dahl). So democracy is not understood as an institutional means to fulfil a social target situation, but rather as a method of preventing any type of autocratic lapse – including the dictatorship of the majority in democratic systems. In this way, the flow of transformation research is fixed on the description of preconditions, opportunities and modalities of more or less regulatory retreats from an authoritarian regime toward democracy. An over-emphasis of liberal civil rights or an analysis based on "input-oriented legitimization arguments", leaves the system-stabilising functions or legitimizing mechanisms of an "output-oriented" viewpoint underexposed (Scharpf 1999). Thus, in the transformation-theoretical standard variations, the discussion about *why* political processes – depending on the achieved material and non-material participation level of the individuals – can attain dynamics which can fundamentally question the acceptance of newly-gained liberal levels of freedom remains superficial. Particularly for post-socialist societies with many years' experience of collectivist-welfare state supply and pronounced social polarization, however, the ability to produce a "system of material opportunities which can be described as fair" by means of economic and socio-political interventions is one of the prime legitimization sources of the political system (Offe 1994). More recent works in the field of transformation research therefore clearly underline the protection of formal civil liberties and the interaction conditions of civil-societal organizations. The safeguarding of *non-material participation*, understood as a comprehensive guarantee of civil rights (to co-determination) and civil liberties is rightly, according to the understanding of West European states, an important determinant for a liberal political system. This view also finds expression in practical politics, for example in the formulation of the Copenhagen criteria of the European Union for the assessment of the democratic capability of the Central European accession candidates required for the eastward enlargement of the EU. This criteria model is used to examine to what extent the Central European states have already implemented political and institutional changes and established a functioning market economy. These criteria also include the guarantee of democratic structures and rule of law as well as the protection of minorities and the acceptance of human rights. The adoption of the *"acquis communautaire"* still requires the recognition of the rights, duties and objectives of the European Union, including the implementation of economic and monetary union and support of the reform process for the creation of political union in the common Europe (cf. Benz, Boeckh, Huster 2000: 113). The European Union has thus laid important cornerstones in the political development of these countries, which will favour the emergence and consolidation of democratic structures. It is to be expected that the attractive prospect of inclusion into the European economic zone will continue to have a disciplining effect on the democratisation process of accession candidates, especially since the formal criteria have so far represented real touchstones for the accession petitions (cf. European Commission (publisher) 2001).

On the other hand, the fixing of such criteria catalogues frequently leads to the omission of a thorough debate concerning socio-economic change as a material substrate of the political changes. However, if one considers the issue whilst largely ignoring *how* the *material participation* in a society or a political system or in a political domain can be guaranteed, the consequence is an omission of any debate concerning the second column on which the (democratic) community rests. For political legitimacy is also a question of how the material sharing is put into practice. A perspective which inadequately reflects this connection runs the risk of drawing premature conclusions, because social balances of power and interest constellations, their ability to deal with conflict and their power of articulation remain unexposed. In this way, transformation societies are subliminally split into two camps. On one side are those who want to participate in the new system and devise the political, economic and social rules of the game of the post-socialist phase. This "visible side" of a system change is primarily the study target of system- and participant-theoretical examination patterns in the scientific mainstream. The group of people who cannot fulfil their chances at non-material participation, and thus in the long-term also see their material participation opportunities questioned, form the "invisible side" of the post-socialist society. As a rule, they receive attention only when they – for example through their voting behaviour – openly display an antidemocratic pattern of behaviour. However, this omits an analysis of the type and extent of the social risks in transformation societies. The contexts of determination as to *why* individuals with certain (weak) social interests remain excluded from the new system and *what*, under consideration of stability-theoretical aspects, the consequences of such a development for the political and social system overall can be, are thus analyzed only peripherally. Socio-political questions are reduced to the associated implications in the implementation of economic reforms; the need for reforms within the social protection systems is barely mentioned; the democracy-stabilising function of the welfare state and its socio-political bodies are also dismissed to the subordinate clause.

Yet it is clear that in Central Europe, as in the entire post-socialist transformation zone, a "stabilisation of the liberal-democratic political regime and its constitutional order can only be expected if, *simultaneously* with democracy and capitalism, far-reaching social safeguards are institutionalised which extend far beyond the level of protection and redistribution achieved in comparable West European cases at the corresponding point in their development as that of the East European countries today." (Offe 1994: 93). The welfare state thus becomes a constitutional precondition for democratic development. This has far-reaching consequences not only for scientific analysis and evaluation of the system change regarding the consolidation level achieved (cf. Götting 1998: 17; cf. Götting, Lessenich 1998: 274). If eastward enlargement is not to be interpreted primarily as an economic project to extend the West European zone of influence, but as a socially-structured system of peace, then it acquires a practical political significance in the socio-political modelling of eastward enlargement, even at the level of EU policy. A purely economic integration will not lead to a durable, socially pacified integration. The rate of socio-economic decline in the new union is too steep for this; plus the expectations of the people in Central Europe of a provider state are still too high after more than fifty years of being provided for by a paternalistic state under socialism.

Moreover, their experience so far with the new political and economic freedoms have left divided societies, in which the winners and losers of the transformation largely stand directly opposite each other. The "equality in poverty" (T. Jarygina) during Soviet socialism has increasingly given way to differentiated social strata with hard social contrasts.

Poverty and Social Exclusion in Central and Eastern Europe

Since May 2004 not only live 450 million people in the European Union, thus forming a huge economic zone, but at the same time, the social and material differences between the individual member states and within their regions are larger then ever before in the history of the European Union. This development present the socio-political complacency of the EU with entirely new challenges. One of the major shaping issues is to what extent socio-political distribution policy can remain within the jurisdiction of the nation states. Can the "European non-welfare state", which bases its integration strategy on the implementation of economic and civil rights, and thus since the end of the Second World War not only lay the foundation stone for a stable European order of peace, but also for a notable level of welfare (Schmid ²2002: 60 f.), be retained? And does the previous "*Differentiation of socio-political responsibilities at the European and nation state level*" suffice in order to continue to guarantee mainly the workers in and through the European Union "a protective function (...) from the effects of globalization" (Kaufmann 1997: 133 f.)? Then the question arises whether the inevitable globalization accompanying the massive enlargement of the European Union, which has now been approved, will not only offer growth opportunities, but also the negative effects of increasing national loss of control, to our own front door. The common economic and monetary zone of the European Union already exerts considerable pressure on the scope of national social policies in its member countries; with the result that social policy is increasingly becoming competition policy (cf. Boeckh, Huster 1998). However, there is nothing to be said *per se* against the sensibility or even historical logic of an enlargement of the European Union. Yet it does point to the urgent necessity of a redefinition of social policy as an instrument for shaping both the enlargement and the consolidation the European Union. For whilst attention is turned outwards toward the undisputed historical chance of a new order in Europe, the integrative power of internal European social policy may too quickly be ignored. This will become highly significant for the stability of the European Union, especially if the social gulf in Europe grows in the long-term, and what belongs together in the European model does not grow together! The social problems of the European Union are already evident. This led to the Method of Open Coordination at the European summit in Nice in December 2000, in which a series of common goals were adopted in the fight against poverty and social exclusion, and thus to a new attempt to lend the economic union of Europe new social legitimacy. In its report on social integration (*Joint Report),* the European Commission recognizes the main danger as social exclusion in the sudden structural changes taking place on the job market, brought about by "rapid economic change and globalization" and the "spread of the knowledge-based society and of information and communication technologies" (European Commission 2002: 7). If however, the comparably highly-developed "old" members of the European Union are already experiencing difficulties in adapting to these conditions, how much more toilsome is the process for the new member states?

General Economic Situation

It is the Central European states, in particular, who had taken their place in the waiting room of the European Union, which can now look back at the (relatively) best macroeconomic developments with relation to the entire post-socialist transformation region. Accordingly, in its annual reports on the progress of the former accession candidates, the European Commission records stable, in some cases above EU-average, growth rates of the real gross domestic products (GDP) throughout, with the exception of Romania. Mainly Hungary, but also Estonia, Latvia to a lesser extent, Poland and Slovenia appear to have steered themselves onto a stable economic path to growth (cf. European Commission (publisher) 2002a). However, two factors must not be overlooked in this observation. Firstly, to this day only Poland has succeeded in significantly overcoming the massive production slumps since 1989. Compared to 1989 (index = 100), the real GDP growth there in 2001 was 129.1; in contrast, Hungary achieved only 108.9, and in the Baltic States the values vary between Lithuania with 67.5 and Estonia with 86.7. The massive production losses at the beginning of the economic system change are still having a distinct effect (cf. UNICEF 2002). Secondly, this means that the gap between the new and the old mem-ber states of the EU remains huge. Even if a more converging trend is becoming apparent, the successes of the economic adaptation strategies are only taking effect very slowly. So far they have failed to significantly narrow the economic gulf between East and West. Thus in 2001, Romania achieved only 25 per cent of the EU average, with an average GDP per capita measured in purchasing power parity. Even Hungary (51 per cent) and Poland (40 per cent) lag significantly behind the average welfare production of the old EU member states. Nevertheless it would appear that the willingness of the people in the transformation countries to make personal material sacrifices is gradually waning, in view of a future macroeconomic stabilization. The European Commission records in its development report for Hungary that, following the structural reforms of the previous years, the government has seen itself forced since the year 2000 to push through an economic policy which aims at "a direct improvement of the living standard through wage and pension increases and the extension of the public infrastructure" (cf. European Commission (publisher) 2002a: 37). This means, therefore, that higher budget deficits must be accepted, which in turn can be problematic with regard to European integration.

The situation in the states of the former Yugoslavia is developing in a particularly grave way. The region is altogether a very heterogeneous entity, with only Croatia showing positive development tendencies. All in all, the region is characterized by limited economic strength. The whole region of Southeast Europe, which corresponds approximately with Romania in surface area and population, yielded a GDP of approximately 40 million EUR in the year 2000. The per capita GDP develops at varying rates and lies between 1,300 EUR in Albania and 4,500 EUR in Croatia. Even if to a varying extent, the whole region suffers from a combination of destabilizing factors. The main structural development problems named by the European Commission in its first annual report concerning the stabilization and association process of 2002 are extensive underground activities, corruption and organized crime, rising unemployment figures, the moving away of young well-qualified workers, and an undermining of the social cohesion caused by massive poverty and social discrimination. For example, in Albania, one fifth of the population lives on less than 1.20 EUR per day and is thus far below the absolute poverty line as defined by the World Bank. Even if the EU records in its report that the take-over of moderate governments in the region has led to a certain level of calm, the unstable constitutional systems, the inadequate pushing through of constitutional principles, weak administration and civil social structures remain the ideal humus for "extreme forms of nationalism" which can flare up again at any moment. All in all, according to the Commission, the countries of the region have a long road ahead of them "before they achieve EU standards in the stability of democracy and socio-economic development." (European Commission (publisher) 2002b: 6, 11).

Regional Disparities

Large regional disparities characterize the economic structures of the Central European states and thus precipitate a steep national decline in welfare. These unbalanced developments typify the entire post-socialist transformation zone. In Hungary for example, the per capita economic strength measured in purchasing power parity (PPP) in the central region around Budapest reached 76 per cent of the average EU value in the year 2001, whilst in the northern lowland plain only 32 per cent was attained. In Poland, which altogether achieves only 40 per cent of the per capita GDP of the EU average, it is mainly the eastern provinces that form the structurally weakest zones. Here, the per capita GDP lies almost 80 per cent below the national average. These extreme disparities in economic strength go hand in hand with corresponding disparities in job availability and income creation. At least, it is questionable whether the financial aid money granted to a limited degree by the EU within the framework of structural adjustment programmes will suffice to dismantle these structural disparities (cf. Jilková 1999; cf. Töpel 1999). The economic development support in the PHARE programme provided by the EU so far constitutes only a fraction of what is contributed in intra-community transfers for structural development in the old member states. This currently leads the Central European countries to the impression that the EU is already able to "fully realize" the advantages of integration, yet in the associated countries profound regional economic segregation effects and consequently unequal opportunities for the population to participate in a positive macroeconomic development manifest themselves. This results from the fact that the economic upturn will "concentrate regionally on just a few industry and service centres in Eastern Central Europe" (Weise et al. 1997: 17, 188). This is where the crucial disadvantage of a policy of conformity lies, which largely relies on the positive effects of private (foreign) investment. For, whilst public funds – under consideration of social interests – can also be employed selectively in structurally weak areas, profit-oriented private investors focus predominantly on regions which are already developed, since here the highest rates of return on capital can be realized with the lowest application of funds.

The Russian economy is of particular importance today, not least due to its sheer size. It is not only decisive for the living situation of some 150 million Russians, through its formerly close economic ties within the former Eastern Bloc, it also influences development in the entire transformation region. In the first years following the change of system, Russian industrial production practically went into freefall. Even in the raw materials sector, the drop in production was extraordinarily severe. Even if today signs of stabilization are beginning to show, the need to catch up will remain enormous for years to come, which at the same time makes Russia a very interesting market for export goods in the future. In 2001, the Russian Federation achieved a real gross domestic product of only 66.5 per cent of the level of 1989. Even under consideration of possible statistical distortions, this can only mean that the economic restructuring and recovery process in the Russian Federation must take place from a very low starting point. It is true that Russia today still represents – thanks to the enormous wealth of raw materials – the economically strongest and thus politically most important power within the CIS; at the same time, this poses an exceptional danger. In the exchange of raw materials for manufactured goods, the pattern of goods traded between the Russian Federation and the EU today resembles the typical pattern of trade between industrial and developing countries. At the same time, a large proportion of raw material profits are not transferred back to Russia, so that, all in all, a considerable impoverishment of the economy as a whole can be observed, with the consequence that urgently needed investment for renewal fails to materialize (cf. UNICEF 2002).

There are three development patterns in Eastern Europe. Whilst in particular the Central European states such as Poland, the Czech Republic, Slovenia, Hungary and Slovakia have steered onto an economic path of growth – albeit at the price of growing social exclusion – the countries rich in raw materials of the CIS can at least stabilize in the mid-term, whilst in the countries of Southeast Europe and the Caucasus new old poorhouses form in Europe.

Unemployment

With the need for restructuring and the ensuing economic crisis, high annual unemployment rates are to be expected. In fact, unemployment has risen in all transformation countries, in some of them considerably. According to the European Commission in 2001, for example, Lithuania officially reported an unemployment rate, especially in the rural areas, of up to 30 per cent. At the same time, the employment rate fell from 62.9 per cent in 1998 to 58.6 per cent in 2001 – and this although the country was able to achieve high GDP growth rates, with the exception of 1999. In Hungary, the country with the most favourable employment situation, considerable regional differences can also be observed. Whilst in the region around Budapest there is almost full employment, in Northern Hungary the official unemployment rate is relatively high at 8.5 per cent. Nevertheless in Hungary, as elsewhere, it is less the level of the unemployment figures than their structure which poses the real problems. Because long-term unemployment in particular presents a growing social problem. With the exception of Hungary and Romania, which show a (nevertheless high) ratio of long-term unemployed of just under 50 per cent of the total unemployed, the ten new EU member countries all lie significantly above the 50 per cent level. Obviously those excluded from the job market hardly stand a chance at successful reintegration (cf. European Commission (publisher) 2002a).

All in all, one can suppose that the actual scale of unemployment in all of the transformation countries of Eastern Europe is still being considerably underestimated. Firstly, it can be assumed that in numerous East European companies there is still a surplus of employees, which will drive the unemployment figures sky-high when a policy of company modernisation is rigorously pursued. Secondly, structural change will bring about further job losses, especially in the areas which are already structurally weak. And on the scale on which EU integration requires them to push ahead budget consolidation on the one hand and to continue the reorganization of large state-owned companies on the other, national governments find that their hands are tied, preventing them from granting public subsidies to make structural change more socially acceptable.

The development of unemployment amongst young people is unsteady. According to UNICEF, the unemployment rate amongst 15- to 24-year-olds in the year 2000 was considerably higher in some places than the respective overall rate. In Slovakia, Poland and Latvia, it is just over 30 per cent and in the Czech Republic it is 26.2 per cent (each referring to the average yearly total unemployment). In Hungary the rate is just under the 20 per cent level at 19.9 per cent, whilst in the Baltic States it is significantly below this level, at an average of 16 per cent. For UNICEF, this paints an overall depressing picture of the job market situation for young people (cf. UNICEF 2002). At the same time, however, one can also assume that young people in particular react quickly to new freedoms and increasingly seek their opportunities in underground or illegal market activities. Whilst this would mean that the material situation of the young people could turn out better than the unemployment statistics would have us believe, the consequence may also be that they are forced into (economic) crime. This can have both negative long-term effects for the standards and value structures of the new elites in developing civil societies, as well as intensifying the feeling of social exclusion felt by young people without perspectives.

Distribution of Income

Reduced industrial production and the growth of unemployment are accompanied by the loss of earning opportunities and sources of income. So it is no wonder that wherever figures concerning income distribution are available, one sees an increase in the disparity of income distribution. In the countries of Central and Southeast Europe, the Gini-coefficient of wages and income (as a measurement of unequal distribution between 0 and 1) has risen considerably since 1989. Obviously the change of system is leading to a modification in the ratio of winners to losers, measured by the status quo ante of income distribution. An income divergence may at first appear favourable from a market economy aspect, since this differentiation can be interpreted as a contribution to the improvement of incentive structures, compared to the formerly egalitarian distribution patterns.

Yet the Gini-coefficient signalizes only a growing or decreasing disparity. It does not tell us where exactly on the income pyramid this takes place. Compare the income positions of rich and poor households, and one will find that, in the entire transformation, region the gap between poor and rich is widening, albeit with greatly varying intensity in some places.[2] In 1989 the income of a rich person in Poland was still around three times that of a poor person; by 1999 this factor had increased to 4.3. In Hungary the disparity grew from 2.5 to 3 times as much and in Estonia from 3.2 to 4.5 times as much. Thus the divide between the economically strong and the economically weak households is constantly growing, even if the jumps are not nearly so sharp as, for example, in the Russian Federation, where disparity rose from a factor of 3.3 to 8.8 (UNICEF 2001: 27).

Altogether – with the exception of the Czech Republic – real incomes have sunk considerably in relation to 1989. Using the real wages of the year 1989 as an index of 100, by the year 2000 only the Czech Republic enjoyed a rise in real wages of 109.7. In contrast, all other Central European countries which are now members of the EU experienced drastic falls. The macroeconomic stability of growth countries such as Hungary (83.9), Slovenia (90.6), Lithuania (46.9) or Poland (98.6) has been paid for in previous years with sometimes massive real wage losses on the part of the workers. However, in most Central European countries, at least since 1995, an almost uninterrupted rise in the real wage can be observed. Yet even if, according to UNICEF, the theory is no longer tenable that it is mainly the countries which have pushed furthest the conversion to a free market economy which also show the largest wage disparities, at the same time it can be observed that particularly the low incomes[3] in these countries have massively increased. Whilst in the Czech Republic the proportion of people on a low income was only just above the OECD median of 14 per cent in 1999 at 16 per cent, in Poland it was 19 per cent, in Hungary 22 per cent and in Lithuania as many as 28 per cent of the people were on a low income. In Russia this portion is much higher again at 34 per cent, just as all of the successor states of the Soviet Union are experiencing an altogether deeper fall and a slower recovery (UNICEF 2001: 30).

These developments make it clear that it is mainly those segments of the population who are already disadvantaged who carry the main material adjustment burden of the upheaval; which can be reduced to the succinct formula that the poor will become poorer, and the rich will become richer. If one is to believe the projections of UNICEF concerning the development of distribution disparities, these tendencies will continue to become reinforced, at least mid-term, since the forecasts concerning the inequality of income and real net output compared with the global economy signalize a widening of the distribution gap for all East Europeans. In this way distribution schema develop, particularly for the successor states of the Soviet Union, which are typical for Latin American and South American newly industrializing countries. But also in the Central European states, the losers and the winners are growing progressively further apart. Macroeconomic improvements diffuse only very slowly via income distribution into the middle and lower income groups. At the same time, the danger is particularly high that small gains in welfare will be swallowed up by crises in economic development.

Poverty

Rising unemployment, growing income disparity and a lack of perspectives invariably lead to life situations generally referred to as *poverty*. Yet their emergence is by no means simply a consequence of the change of system, even if the former Soviet socialist states had not officially recognized this until well into the mid-1980s. Whilst the system of guaranteed employment, price subsidies and all-round social safeguarding provisions, such as free access to health and education, prevented crass appearances of poverty, it nevertheless failed to completely eradicate them as a phenomenon (cf. Ahlberg 1990).

As is evident from the studies carried out by UNICEF, there were some grave increases in the poverty rates in Eastern Europe in the years following 1989. However, collecting reliable, up-to-date empirical material is considerably difficult. Some methods of collection and statistical concepts for recording poverty differ considerably. Nevertheless, the UNICEF MONEE Project shows that in the Central European countries mainly children and young people are most commonly affected by poverty and that they have thus become one of the main poverty risks – besides the loss of employment. From the UNICEF background papers for the eighth report concerning the situation in the transformation countries of Eastern Europe a clear increase in the poverty figures can be observed for all household types in Poland between 1994 and 1998. Measured by the relative poverty line ("50% of average (equivalent) expenditure of households"), 4.1 per cent of the households without children were below this line in 1998, of the households with 2 children the number rose to 12.3 per cent, and in households with four or more children to 42.2 per cent (UNICEF 2001a: 25). Based on the absolute poverty line as defined by the World Bank (US $ 2.15 or 4.30 per person per day), 1.9 per cent of the children between 0-15 years in the Czech Republic were living on less than US $ 4.30 per day in 1996. In 1998, 2.0 per cent of Polish children were even living below the US $ 2.15 level and 30.7 per cent below the US $ 4.30 level! In Hungary the situation was almost identical in 1997 at 2.4 and 28.8 per cent. At the end of the 1990s, in the Czech Republic, Slovenia and Croatia less than 5 per cent of the children were living in absolute poverty; in Hungary, Poland and Bulgaria it was between 25 - 30 per cent, in the Baltic States and the Western CIS the figures were 30 - 50 per cent, in the Caucasus around 70 per cent and in the Central Asian Republics over 75 per cent (UNICEF 2001: 32).

This sudden mass impoverishment in Eastern Europe can be explained in the first phase of upheaval until around 1993 mainly by the massive drops in production, real wages and incomes. In a second phase, the rapidly growing income disparity was especially to blame. Deregulation, liberalization, privatization and increasing wage gaps are key words behind this development. However, not all people lose their source of income to the same extent. For the rapid development of wage disparity can be explained to a certain extent by considerable wage increases for highly qualified workers. Here, the emerging structural (poverty) problems are largely due to the fact that, during the change of system, jobs were, and will continue to be, lost in considerable numbers and, as with developments on the West European job market, it will be mainly the poorly qualified workers who must fear (long-term) unemployment and thus considerable losses in wealth; whilst highly-qualified workers in the growth industries can attain significant income growth. For the UNDP Regional Director, Anton Kruiderink, this development is a consequence of a too rapid and thorough abolishment of the state administration of the macroeconomy which could – along with the increasingly precarious social situation in the former Soviet socialist states – turn out to be the "greatest parting mistake of the millennium".

On the other hand, the Polish and Hungarian examples show that with a radical market policy over rising production, new scope for distribution can be created. However, their use must be legitimately and democratically discussed. For it can also be observed there that the market alone does not create balanced distribution currents.

Social Disintegration Trends

All in all, the socio-economic figures for Eastern Europe – independently from the chosen path of transformation – signalize so far a dangerous level of social exclusion and social polarization. Hardly a day goes by when the media do not print examples of a decompensating social situation in Eastern Europe. And as a rule, it is the most vulnerable in society who are exposed to the most extreme life risks. Children, the elderly and infirm, the homeless, ethnic minorities and other groups: the list goes on. Since 1989, UNICEF has been studying at regular intervals the change in living conditions in the Central and East European transformation societies. The social indicators chosen record changes in the field of income and its use, demographic factors such as marriage and divorce rates, death rates, health indicators, and information regarding social cohesion and the participation of children and young people in education. Even if generalized statements about the complex conditions in Central and Eastern Europe can only be made with great caution, socio-economic studies hitherto indicate only sporadic signs of an improvement in the living standards through the change of system – at least as far as the large majority is concerned. In contrast, new problems have emerged, which unfortunately point to an acceleration of the downward social spiral. Social and ethnic tensions, the re-emergence of diseases associated with poverty which had been considered eradicated, rapidly increasing drug abuse and the sex slavery of women and children are only spotlights on issues which will not disappear of necessity when economic growth improves. There is a danger that in certain transformation countries or regions socially disparate, politically unstable and criminal structures will establish themselves permanently (cf. UNICEF).

Visions for a Social Europe

Through the eastward enlargement of the EU, at least, some of the Central European states have become part of the community. But not only the new members, also the countries which have had to take their place in the EU waiting room or which do not want to join at all, have an effect on the EU European integration process, just as their own development will be determined by it. Besides direct social movements arising in the common house of Europe from migration, there are above all indirect movements which will increasingly determine the framework conditions of the actions of the national welfare state in the future. These indirect movements are clearest at the moment on the national job and finance markets, but also in the field of social policy. By introducing a uniform economic and monetary zone, the member states of the EU have given up the classic instruments of foreign trade policy. To achieve competitive advantages, they have come up with a wealth of different agreements and laws, which they have used for example to lower labour costs at the expense of the social safeguarding system (cf. Benz, Boeckh, Huster 2000).

The Central and East European transformation countries are not the cause of this process, yet they can certainly accelerate competition for lower social standards. Firstly, particularly border regions use low social, wage and environmental standards along with a relatively plentiful supply of qualified workers to attract foreign investors. At the same time, they themselves can push ahead, if at all then only cautiously, the enlargement of the social safeguarding system – which is urgently needed considering the social situation – to retain their locational advantages, which can have a destabilizing effect on domestic politics. And secondly, the loss of competition between the systems means that the capitalist system no longer needs to prove its superiority over the Soviet socialist system through a well extended welfare state, so that its economic justification is questioned much sooner. This *double transformation in Europe* has been bound firmly to a neoliberal economic reform, as if there had been no alternative. The consequence is a simultaneous economic and political transformation by no means just in Central and Eastern Europe, but also in the Western Europe of the European Union itself. Because there the objectives and implementation forms of the nation state have indiscernibly, but effectively, changed and thus intensified the dilemma poignantly characterized by Fritz W. Scharpf: "The capacities of the Union to fulfil its own policies have been reinforced not nearly as much as they have been reduced at the level of the member states." (Scharpf 1994: 220) Developed welfare states mutate to "competition states" (Heinze et al. 1999), slimming down in the area of dealing with social problems, yet very much gaining in significance in the area of reinforcement of major economic suppliers. However, important voices certainly have warned of the dangers of no longer dealing with political tasks appropriately in the interplay between now functionless nation states and a supranational level of action which was not equipped with sufficient competencies. Because an economic and monetary union (EMU) will "very probably only function if it is supplemented with a centralized fiscal system, as well as a system of unionwide public financial transfer. This requires (...) a political union. (...) Every monetary union which is not anchored in an evolved – in a tried and tested – political union threatens to break up sooner or later." (Lusser 1996: 192 f.) However, if an EMU between highly developed industrial countries requires such supporting measures, how much higher then will be the (socio)political need for action, considering the inclusion of the new Central European countries?

However, it would be missing the point to consider all the socio-political developments as damaging (social) dumping. Nevertheless, it remains in the logic of the European Union that these dumping races to secure supposed competitive advantages – at least in the ambits organized according to the subsidiarity principle – can take place at any time as long as there are no uniform minimum standards in place to prevent this. Considering how controversial the positions are, particularly in this point, total European harmonization would be very difficult to attain. Nevertheless, for this very reason the national minimum safeguard systems and their alignment are all the more imperative. Richard Hauser defended and urgently called for the necessity of national minimum standards and their development (cf. Hauser 1995). This demand has already been developed in models such as the "European Social Snake", which is supposed to assure common upper and lower limits for social standards in a defined adjustment procedure, besides other theoretical projections (cf. Kowalsky 1999).

In all this it must be remembered, however, that Europe is too broad a term to be operationalized implicitly. Whether or not one wishes to imagine EU-wide minimum safeguards: a demarcation must be drawn. But which political entity will step into the place of the former nation state and is it capable of mobilizing the form of solidarity required for the legitimization of massive socio-political redistribution procedures? There is no convincing answer to this question yet; solidarity can only be organized within borders, especially when – as in the case of the EU enlargement rounds – it is supposed to extend beyond borders. But what will become the criteria for Europe? The national interest of Western European states? Geography? An existing or required system of values? A constitutional system? The changes in Europe have put into question what hitherto existed, albeit in varying intensity, namely a "collective identity" (Habermas). In this respect, the actual upheaval in Europe has yet to take place and did not take place in 1989/1990.

What happens, however, if the current growth and EU enlargement strategy with its consequences of social exclusion is continued? The East European transformation countries will then very probably experience what the "newly industrializing countries" experienced and are still experiencing: namely, that despite high debts on the international financial markets, it is quite impossible to be promoted to the circle of the wealthy economic powers. But with that, the potential of the losers, those excluded from participating and those hindered in their ascent, massively reinforced in Western Europe through developments in the Eastern transformation countries. Social structures collapse which were essential for the hitherto wealthy societies. In this context, Bourdieu applies the term "structural violence" (Johan Galtung) and links this to the social segregation processes as a consequence of current policies. He comes to the following conclusion: "Violence never gets lost, the structural violence practised by financial markets, the compulsion for redundancies and the far-reaching uncertainty of personal circumstances hits back in the long term as suicide, delinquency, drug abuse, alcoholism, in all the small and large everyday acts of violence." (Bourdieu 1998: 49) Individual and social, national and outward conflicts detach themselves from the web of problems arising from the removal of national borders, and the fears and threats of social descent associated with them; and it always tends to be outsiders who ask about the connection between violence and social situation. Even this striking contradiction is seldom discussed publicly: how many of our financial resources are spent on forcibly solving social and/or international conflicts, and how many for solving the social problems that are the cause of these conflicts?

It becomes obvious: the question of the "European House" is always ruled by interests: at present, one cannot avoid the impression that the Western European states are doing much the same in Central Europe as what the Soviet Union asserted on its part after 1945, i.e. the formation of a *cordon sanitaire* of states which were sympathetic to, and in the end dependent on it. No concepts for solving the domestic political problems of the new members have been developed, and there are no visions of the total European architecture, not to mention attempts to seek a consensus with the remaining states. In particular the social structures in Europe are less certain and less clear than ever. Contrary to expectations, solid economic and social development processes in the West European part would have a stabilizing effect on the eastern transformation process, since the states of Western Europe themselves are currently undergoing an economic and political transformation process, the outcome of which appears uncertain. Rightwing populists in Austria, Italy, France, The Netherlands, Belgium and Denmark took advantage of this for electoral success after the end of the "social democratic decade" in Europe. And not least the current developments concerning the war of the USA and the Western community against Islamist terror illustrate that the material distribution structures which accompanied the "wave of democratization" (Samuel Huntington), have led to an unstable world-political situation. Thus the recognition that no peaceful coexistence is possible as long as there are people who literally have nothing to lose, also provides the deeper reason for a plea for an active socio-political shaping of European integration.

A Europe of transnational regions, interlinking rings and circles and the most varied paces along with commonly shared norms and fundamental values, which must also include social basic rights: this could be a model, on condition that it is developed, discussed openly and also understood as a chance for those currently standing in the shadows. Europe is not a homogeneous entity, nor a homogeneous political power and definitely considerably socially varied. But in this Europe, a great many countries in East and West have discovered that democracy requires social underpinning. Therefore this Europe can only be a democratic Europe if not only the cultural and political domain, but also the social domain is organized. This is not a contradiction to existing economic interests and concepts, but a necessary relativization.

Annotations

1 In the context of this essay, Central Europe mainly refers to the Central European new EU members. Southeast Europe encompasses the western Balkans (Albania, Bosnia, Herzegowina, Croatia, the Federal Republic of Yugoslavia and the former Yugoslav Republic of Macedonia). Eastern Europe descibes essentially the Community of Independent States (CIS) and here in particular the Russian Federation.
2 In its MONEE Project, UNICEF defines "a rich person as someone found 10 percent down from the top of the income distribution and

a poor person as someone 10 percent up from the bottom." (UNICEF 2001:27)

3 Low income recipients are defined here according to the OECD standard as: "employees with monthly earnings below two-thirds of the median." (UNICEF 2001:30)

References

Ahlberg, René (1990): Armut in der Sowjetunion [Poverty in the Soviet Union], in: Osteuropa, Heft 12, S. 1159-1174, Stuttgart

Biskup, Reinhold (Hg.) (^{2}1996): Globalisierung und Wettbewerb [Globalisation and competition], Bern et al.

Benz, Benjamin / Boeckh, Jürgen / Huster, Ernst-Ulrich (2000): Sozialraum Europa. Ökonomische und politische Transformation in Ost und West [Social Area Europe. Economical and political transformation in East and West], Opladen

Beyme, Klaus von (1994): Systemwechsel in Osteuropa [Transformation in Eastern Europe], Frankfurt a.M.

Beyme, Klaus von (^{2}1996): Ansätze zu einer Theorie der Transformation der ex-sozialistischen Länder Osteuropas [Attempts for a theory of transformation in the postcommunist countries of Eastern Europe], in: Merkel, Wolfgang (Hg.), Systemwechsel 1. Theorien, Ansätze und Konzepte der Transitionsforschung [Transformation 1. Theory, Attempts and Concepts of Transformation Studies], S. 141-172

Boeckh, Jürgen / Huster, Ernst-Ulrich (1998): Politische Steuerung des Arbeitsmarktes angesichts Europäisierung und Globalisierung [Political labour market policies in the scope of Europeanisation and Globalisation], in: Politische Vierteljahresschrift Heft 4, S. 845-858, Opladen

Boeckh, Jürgen (2003): Regionalisierung im Systemwechsel, Rahmenbedingungen dezentraler Sozialstaatlichkeit am Beispiel zweier nordrussischer Kommunen [Regionalisation in Transformation, Framework of decentralised social policy in case of two North-Russian communities], Opladen

Bourdieu, Pierre (1998): Gegenfeuer. Wortmeldungen im Dienste des Widerstands gegen die neoliberale Invasion [Counter Strike. Requests to speak in service for resistance against the neoliberal invasion], Konstanz

Döring, Diether / Hauser, Richard (Hg.) (1995): Soziale Sicherheit in Gefahr [Social security in Danger], Frankfurt a.M.
Europäische Kommission (Hg.) (2001): Die Erweiterung erfolgreich gestalten. Strategiepapier und Bericht der Europäischen Kommission über die Fortschritte jedes Bewerberlandes auf dem Weg zum Beitritt (SEK (2001) 1744 bis 1756) [To create enlargement sucessfully. European Commission strategy paper and report on the improvements of the candidate states], Brüssel
Europäische Kommission (Hg.) (2002): Mitteilung der Kommission an den Rat, das Europäische Parlament, den Wirtschafts- und Sozialausschuss und den Ausschuss der Regionen: Entwurf zum Bericht über die soziale Eingliederung: Teil I – Die Europäische Union [Commissions annoucement to the Council, the European Parliament, the Economic and Social Commitee and the Commitee of Regions: Draft Report on Social Inclusion: Part 1 – The European Union], o.O.
Europäische Kommission (Hg.) (2002a): Regelmäßige Berichte über die Fortschritte der Beitrittskandidaten auf dem Weg zum Beitritt [Periodical report on the improvement of candidate states], diverse Berichte vom 09.10.2002, Brüssel
Europäische Kommission (Hg.) (2002b): Der Stabilisierungs- und Assoziierungsprozess für Südosteuropa. Erster Jahresbericht [The process of stabilisation and association in South East Europe. First Annual Report], Brüssel
Frankfurter Rundschau (2003): Die EU besiegelt ihre Erweiterung [EU seals its enlargement], Ausgabe vom 17./18.04.2003, Frankfurt a.M.
Götting, Ulrike (1998): Transformation der Wohlfahrtsstaaten in Mittel- und Osteuropa. Eine Zwischenbilanz [Transformation of welfare states in Middle and Eastern Europe. A mid-term review], Opladen
Götting, Ulrike / Lessenich, Stephan (1998): Sphären sozialer Sicherheit. Wohlfahrtsstaatliche Regimeforschung und gesellschaftliche Transformation [Spheres of social security. Analysing welfare state regimes and social transformation], in: Lessenich, Stephan / Ostner, Ilona (Hg.), Welten des Wohlfahrtskapitalismus. Der Sozialstaat in vergleichender Perspektive [Worlds of welfare state capitalism. Social State in comparative perspective], S. 271-320
Habermas, Jürgen (1998): Die postnationale Konstellation und die Zukunft der Demokratie [The postnational constellation and the future of democracy], in: Blätter für deutsche und internationale Politik, Heft 7, S. 804ff.
Hauser, Richard (1995): Reformperspektiven des Systems der sozialen Sicherung bei veränderten Rahmenbedingungen [Changing frame-

work and perspectives of reform in the system of social security], in: Döring, Diether / Hauser, Richard (Hg.), S. 51ff.

Heinze, Rolf G. / Schmid, Josef / Strünck, Christoph (1999): Vom Wohlfahrtsstaat zum Wettbewerbsstaat. Arbeitsmarkt- und Sozialpolitik in den 90er Jahren [From welfare state to competition state. Labourmarket and social policies in the 90ies], Opladen

Huster, Ernst-Ulrich (1996): Armut in Europa [Poverty in Europe], Opladen

Huntington, Samuel P. (1991): The Third Wave: Democratization in the Late Twentieth Century, Norman

Jarygina, Tatjana (1994): Armut im reichen Rußland [Poverty in rich Russia], in: Osteuropa, Heft 12, S. 1146-1157

Jilková, Jiøina (1999): Osterweiterung der EU und die Rolle der Strukturfonds – Das Beispiel Tschechische Republik [The enlargement of the EU and the role of the Structural Funds – The case of the Czek Republik], in: WSI-Mitteilungen, S. 390-396

Kaufmann, Franz-Xaver (1997): Herausforderungen des Sozialstaates [Challenges on social state], Frankfurt a.M.

Kowalsky, Wolfgang (1999): Europäische Sozialpolitik – Ausgangsbedingungen, Antriebskräfte und Entwicklungspotentiale [European social policy – Initial situation, driving forces and developing potentials], Opladen

Lessenich, Stephan / Ostner, Ilona (Hg.) (1998): Welten des Wohlfahrtskapitalismus. Der Sozialstaat in vergleichender Perspektive [Worlds of welfare state capitalism. Social State in comparative perspective], Frankfurt a.M./New York

Lusser, Markus (^{2}1996): Nationale Geldpolitik zwischen Regionalisierungs- und Globalisierungstendenzen [National Monetary policy between regionalsational and globalisational tendencies], in: Biskup, Reinhold (Hg.), S. 184ff.

Menzel, Ulrich (1998): Globalisierung versus Fragmentierung [Globalisation versus fragmentation], Frankfurt a.M.

Merkel, Wolfgang (Hg.) (^{2}1996): Systemwechsel 1. Theorien, Ansätze und Konzepte der Transitionsforschung [Transformation 1. Theory, Attempts and Concepts of Transformation Studies], Opladen

Merkel, Wolfgang (1999): Systemtransformation [Transformation of political systems], Opladen

Offe, Claus (1994): Der Tunnel am Ende des Lichts: Erkundungen der politischen Transformation im neuen Osten [The tunel at the end of light: research on the political transformation in the new East], Frankfurt a.M./New York

Reißig, Rolf (1998): Transformationsforschung: Gewinne, Desiderate und Perspektiven [Research on transformation: Benefits, enquiries and perspectives], in: Politische Vierteljahresschrift, 39. Jg., Heft 2, S. 301-328

Scharpf, Fritz W. (1994): Optionen des Föderalismus in Deutschland und Europa [Options of federalism in Germany and Europe], Frankfurt a.M.

Scharpf, Fritz W. (1999): Regieren in Europa [Governance in Europe], Frankfurt a.M.

Schmid, Josef (^{2}2002): Wohlfahrtsstaaten im Vergleich [Welfare states in comparison], Opladen

Töpel, Kathleen (1999): Förderung der grenzüberschreitenden Zusammenarbeit an den Außengrenzen der Europäischen Union [Supporting cross-border cooperation at the EU external frontiers], in: DIW-Wochenbericht 33, http://www.diw.de

UNICEF (Hg.) (1999): Generation in Jeopardy. Children in Central and Eastern Europe and the former Soviet Union, New York

UNICEF (Hg.) (2001): A Decade of Transition. The MONEE Project. Regional Monitoring Report No. 8, Florenz

UNICEF (Hg.) (2001a): Trends and indicators on child and family well-being in Poland, Background paper prepared for the Regional Monitoring Report No. 8: A Decade of Transition (2001), Florenz

UNICEF (2002): Social Monitor 2002. The MONEE Project. Regional Monitoring Report No. 9, Florenz

Weise, Christian / Brücker, Herbert / Lodahl, Maria / Möbius, Uta / Schultz, Siegfried / Schumacher, Dieter / Trabold, Harald (1997): Ostmitteleuropa auf dem Weg in die EU – Transformation, Verflechtung, Reformbedarf [Middleeast Europe on the way into EU – Transformation, interweaving, reform necesseties], in: Deutsches Institut für Wirtschaftsforschung, Beiträge zur Strukturforschung, Heft 167-1997

Peter Pavlovic

The churches and the poverty in Central and Eastern Europe

Dealing with poverty is one of the central roles of the Church. This basic fact is also a part of the reality of church life in Central and Eastern Europe. The whole region currently faces a number of challenges, including poverty, which is becoming a problem of increasing importance. There are several reasons for this:

• *Transformation of society*
After the development of an egalitarian society, which characterised life under the previous regime, nowadays the situation in the region is marked by a rapidly deepening gap between the wealthy and the poor. It is not that there was no poverty in those countries before. The poor can be found at all times in every society. The new social order, however, brought less state control and interventions into the lives of the people. In the changed situation, it is no longer possible for people to rely on the role of the state in the way that they did before. This has a positive effect in that there is increasing awareness of the individual taking responsibility for how their own lives and those of their family are organised. On the other hand, the income of an individual and his/her family is not guaranteed any more by the state but is fully in his/her own hands.

• *Transformation of the economy*
Transformation of the economy has as an aim the improvement of the quality and quantity of production, which should consequently lead to improvement of the living standards of the population. This process has, however, an effect, not only on the material side of the economy, but also has human and social implications. Employment is not guaranteed by the state any more. One's job is in the hands of the individual. Unemployment as a new phenomenon goes hand in hand with an increase in poverty. In

most of the countries of Central and Eastern Europe, economic transformation is an aim which is still far from being fulfilled. It has an impact, which may be temporary but still significant, particularly on the weakest in society.

• *Transformation of the social systems, particularly pension schemes*
The old systems are not able to provide sufficient benefits in the new conditions which have been influenced by the transformation of the economy and also by the negative demographic development. A danger, often changing rapidly from a potential to a real one, is that elderly people, dependent on pension benefits, increasingly constitute a growing group which lives on the edge of poverty.

The task of summarising the attitudes and activities of churches which respond to the problem of poverty in the region, faces a number of difficulties. There are significant differences among countries of the region regarding economic and social indicators, as well as in the position and the role of the churches in the society of each country. The strong and far-reaching tradition of most of these churches in dealing with poverty, has been part of the common aspects of church life in the region, particularly before the 2nd World War, and was violently interrupted by the political regimes afterwards. After the War, churches were forbidden to be involved in one of their main activities, which is symptomatic for the Church: social work for the people and with the people. Under the new conditions, since the collapse of totalitarianism, churches have been trying hard to revitalise this part of their tradition as much as possible. In practical terms, these efforts were marked by building up the material and administrative structures of the churches and their diaconal institutions, as well as by the state restoring church property, which had been used for church social work in the past. In some countries this process has not yet been completed. The results of property restitution vary from country to country and depend on many conditions. The relationship between church and state is not the smallest of them. Church run social work still shows marks of transition.

The current situation is, however, characterised not only by the restoration of history. It is a mixture of tradition with the churches' response to challenges characteristic of modern and post-modern society. It mirrors the genuine mission of the Church under conditions strongly influenced by the transition of the economy and the whole of society in each country. Most of the churches in Central and Eastern Europe are, despite manifold internal difficulties, active in providing help of various kinds for those who suffer and need this help.

The information and facts described in the following do not aim to provide a comprehensive picture of the situation in Central and Eastern Europe. First of all, the scope of this text is limited to the description of those countries which stood at the door of accession to the European Union till May 2004. It would require much more space and analyses to include other Central and Eastern European countries, where life marked by poverty and social problems is a significantly more wide-spread reality than it is in the countries described.

Not all churches of the region are taken considered in this overview. Attention is limited to the churches which are linked to the Conference of European Churches.[1] Most of them are minority churches. Only Romania and Bulgaria in this group, are countries with a strong majority of Orthodox churches. All churches in Central and Eastern Europe have had to go through the period marked by economic difficulties experienced by the whole of society. In this situation, churches had to manage the basic task of self-organisation while looking for an identity in the new situation, which was marked by the magnificent effort, often connected with a lot of sacrifices, among the people within the church. Not all churches in the region fully incorporated social activities into their agenda and, in particular, work for the poor. Lack of capacity is the explanation most often given. Many, however, did. Their work with the poor is in most cases characterised as practical work which aims to alleviate the negative impacts of poverty and has the character of immediate help.

It is of utmost importance to note the social work, and especially the work with the poor, carried out by the minority churches of the region. Particularly the fact that, despite the given conditions, the activities of a number of the churches oriented towards society have been considered by them, not as something 'added' to their main mission, but as something fundamental, something that is an integral part of the existence of the church. The size of the church obviously determines the size of their social activities. However, one characteristic of a number of minority churches is that their social involvement is much bigger than would be expected purely on the basis of their membership numbers. The figures in the attached table can help to illustrate the religious affiliation of the population in the countries of our interest.

	Protestant[%]	Orthodox [%]	Roman Catholic +Uniat [%]	Non-religious [%]	Others [%]
Poland	0.4	1.4	78.0	9.7	10.5
Czech rep.	2.3	0.2	26.8	59.0	11.7
Slovakia	9.0	1.0	73.0	13.0	4.0
Hungary	20.7	0.3	60.3	7.0	11.7
Lithuania	1.3	4.9	68.1	23.6	2.1
Latvia	19.4	4.4	20.0	41.1	15.1
Estonia	14.1	3.5	0.3	60.4	21.7
Romania	6.0	70.0	9.0	1.0	14.0
Bulgaria	0.3	85.0	0.5	0.4	13.8
Slovenia	1.1	2.2	81.6	13.3	1.8

Tab.1: Church affiliation in the selected countries of Central and Eastern Europe.

Unfortunately, not all churches from the region have been ready to share information about their activities with the poor. The following description cannot therefore serve as a full summary with reference to all the existing work. It illustrates the general approach of the churches to the problem of poverty.

There are various ways in which poverty reveals its face. It is not possible to include all of them in a short article. Regarding the situation of Central and Eastern Europe, much more could be said about the links relating poverty to migration and trafficking of human beings, which are very specific problems of those countries,[2] as well as about the links of poverty to other specific features which drastically increase its impact, as, for example, for the disabled, elderly, and orphans etc. Much more could also be said about the activities which indirectly help to overcome the impacts of poverty and which deserve a specific description, e.g. education. All these are not the subject of this text. The situations in various countries and various churches differ. Regarding their involvement with social tasks, churches in the region have their own priorities depending on their own specific situation, traditions and their practical possibilities.

Poland

The starting point for church social work after the collapse of the previous political regime, differed from church to church. Soon after the political changeover, churches began to build new organisational structures for social care activities. Attention to poverty and the organisation of help for poor people was, from the start, very high on the priority list of those activities. In the Orthodox Church that activity was initially limited to youth programs (e.g. summer holidays for poor children). The church took over a few deserted schools from the local authorities, where it organised care and youth homes. This later developed into an organisational structure for the whole church, which supervises the charity work of the church. In the Evangelical Lutheran Church, commissions for diaconal work were created in every diocese, which later stimulated the development of practical diaconal work for the whole church and the organisation of Evangelical Diaconia. A Committee for Social Affairs, responsible for the social work of the church, was also created in the Evangelical Methodist Church.

Examples of activities

In the Orthodox Church:
- Social Care Homes and the Youth Home
- deliveries of cost-free equipment to the Social Care Homes and public hospitals
- centres of psychological pastoral counselling
- a scholarship program for talented students from pathological and poor families.

In the Evangelical-Methodist Church:
- summer camps for children from poor families
- collection and re-distribution of second-hand clothes in the "Surprise Christmas" project, which consists of delivering gifts to poor children.
- assistance to addicts and their families

In the Polish Catholic Church:
- support for congregations and medical centres with the "Medical Bridge for Poland" project.

In the Evangelical Lutheran Church:
- support for elderly people
- programs for children from poor families
- financial support for the unemployed
- offer of meaningful work for poor and unemployed people in exchange for lunch and second-hand clothes
- free medicine for those who need it and cannot afford it
- the rehabilitation and resocialisation centre for the socially excluded (long term unemployed, poor, alcoholics).

Long term strategy

One of the major problems of work with the poor, besides helping to provide basic needs, is to deal with the social consequences of poverty. Very often a lack of meaningful work and a life in poverty is related to lack of prospects, depression and alcoholism. This has been recognised as a strong challenge for the work of the churches. In the long term perspective, churches mainly recognise that they can be much more effective in their social work if they combine their resources and work on joint projects. Some examples of the existing co-operation between churches in some social projects (e.g. co-operation of the Lutheran, Orthodox and Roman Catholic churches) can be given. Work with the poor is characterised by increasing motivation at the congregational level. Improvement of the co-ordination and co-operation between various church centres, as well as work on church strategy, is the challenge for the future.

Relations with the state and municipal authorities

The relationship between churches and the state is considered by most of the churches as unsatisfactory. It is considered difficult for minority churches to influence the policy of the state. In spite of this, some churches make a continuous attempt to lobby state institutions for the sake of the poor. Those relations are, however, better at local than at central levels. Often it is possible to establish reasonable co-operation on social projects between churches and local authorities, in the framework of which the local authority provides the running costs of the project and the churches the know-how and the actual work. The size and effectiveness of such projects, however, often depends on personal contacts rather than on formal structures of mutual co-operation. The fact that the churches have not had all property owned before the War restored by the state, has an impact on the social work of the churches.

Vision

There is wide spread conviction that the churches in the country have a large spare potential, in particular in human resources, that can be engaged in social activity. Lack of financial resources is an obstacle to setting the activity in motion. There is especially much to do in the area of advocacy and individual activation of people in difficult situations. It is also recognised that more attention should be given to social problems in the church educational system. A substantial role for the churches in their work with the poor and unemployed is seen particularly in providing assistance in overcoming a spreading tendency to seek an easy escape from the problem of poverty in alcoholism.

Czech Republic

Before the War, churches in the country ran a number of shelters, orphanages and houses for the poor, as well as various programs helping the poor. New conditions did not enable the churches to renew this work on the same full scale as in the past. At present, the work concerning poverty aims mainly to focus on the unemployed and homeless. The work with the poor is in particular developed in the Silesian Evangelical Church of the Augsburg Confession. The church is located in the north-eastern corner of the country in a highly industrialised region stricken by economic transformation and restructuring. The region is characterised by a rapid increase of unemployment. The church is confronted with increasing direct or indirect requests to help the unemployed and to deal with secondary signs of unemployment. Poverty is the first of these. The church social work is organised by the Silesian Diaconia founded in 1990. Today the Diaconia runs 24 centres grouped in three thematic sections. Work for the poor and homeless are part of the basic activities of the Silesian Diaconia.

Examples of activities
- 5 centres for the unemployed and homeless
- collection and redistribution of second hand clothes
- relief help during the floods in 1997 and 2002 with particular attention for to the poor
- practical ad hoc help in the congregations
- organising of regular trips with material help, e.g. food, clothes and medicine, to southern and eastern European countries (Ukraine, Albania).

Relations with the state and municipal authorities
Church social work is accompanied by reasonable co-operation with the state authorities at the central as well as local levels.

Vision
The Silesian Lutheran Church is a very tiny minority church. The social work of the church is a significant part of its self-identity. Economic and social development in the region makes the connection between the Gospel and social involvement even stronger. Education for this work and the increase of volunteer activities for the poor in congregations are priorities for the days to come.

Slovakia

Caring for poor and needy people has also a long history in Slovakia and in the Protestant churches goes back to the pre-War period. After the political changeover, the new situation in society was mirrored by the churches by establishing the new diaconal organisations: Evangelical Diaconia in the Evangelical Lutheran Church and Philantropia in the Orthodox Church. Social services in the Reformed Christian Church as well as in other Protestant churches have been organised through the work of the church parishes and specialised church centres, e.g. for people with disabilities, orphans etc. Centrally organised work, which would focus on help in poverty, was particularly developed in the Philantropia of the Orthodox Church. Work with the poor in the Evangelical Lutheran Church has been done separately from the structures of the Evangelical Diaconia, on the congregational level. The situation in other Protestant churches is similar. The work with Roma people has had a particular importance in church activities with the poor. This is a special example of the existence of wide spread poverty and social exclusion.

Examples of activities
- providing food for the socially weak and food service with delivery for poor and immobile people – Philantropia at various places
- a shelter house for homeless – Philantropia
- congregational activities for helping the poor, which includes financial and material support
- organising meaningful work for the unemployed
- work with the Roma at the congregational level
- collections of food, clothes and medicine for poor in the countries of southern and eastern Europe

Relations with the state and municipal authorities
There is reasonably good co-operation between the churches and the state, which is also mirrored in organising the social work of the churches. Churches have been seen by the state as an important partner in providing social services. In a number of cases, projects run by the churches are

dependent on financial contributions from the state and/or local municipal authorities. Co-operation with local authorities is of particular importance. Transformation of the social and tax system in the country, which is currently underway, can be a challenge and will determine the form and content that the partnership between state and church will take in the future.

Education
Social work has become a part of the curriculum in theological faculties and other schools run by the churches. Several conferences and seminars have been organised in the churches and also at the ecumenical level. The Evangelical Theological Faculty published a book "Social problems in Lutheran theology" in 2001.

Vision
When providing social services in the country, the discourse gradually shifts from quantity of services to their quality. By offering their services in the social field, churches can be an even more important partner for the state than they were in the past.

Hungary

A significant network of church social institutions was already functioning in the period before the 2nd World War. Some of those institutions continued to be managed by the churches even in the post-War period, during communist rule. Today, Protestant churches in the country again run a developed network of social and diaconal centres and provide a number of social services. Demographic development in the country indicates that there is an extremely great need for institutions to take care of the elderly. In the current economic situation, elderly people fall into one of the first categories of society which have to face the challenge of poverty. Co-ordination of social work in the Protestant churches is managed through appropriate national structures at the level of synod commissions. Diaconal institutions are an important part of the structure of the

Protestant churches in the country. Independent local initiatives play an increasingly significant part within the complex system of social services provided by the churches.

Examples of the activities
- 21 old people's homes run by the Lutheran Church
- 52 varying institutions for those who suffer from poverty, social inequality and social exclusion (homes for elderly, the disabled, homeless, drug-addicts, alcoholics etc.) run by the Reformed Church
- social work with alcoholics
- social work with Roma people.

Relations with the state and municipal authorities
There is reasonable co-operation with the state on the national, regional and local levels. The state recognises the churches as an important contributor providing social services in the country. From the side of the churches, however, the complaint is made that the financial support allocated from the state budget for these services is more symbolic than efficient.

Education
In the Hungarian protestant churches, great attention is traditionally given to education. Training for social workers is provided by the churches at university, as well as at secondary school-level.

Documents
In the Reformed Church, the handbook on Christian social work was published in 1986 and is still the valid document regulating social work in the church.

Vision
The church social services are an important part of the social institutional network of the state. Churches are proud of it. Their growing importance has also increased the interest for social work at the congregational level.

Latvia

Although Latvia has achieved considerable results in the transition to the market economy since 1991, the country is still struggling with decreasing living standards and poverty in society. For the Evangelical Lutheran Church in Latvia, work with the poor is organised by the diaconia. There was no previous history or tradition of diaconia in the Lutheran church in Latvia. In 1994 the first training programs were initiated and in 1996 the first projects started. In order to support poor people, diaconia in Latvia have organised their work in the following directions:

A) preventive measures:
    – support groups;
    – day centres for specific risk groups and crisis centres.
B) practical aid and feeding of the poor
C) night shelters.

Examples of activities

- ten diaconia centres around Latvia: Each of them works with poor people in its own way: night shelters, children centres, soup kitchens, clothes stocks, possibility to wash clothes etc.
- help for poor people at the parish level
- three soup kitchens and one food distribution spot in the capital: The Evangelical Lutheran Church was one of the first in Riga and Latvia that opened soup kitchens. Diaconia soup kitchens serve in other parts of Latvia too. The feeding of the needy is necessary, moreover, it is an ever-increasing need.
- collection and distribution of clothes and footwear: All the regional diaconia centres and the biggest churches have clothes stocks
- spiritual and pastoral support for the poor, people in crises and difficulties
- street children are one of the crucial social problems in Latvia closely related to poverty. Street children and their parents are mostly from very poor families. The church project opened in 1998 "Day centre for street children" was the first of its kind in Latvia.

Long term strategy
Diminishing of the poverty problem in Riga is one of the main aims and plans for this kind of work. The church plans to continue helping poor and needy people by providing food and clothes. The church diaconia prepares the projects in which increased co-operation with the state government will be expected.

Relations with the state and municipal authorities
Although the church is trying to influence state policy, it still does not get acknowledgement and recognition for its work from government. However there is, in a number of cases, fruitful co-operation with the local and municipal authorities. The relationship with local authorities is usually much better in the countryside, because in a number of cases the church is the only organisation that does something about poverty. The municipality is, in these cases, ready to provide a property in order to establish some social activities.

Church documents
During recent years, a significant effort has been undertaken to make social work known to the members of the church and wider society. A number of books about diaconia have been published, focusing on spiritual and theological aspects as well as on practical help. The archbishop of the church sent out several letters to pastors motivating them to take part in activities and to popularise diaconia activities in helping needy people in the country.

Vision
The involvement of the church in poverty problems is the main priority of church activities. The church is, however, dependent on the support of partners from abroad for all activities. Overcoming the passive approach of government to dealing with poverty, is part of the challenge. The other challenge is the education which church and diaconia workers dealing with poverty need for their work. Education and training are the focal points in future development of church work with the poor.

Romania

All churches in Romania are very interested in diaconal ministry and very soon after 1990 developed diaconal structures that grew into diaconial departments. Diaconial structures address the majority of their services to poor people and people in need. The church has a long history of dealing with poverty in Romania. Modern practices in working with poverty started at the end of the 19th century. The churches in Romania established not only asylums, orphanages, social canteens, but also small enterprises that unemployed people could easily access like carpentry shops, construction companies, printing houses, paper factories, sewing shops, icon and church staff factories and so on. For rural people working in agriculture, the Orthodox and the Uniat Church had Folk Credit Programmes for agricultural development and credit provision for small businesses. All these programmes were suspended when the communist regime came into power and, because of lack of resources, cannot be re-established. For the moment, credit for development programmes in Romania are carried out with the help of various foreign partners. Direct programmes for poverty have been addressed since 1990 by the churches as well as by the AIDRom.

Examples of activities
- at least two social canteens in every bishopric of the Orthodox Church in Romania
- programmes for supporting students from poor families to continue to attend school
- vocational training programmes for youth reintegration
- unemployed women reintegration programmes
- all Orthodox Church deaneries developed their capacity for addressing the issue of poverty, by employing at least two social workers to assess the needs of the poor and to develop projects.

Long term strategy
The member churches of AIDRom have developed an Action Plan for Diaconal Services that serves as a basis for educational planning and

human resources development projects within the churches. The plan focuses, among other things, on development of practical activities addressing the primary and secondary needs of the poor.

Relations with the state and municipal authorities
The framework of state - church relationships has been improved since the state invited churches to take part in the consultation process regarding the National Anti-Poverty Action Plan and Promotion of Social Inclusion. AIDRom played an important role in this process as a resource organisation and as a consultant participating in the elaboration of the strategic objectives of these programmes. Churches have a good responsive attitude whenever the state institutions call upon them. They, however, do not initiate any state policy.

As far as the restitution of church property by the state is concerned, a part of the former properties that can be used for programmes related to alleviation of poverty have been given back. Churches, however, do not have the necessary finances to invest and prepare such properties for this purpose.

Documents issued
Some church pastoral letters mention poverty as the cause of many anti-social phenomena such as; trafficking in women, domestic violence, abortion, youth disorientation and violence. A comprehensive book addressing the issue of poverty: "The Destiny of Social Doctrines in the Romanian Orthodox Church. The radiography of a dilemma" was published in 2000.

Vision
The main challenge for the future is to solve the dependency on foreign funds and to develop anti-poverty programs and self-sustainable structures. Another serious need would be education for social work and related management skills.

Bulgaria

Political changes and economic transformation have had a heavy impact on the country. They caused a rapid rise of unemployment and poverty. These phenomena are particularly strong in the countryside and among ethnic minorities in the country: Roma people and Turks. Two other special groups of the population, which have to be specially mentioned while speaking about poverty in the country today, are elderly people and orphans. Funds allocated by the state for pensions and the running of orphanages are, in a high number of cases, not able to cover basic needs. Churches started to get involved in social work immediately after the political changes. Most of them are active in helping the poor in their various needs. An important part of church work in this field is that churches are actively present in their struggle with poverty in the Turk and Roma inhabited areas.

Examples of activities
- social kitchens run by churches exist in the capital and a number of other towns
- distribution of food packets and medicine, particularly in the winter period
- collections of food, second-hand clothes for orphans and poor elderly people
- material help for state run hospitals including medicine and equipment
- organising of medical teams visiting poor villages
- special attention to basic education in the poor Roma villages.

Relations with the state and municipal authorities
In this respect, it should be mentioned that co-operation with local authorities is reasonably good. However, it does not include financial support for the church social projects.

Vision

Social work activities of the churches are run mostly thanks to the help and support of partners from abroad. In the current situation in the country, this is the basic presupposition for further existence of the services, at least on the scale they are on now. Care for the poor in the country is a service of enormous need. Churches, particularly very tiny protestant communities, are proud that they can be part of this mission, in spite of their own poverty. Providing and organising help for the poor is part of their own identity.

Conclusion

The situation in Central and Eastern Europe provides a number of challenges for the life of the churches. One of the most profound is the question of the development of future relations of the churches to society. It deserves profound recognition that, in many cases, very small churches are in a position to respond to this challenge in a constructive way. Many of them already took the challenge of poverty seriously and they are ready to demonstrate in practical ways for everyday life what Christian solidarity means in reality. These communities are very often a living demonstration that Jesus' words: "as you did to one of the least of these my brethren, you did it to me" (Mt. 25:40) are understood, not in their verbal, but in their full, life-transforming meaning.

Annotations

1 Conference of European Churches includes 126 member churches of Protestant, Orthodox, Anglican and Catholic traditions from all over Europe (www.cec-kek.org). Activities of the Roman Catholic Church in the which deal with poverty are described in the various reports from the national organisations Caritas and Caritas Europa.
2 In this respect see e.g. activity of the Churches' Commission for Migrants in Europe (CCME) working on behalf of its members on the European level.

III. Country reports

Martin Schenk

Austria

Data and Socio-political Discussion

According to the Household Panel(ECHP), 12% of the population (930,000 persons) had less than 780 EUR per month at their disposal in the year 2000, that is 60% of the weighted median income. In Austria, this is seen as the risk threshold.
310,000 (4% of the population) of these are acutely poor. In addition to their limited financial resources, these people suffer from noticeable limitations in covering their basic needs. Poor people are not just those who sleep in cardboard boxes at the station, but also those who cannot take part in everyday life. That means that, (1.) they live in sub-standard or overcrowded housing, (2.) that they have financial problems with clothing and feeding themselves and paying for heating, (3.) they don't see themselves as being in a position to invite guests to their homes once a month and (4.) they have rent or loan repayment arrears. The definition of acute poverty in Austria is described not only in terms of money, but also in terms of living circumstances. Poverty does not just mean having too low an income, but means having a lack of opportunities to participate, at least at a minimum level, in the main areas of society: i.e. accommodation, health, employment market, social contacts, and education. Poverty is a lack of chances for a person to achieve fulfilment, a loss of fundamental freedom.

Poor people are ill twice as often as people who are not poor. The so-called "manager sickness", with high blood pressure and risks of heart attack, occurred three times more often in poor people than in managers. The enormous pressures suffered by people in precarious living situations makes them ill. Data about mortality in Austria shows us the extremes of inequality in death. People with a low income and a low level education, die on average five years earlier than those with a higher income and a higher level of education.

Women (13%) are more at risk of suffering from poverty than men (10%). The over 60s (18%)are most at risk; for children and young people up to the age of 20, the rate is 13% and for people of employment age it is 9%. People who only have the minimum school leaving certificate or less are more than twice as likely to become poor than people with a higher school leaving certificate (8%). People in households with disabled family members show a 20% risk of suffering from poverty. The risk level for non-EU citizens (17%) is higher than that of Austrians and EU citizens (11%). According to household type, single parents (16%) are most at risk, followed by households with three and more children (15%), the level of risk for households with two children (10%) and one child (5%) is less than average. The level of risk for people of employable age is not only dependent on family size, but much more dependent on participation in employment. State transfer payments in Austria make up a third of the available total income of the total population and as much as half of the income of the socially disadvantaged population groups. The welfare state benefits result in the poverty risk rate decreasing from 23% (without state transfer payments) to 12% after state transfer payments. After this redistribution, the bottom 10% receive 60% more than the market income. If we only consider transfer payments, 40% of the funds go to the lowest fifth income group and only 6% go to the highest fifth. In an EU comparison of social structure indicators, Austria is in the top league and is one of the states with the least poverty.

There are several areas which show signs of growing problems. Despite being in work, more and more people don't have enough to live on. More and more people with psychological problems fall through the social net. An increasing number of people cannot find a foothold on the employment market (any more). This is particularly dramatic for young people without the minimum school leaving certificate. Many women do not have any independent subsistence protection in old age.

Poor in spite of Work
In spite of being in work, 57.000 people in Austria do not have enough to live on (1,6% of the employed). If dependants and children who live in the

same household are included, the number of the working poor increases to 178,000 people. Employment does not protect people from poverty.

This affects, above all, families with many children and immigrant households as well as single mothers. What they all have in common, is that there is only one earner in the family and that they have atypical or low wage occupations. A considerable part of the employment market data is made up of jobs that are precarious or below subsistence level. For some, mini jobs or part-time employment mean an increase in personal scope but for many, they are an involuntary limitation. Thus there are winners and losers. Having a low wage or salary also leads to having less subsistence protection from social benefits in illness, unemployment and retirement. Giving in to the interests which are forcing through a low wage sector with work at any price, is a socio-political time-bomb. Not insignificantly, an increase in atypical employment situations led to a rise in the working poor in the USA. In Austria, this connection between atypical employment forms and the risk of poverty or even acute poverty can also be proven. The poverty risk level of people in long-term employment is at 4% only half as high as for people with short-time employment contracts (9%). If the contract is limited to less than a year, then the risk of poverty increases again. Part-time work is also connected with high poverty risk. Part-time employees with up to 20 hours per week have a three times higher risk and those with 21 to 30 hours have twice as high a risk of being poor, as those people who work 31 to 40 hours.

Income Gap: Social Polarisation
The gap between the top and the bottom is widening. If we cast a look at income tax statistics of individuals we can see increasing social polarisation in Austria: There is a lower than average increase of lower incomes and an above average increase in higher incomes. Reliable data for wages and salary income is available but only limited data about incomes of the self-employed and there is no data about individuals with income from property or capital.

Since 1995, the net wages of the lowest 30% of income earners have risen by 2.3%, whereas the top 5% earners have been able to increase their income by 17.4%. An average earner in the top 5% bracket earns 13.2 times as much as someone in the bottom 30% bracket. In 1995, someone in the "richest" group earned eleven times as much as one of the "poor". The top 10% receive net income which is higher than that of the bottom 50%. If the extra profits on top of the income of the self-employed and of property/capital owners were taken into consideration, then the gap would widen even further.

The disproportionately high rate of income growth for the top 5% represents an additional gain of more than 500 million EUR. If the net income spread of the salary and wage earners had stayed at the already high level of 1995 then there would be over 500 million EUR left over. That means that we would just have to reinstate the income distribution levels of 1995 and there would be 500 million EUR left over for social investment.

In recent years, financial income has been favoured over production profits and fixed investments. While profit and investment quotas ran parallel up to the 1980s, since then the profit quota has risen dramatically and the investment quota has stayed behind. Income from the financial markets is more lucrative than investment in real capital.

In the same way, over the last two decades, the part of national income made up by wages has reduced markedly while the income from property and from financial wealth has increased dramatically. The state has not only not taken this shift in its tax policies into account, it has actively supported it. Whereas the tax burden on "work" increased constantly, the wealth tax was disposed of, in spite of a dynamic increase in wealth values. Austria takes up the last place in the OECD comparison of wealth tax. As far as revenue from tax on profits is concerned, Austria takes up the penultimate position in the EU. The one-sided burden of the economic factor "work" over the last 20 years, has lead to a massive imbalance in the financing of social compensation and has placed a considerably greater burden on low income people. Therefore a considerable sum is now not available for causes for the common good, instead the tax screw has been tightened on employees and on mass consumption. Low income groups do not have the opportunity to increase their wealth. The Austrian economic research institute, WIFO, estimates that the lower third income group receives 6.5% of the total income from interest, the middle group receives about a quarter and the top third income group receives around two thirds of the interest.

Elevator going up, safety net below
New social challenges require new social solutions. Fighting poverty and avoiding poverty go hand in hand. We need a net at the bottom so that no-one falls into the cellar. We need an elevator going up and open stilt houses so that whole groups of the population don't get stuck on the bottom floor. This is subsistence protection at the bottom and integration going up. Poverty researchers are agreed that basic laws and rights for all are more effective than handouts for just a few and that social balance is a more effective basis for avoiding poverty than the privatisation of social risks.

People who are not "safe" because they don't have a gap free curriculum vitae, are not married or do not have the correct passport, are at a high risk of being left outside. The need for a reform of the lower social net is large. The current statistics on poverty show three groups which are especially at risk, which represent exactly the "three pillars" for access to the welfare benefits: single mothers, unemployed and immigrants.

After the war, the welfare state was built on three fundamental pillars: the male breadwinner household, paid work and citizenship. Since then, quite a lot has changed. Many women are the breadwinners for the family and there are many different forms of co-habitation. Curriculum vitae often show gaps, and uncertain "Mc-Jobs" are on the increase. Many people have immigrated into Austria. Holding on to the principle of the "male breadwinner household" leads to a high risk of poverty and to a minimum pension for a third of all women. Fixing ourselves to the classic model of paid work, overlooks the increasing number of working poor and the social deterioration of the (long-term) unemployed. The history of concentration on a person's origins, leads to social exclusion and a lack of chances to climb the ladder for immigrants. An independent subsistence protection system for women is needed, basic protection systems that are independent of work biografy and equal rights for all, irrespective of origin.

Social security needs unified standards. There should be investment in bridges to the employment market for the disadvantaged. The, at present, legal discrimination against immigrants regarding access to housing, the employment market and co-determination must be abolished. Political and legal measures which contribute to the stigmatisation of addicts, former prison detainees, or the homeless must be removed. It is possible to minimise the high risk of illness for people on low income. An education system based on equality and the possibility to learn something new in the difficult employment market helps poorer people. Jobs, where you can earn enough to live on, ensure independent income. A good provision of child-care and family-friendly work conditions is of great advantage to women (and their children). In addition, a lively civil society which can commit itself to solidarity with fellow humans, produces the values which the welfare state cannot manage to provide itself but which it needs for the protection of its weakest members.

Interpretation and argumentation of the Church and Diaconia

Chances of fulfilment: the freedom of the weak

For a long time, poverty was defined as lack of property. The economist Amartya Sen, who was awarded the Nobel prize for his work, argued that it meant the ability to transform these goods into freedom. That is, into freedom for people to realise their idea of what a good life is. Property is desired because of the freedom that it enables one to achieve. One needs goods, but it is not the quantity of these goods that determines whether this freedom is present or not. The possibility of realising what one considers to be a good life, also depends on social structures, living habits, social skills and general wealth. A good welfare system makes it more freedom possible for the individual. It is a prerequisite for this, that the values of individuality and freedom are not just a privilege for high income and wealthy members of society. These straightforward thoughts have a an enormous effect on the battle against poverty. 1.) Poor people are subjects, not objects, of economic actions. 2.) We can only talk about freedom when the freedom of the disadvantaged is included. 3.) Just increasing the amount of property owned does not fight poverty. Liberalisation, which limits the choices and chances of freedom of those with the lowest income, is only semi-freedom. When analysing social justice, the individual use of chances of fulfilment for the poorest must also be evaluated.

Priority option for the poor

In the guidelines for diaconia from the general synod in 1997, the evangelical churches of Austria emphasize "the main priority for the poor." That means "developing economic strategies to strive towards social justice. The church must look for cooperation partners in society to help achieve this. The church will not be able to achieve solutions on its own, but its responsibility to stand up for social justice must not be given up."

The same direction is taken up by the wish expressed for a "social toleration test" of legal policies. Here too, there is the socio-ethical conviction that all political policies must be measured against their effects on the poor.

"The social institutions and initiatives of the church see social developments before they have been documented by social scientists", argues Herig Sturm, Bishop of the Evangelical Church A.B, as part of the initiative for an ecumenical Sozialwort in Austria. The churches contribute their experience from the bottom up, like a seismograph of society. They experience the results of political or economic policies very directly.

The strength of the weak

"The primary task of the diaconia is to turn especially to those areas of need that are not really noticed by the network of public social institutions. Diaconal action is always a protest as well, because it alleviates need, but at the same time calls out for a change in the conditions which lead to that need." It continues in this way in the guidelines of the general synod of Austrian Churches. It is all about help and about protest. Sometimes it is about help under protest.

Solidarity was originally developed as a direct alternative to charity – practised by the "weak" against "the Strong". Solidarity always means distrust of charitable people/institutions from above and from outside. "The Weak" broke away from dependence and refused recognition by "the Strong". In the "vale of tears", the morals of appeal mean that the weak stay weak and still have to be compared with the strong. The central history of helping and of humanitarian and charitable commitment in these areas that has legitimised and motivated charity for centuries is the parable of the Good Samaritan. Robbers leave a traveller half-dead in a ditch. Now the story has started again: one person stops. He gets him onto his donkey and takes him to the next inn. He pays, makes sure everything is taken care of and announces that he will check on him on the way back. Then the Samaritan goes on his way. So this is no self-worrying helper type of person, no goody-goody acrobatic exercise in conviction. Simply: our paths have crossed, I have done what needed to be done, I have secured the framework conditions so that you can get back on your feet, I'll come round again. And then the Nazarene man's question: "Who was the victim's neighbour?" Not: to whom should I show brotherly love? There is a radical change of perspective here, another view of the story has broken in on us. The question is asked from the point of view of the person in need: "Who is my neighbour?" – with the eyes of the victim.

This differs radically from the Samaritan of the nationalist West, which needs a victim – a scapegoat-victim – in order to see. This differs greatly from humanitarian conviction, that decides for others, that needs victims as a constant object of captive welfare.

Whoever speaks has something to say. We can only find out who someone is or was by listening to the story of which they are the hero or heroine. Speaking up does not mean speaking on somebody's behalf but speaking for yourself. When excluded persons give their world visibility they create a place from which they can speak. The curtain opens on a stage on which one's own story gets its own interpretation, and at the same time meaning. Your own unspectacular life gets a platform and becomes special. The people who speak can speak out and tell us who they are and who they can be. The first step is mostly to make identity visible and noticeable, which denies a comparison with the winners. Nobody likes to define him/herself as "poor" or as a "loser" in the long-term.

So places are created where excluded people can begin to speak and act in forms of collective action, which take place in the real-life situations, and in specific cultures and lifestyles of the persons affected. Homeless people and their friends gather around the street newspaper Augustin, immigrant kids perform hip-hop, immigrants put on film weeks and give lectures, unemployed youths present themselves on video, single mothers get together to help each other. Places are conquered and interpreted. Public rooms are lit up as stages – and they are performed on together. In order to break the monopoly on definitions held by the powerful, opponents' terms are redefined and taken on by their own groups. Foreign musicians perform as "Tschuschenband", homeless alcoholics call their hostel "Tschecheranten Home" ("Tschusch" is a derogatory term for foreigners and "Tscheranten" are drinkers).

The laid table

Diaconia from the Greek means "to serve at table". Everyone is invited to table, no-one is excluded. The laid table is the centre of Christianity. The table at which all will be satisfied, is the central symbol of the community of solidarity that Christians celebrate at communion.

"Our faith is at stake." As expressed by the general synod 1999 in its declaration on xenophobia and racism. "God has put us on the side of the poor and those who are excluded. Whoever (...) looks down on the outsiders, is opposing God." "Commitment against racism is a central question of faith." The declaration concludes: "We will begin with ourselves."

Church and Diaconia in practice

The Evangelical Church in Austria is a minority church. Around 90% of the population is Catholic, 4% profess to be members of the Evangelical Church. The Evangelical Church shows a disproportionately high amount of diaconal commitment. The Catholic organisation, Caritas, has 8,000 co-workers and the Evangelical diaconia has 4,000. The work of these diaconal initiatives and institutions includes work with the homeless, refugees, addicts, disadvantaged youths and disabled people.

The diaconia is a co-founder of the Austrian Conference on Poverty, a network of 25 social organisations. In 1995, the first Austrian-wide poverty conference took place. At this conference, a wide spectrum of civil society bodies were present; charitable associations, umbrella organisations of social initiatives, church and trade union organisations, educational and research institutes and cooperation groups of single parents and unemployed at risk from poverty. Since then, they have been acting under the name "Die Armutskonferenz" (The Poverty Conference) to analyse the widely hushed-up problem of poverty and social exclusion in Austria and to improve the lives of people affected by this. Regional networks and platforms have been set up in numerous states. An all Austrian Action week against poverty and exclusion has already taken place four times. Diaconia and the church finance the work of the coordination team of the Poverty Conference and take part in their common activities. The Poverty Conference see themselves as a lobby for those who have no lobby; so takes up the conscious position of standing up for certain interests. The church, with its civil society initiative, does not only supply ethical orientation here, but actually intervenes in favour of disadvantaged people. In the eight years since it was founded, the poverty conference has worked on concepts for subsistence protection, reform proposals for social benefits, campaigns for the improvement of health care for the poor, analysed the effects of government budgets on the weakest income group and brought attention to negative socio-political developments by means of public campaigns. One main focus in the last few years has been the monitoring of the European-wide initiative "National Action Plans Against Poverty". In order to get this comprehensive work into perspective, two conferences on wealth took place that dealt with questions of distribution of opportunities and the almost non-existent wealth data.

Evangelical work in the field of refugee care is particularly strong. The Evangelical Church next to the largest Austrian refugee camp in Traiskirchen was the starting point for a considerable initiative on legal advice, emergency night hostels, healthcare and imprisonment prior to deportation. The "mobile emergency hostel" campaign for example, provides asylum-seekers with temporary accommodation in the parishes.

After the predicament of homeless asylum-seekers escalated in the winter of 2002/2003, a campaign was started – "existence for refugees." It gets the affected people to join in, turns to the population with signature lists and organises public campaigns in front of the ministry. In this field, diaconal political practice does not limit itself just to lobbying but chooses stronger forms of opposition. As for example, taking legal court action against ministerial decisions. This brings them into potential conflict with the government, parts of the population and some of its own members.

By supporting the petition for a referendum, the Evangelical Church also proved conflictive. This was a referendum for a welfare system based on solidarity in Austria. There was great public support for this, and it was signed by 700,000 people, but it was also apparent that there was opposition from the lobby which is pushing for privatisation of social risks. The church leadership argued remarkably clearly that the church initiatives see themselves as legitimate protagonists because of their concrete solidarity, often performed by voluntary workers, and claim to have a right to demand social solidarity in society. Brotherly love and social solidarity cannot be played against each other.

"Welfare state and freedom, solidarity and individuality are not mutually incompatible, but complement and depend on each other. The welfare state is necessary if the values of individuality and freedom are not just to be a privilege for people with high incomes but something that is available for all people." This was how the ecumenical social mission statement ("Sozialwort") was formulated at the first advent Sunday 2003.

The ecumenical social mission statement was worked out over a period of three years. It is a world premiere for 14 Christian churches of catholic, protestant and orthodox tradition to have published a common social mission statement. The first stage consisted of developing a social report. The starting point for this was formed by a broad survey of the social practices of the different churches. The results of this survey were summarised in the social report. It was then possible to see the manifold nature of the social initiatives of the churches, to see the difficulties of the work and to examine the demands of politics and church leaders. 550 social initiatives and establishments within the Christian churches contributed to this social report. In comparison to other social reports, this 192 page report is based solely on experience gained from social practice. It mirrors the experience of social initiatives and is the first overall view of social commitment in the Austrian churches. On the basis of the social report, subject areas were developed which were of importance for the content and socio-ethical structure of the social mission statement.

The ecumenical social mission statement cannot be assigned to the wall-builders who want to set up walls around the status quo of the welfare state, nor does it sing in a church chorus to the triumphant fanfares of reformism. The social mission statement provides a critical analysis of current social security systems but it does not allow itself to be used as a tool to destroy such social structures, for those who see individual freedom as an opponent of institutional solidarity: "Access to high quality social services must be secured for all, independent of income or origin. Public services attain their legitimacy and recognition in society because, financed by all, they are available to all to the same degree." (Social mission statement)

And it continues: "Social security does not make society poor but is a fundamental element of social solidarity. Social investments also have a positive effect on the economy.

A well organised system of schools and educational establishments ensures a good level of education. A health system available to all and a well-functioning infrastructure form the basis of a successful economy. The provision of a safety-net for risks like unemployment and old age are indicators of wealth and affluence in a society. This affluence, that should exclude no single group, but aims at including as many people as possible, is a positive element of the economic location of Austria and is the basis for ensuring quality of life for all, the maintaining of which should be seen as a fundamental task." (Social mission statement)

The demand for participation and democratisation of the welfare model is the central theme of the social mission statement. The aim of increasing the chances of people to achieve fulfilment, particularly for poorer and disadvantaged people, is a subject which is discussed in all chapters. Autonomy should be strengthened; autonomy which is open and does amount to more than just being able to pay into an insurance fund.

Throughout, there is also a constant demand for independent subsistence insurance for women, and concerns the distribution of income and work, recognition of broad work and economic terms as well as independent pension insurance. Particular attention is paid to the basic security elements not only of social welfare but for all systems of social protection such as pensions, health and unemployment benefits. Because "the churches are convinced that the real material and legal requirements for the participation of people in a life of freedom and community, with responsibility and dignity, can be created." There is enough for everyone. Everyone is invited to table, nobody is left out.

The church leadership and the diaconia feel obliged to tackle this task of public intervention.

The welfare state and freedom, solidarity, and individuality do not exclude each other, but confirm and complement each other. Strong economies in Europe have a strong welfare state – weak economies have a weak welfare state. A welfare state makes society rich, not poor. High social rates do not indicate economic backwardness but the opposite: high prosperity.

In accordance with this, there were several public interventions by the church leadership and the diaconia. The attempt to influence social policy leads, on the whole, to a toning down of planned policies but seldom leads to a new version being created in the interests of the weakest. The diaconia has no other means of putting pressure other than the word, social practice, believability and public interest. In a situation where poverty is not seen as avoidable, but as an acceptable evil, the basic foundations collapse; the foundations that are necessary to fight poverty, to make it a common cause and to make it a res publica and a political priority.

References

Bundesministerium für soziale Sicherheit und Generationen (2002): Federal Ministry for Social Security and Generations: Report on the Social Situation 2001-2002, (www.bmsg.gv.at)

Die Armutskonferenz (2001): The Poverty Congress (2001): And you are out! Social and spatial exclusion, publication from the 4th Austrian Poverty Congress, (www.armut.at)

Die Armutskonferenz, Attac, Beigewum (2002): The Poverty Congress (2002): The inheritance of affluence. Winners and losers in European welfare. Mandelbaum Verlag

Die Armutskonferenz (2003): The Poverty Congress (2003): Poverty can damage your health. Social inequality and illness. Information, data, connections, (www.armut.at)

Die Armutskonferenz (2003): The Poverty Congress (2003): Social tolerance test. Poverty testing, in: Der Nationale Aktionsplan gegen Armut und soziale Ausgrenzung 2003-2005, p. 29, The national action plan against poverty and social exclusion 2003-2005 (www.armut.at)

European Anti Poverty Network (2002): A decisive contribution to the battle against poverty and exclusion? The European strategy towards social integration. An interim report. (www.eapn.org)

Generalsynode der evangelischen Kirchen (1997): General synod of protestant churches(1997): Diaconia – locations and challenges – a principle report. (www.evang.at)

Generalsynode der evangelischen Kirchen (1999): General synod of protestant churches (1999) Declaration on hatred of foreigners and racism. (www.evang.at)

Guger, Alois (1996): Redistribution by public budgets in Austria, Economic Research Institute, Vienna WIFO

Ökumenischer Rat der Kirchen (2001): Ecumenical Council of Churches (2001): The social report. Experience and practice of social commitment. (www.sozialwort.at)

Ökumenischer Rat der Kirchen (2003): Ecumenical Council of Churches (2003): Social Memorandum. (www.sozialwort.at)

Schenk, Martin (2002): The shame of failure: Historical Museum Vienna, Poverty, exhibition catalogue, p. 41- 55 (Die Scham des Versagens, in: Historisches Museum Wien (Hg.), Armut. Ausstellungskatalog, S.41-55) , (www.museum.vienna.at)

Herwig Hermans

Belgium

Poverty and Poverty Policy in Belgium

The coalition agreement of July 2003 determined that efforts will be made to give all citizens the chance to benefit in the prosperity of our country. Indeed, Flanders and Belgium rank among the best in the world standard of living charts. Yet, those figures don't mean anything to a substantial proportion of our inhabitants, who, day by day, are aware of what exclusion and survival mean to the poor.

In the following, we will give a survey of poverty in the Belgian context, we will describe some trends and challenges concerning poverty reduction, recent policy and available policy instruments.

Poverty in Belgium
The estimated number of people who can be classified as poor is now more than 700,000 or 7 per cent (according to the EU-standards) in a population of 10 million. A great many of them are people who just manage to survive, thanks to a minimum benefit-allowance. In 2003, the minimum subsistence-system was changed slightly and it is now called the "leefloon" or "lifewage". During the last few years, the number of people drawing the minimum allowance has decreased. By 01 January 2002, the estimated number was 67,789; this is a decrease of 6% compared to 01 January 2001. However, this does not automatically mean that poverty is decreasing. Maybe there are more people who don't claim the allowance. Statistics on gaps in social insurance show that, over the last three years, about 10% of the population have actually been living below the subsistence level. Moreover, some of those minimum earners have to share their income. A little more than a quarter (27%) of them had one or more persons to support. That means that, at the beginning of 2000, in families having to make both ends meet with the so-called "life wage", at least 40,751

children and adults were supported by the person receiving allowance. Besides, there are other people living on the minimum income, such as the elderly. They can appeal to the Old-Age Security Income (Gewaarborgd Inkomen voor Bejaarden), today called the Old-Age Income Guarantee (Inkomensgarantie voor Ouderen).

Summing up

We can conclude that, despite the decrease in the number of beneficiaries of minimum allowances, in 2002 more than 200,000 people had to get by on a "lifewage" (minimum subsistence/ "lifewage" or old-age security income/old-age income guarantee). Some categories should be added to this number which are hard to calculate, such as people living below the minimum or having just a bit more (due to unemployment, illness, invalidity...)

Trends and Challenges
• Unemployment increasing again

The engine of our "active welfare state" is misfiring. Industrial activities and businesses are no longer growing. In 2002, unemployment increased again and, on the whole, the same groups as always suffered from exclusion. The risks of becoming unemployed are unequally spread out. There are huge differences among individuals, as well as among regions. The vulnerable position of the poorly-educated and migrants is a striking example of that structural exclusion, with no regard to cyclical fluctuations. Low level schooling increases the risks of long-term unemployment. The level of schooling for those who are unemployed for more than a year proves to be considerably inferior to the education level of the short-term unemployed.

• Income gap increases

It's clear that the problem of poverty implies more than (not) disposing of a (poor) income. Nevertheless income level and income spread remain a good indicator of poverty and social exclusion. Tax statistics show that the proportion of the lowest (drawn) incomes has decreased since 1993. In 1999 the lowest 30% disposed of 10.6% of the net taxable income, while the richest 10% disposed of 29.3%; after tax deduction it was still 13.4% for the poorest 30% and 24.3% for the richest 10%.

- The excessive burden of debt increases

Ever growing debt problems are a major cause of concern. In the second half of 2001, the total amount of outstanding debts added up to 13229.80 million Euros. The number of people who fail to pay off their loans increased again in 2001, compared to the year before. Since the mid-nineties, the number of registrations and the total amount of overdue debts known by the Centre for Credits to Private Persons (Centrale voor Kredieten aan Particulieren) has kept increasing. In 2001, there was also a rise in the number of people who could not pay their gas or electricity bills. In 21,790 households – each owing the average sum of 967 Euros – the energy supply was cut off. Moreover, 15,540 "potential limiters" and 8,710 "pay slots" were installed. A striking increase!

For some – especially for a lot of young people – debts lead to poverty. In 2001, there was a new rise in the number of people unable to pay several instalments of their loans. Among them, are both people living in poverty with several debts and the new poor, facing poverty for the first time because of debt. Debts on loans – consumer and bank debts – make up a quarter of the total debt burden. The energy-linked debts represent a debit item of 17%. Rent arrears and medical care related debts are the fourth and the fifth cause of debt.

- Education

Flanders is known as a country with a top quality education system. In spite of that, there is a substantial educational gap between children performing up to average and those performing poorly. Although education can be a major stepping stone for children of deprived families, they are always found in schools that curtail those children's options drastically.

- Health

With regard to health and access to health care, there are important differences between the higher and the lower socio-economic classes. Data from the National Data Bank Mortality (Nationale Bank Mortaliteit) and the Belgian Health Inquiry 1997 (Belgische Gezondheidsenquête 1997) reveal that there are socio-economic differences regarding illness and mortality. For example: the life expectancy of an unqualified man aged 25 is 5.5 years below the life expectancy of a man of the same age, with a higher education certificate.

The Belgian Health Inquiry shows that, for one third of Belgian households, the costs of medical services are hard to bear. In the year preceding the inquiry, 8% of households had to postpone a medical consultation or the purchase of medicine. We know that households with an unqualified householder have to delay their use of medical care five times more often than households with a highly qualified householder.

• Housing
The housing problem remains a permanent source of concern in the struggle against poverty and social exclusion. Low-income people hardly have any chance on the private rent market. The social rent sector is but a marginal phenomenon and it is almost impossible to buy a house, so low-income people have to rent in the private sector and are the victims of instability, i.e. the market price increases.

Between 1976-1997, tenants, after paying their rent, had a 20% loss of spending power, while the proprietors' spending power remained almost the same. This decrease of spending power is not due to a decrease of real income but to the evolution on the housing market. By analogy with the poverty-trap and the unemployment-trap, this can be called the housing-trap: all efforts to increase the income of the poor are undone by permanently increasing rents. An adequate social policy has to take into account what is occurring on the housing market.

• Into and out of poverty in Belgium
Research concerning the dynamic aspects of poverty sees through the image of income poverty as a marginal social phenomenon. Long-term evaluation of the situation of the poor revealed that poverty often appears in the middle classes as well, maybe as a short or one-off experience. Long-term research shows that actually many more people face poverty for a certain period of time, unlike the results of short-term investigations.

When 60% of the median (standardized monthly available) household income is considered the limit (621 Euros), we see that over a period of 5 years 23% (!) of the population have to face income poverty. About 4 to 10 of them lived in poverty for one year or more. Income poverty mostly appears for short periods of time, but the longer a person is poor, the smaller the chance that he/she will manage to escape from poverty. About one tenth (11%) of the households with a working householder (normally the last group to be struck by income poverty) become poor at least once every five years.

Getting into or out of poverty (or staying permanently poor) often happens at particular key moments in the course of one's life, so-called "life events". These events can be a demographic phenomenon, being part of the "normal" course of human life, such as entering into or breaking off a relationship, or the birth of children. But there are also life events which cause a change in income, such as retirement or unemployment. These key events have striking consequences for any member of our society, but for people living just below or above the poverty line, they can lead to a big (positive or negative) difference in the quality of life.

• Poverty in the countryside

Several macro-social tendencies have an effect on the financial situation of farmers.

On the basis of agricultural and accounting data, we learn that 26.8% of Belgian farming enterprises provide a yearly household income that doesn't go beyond 10,000 Euros. On average, 22% of the Flemish farms and 30% of the Walloon farms find themselves below the threshold income of 10,000 Euros.

Policy: intentions and action

The federal policy debate during the previous legislature was held under the banner of "activating". That policy led to some measures in the fields of employment, social security and assistance.

– A number of allowances were increased, for example: the minimum unemployment allowances, the disablement benefits for employees, the oldest (most senior ranking) pensions, contributions for invalids, the subsistence level or "lifewage".

– In the area of health care, there was the extension of the application of the Maximum Health Care Bill. (Maximale Gezondheidsfactuur)

– Regarding employment, a lot of attention was given to the redefinition of the employment projects and the improved protection of older employees. The National Action Plan for Social Inclusion (Nationaal Actieplan Sociale Insluiting / NAPInc), adopted by the Federal Government in June 2001, contains a great deal of measures meant to improve the employment chances of high-risk groups: "Runways for youngsters", the "Spring Programme" for "lifewage" beneficiaries and for people on the dole, the specific regional training and involvement routes.

As for the period 2001-2003, the authorities brought the four fields of social exclusion outlined by the EU conference in Lisbon into focus: income and employment, housing, education and health. Under its EU chairmanship in the second half of 2001, the Belgian Government managed to have some indicators outlined, which will ensure a better observation of the evolution of the struggle against poverty in the member states.

The recent "purple" coalition agreement also considers the creating of new employment (the ambitious aim is to create 200.000 new jobs!) the main weapon against social insecurity, poverty and exclusion. One of the measures is the gradual introduction of a job bonus to increase the income span between dole and lower wages. However, the planned restructuring of public enterprises will be a major challenge for the new government. It is to be feared that the inevitable reorganization will have financial consequences, in particular for the thousands of low-qualified workers, who today have a job with the Railway Company or the Post Office. Though an active re-involvement policy, accompanying the reorganization of the public sector, is promised and one intends to stimulate the social economy, it is clear that the employment of the lowest qualified will be a tough job during the years ahead.

The coalition agreement also foresees the increase of participation via the promotion of the accessibility to socio-cultural activities, the fight against functional illiteracy, the creation of more chances to dispose of comfortable housing and the reduction of debt.

Yet, the coalition agreement is quite vague, except for the last question, where the options of civil bankruptcy and the amendment of seizure regulations are mentioned.

Finding good alternatives for the unemployed is something the Communities and the Regions have to cope with. As for the allowances, it has been reported that the lowest social allowances and the "lifewage" will gradually be increased ... within the limits of the budget. And the local Public Social Work Centers (Openbaar Centrum voor Maatschappelijk Werk /OCMW) will be asked to do a bigger part of the job. To meet this objective, they should be able to work more efficiently, thanks to less complicated administration and the punctual payment of subsidies.

There were some changes in Flemish policy as well. At the end of 2002, the Social Impulse Fund (Sociaal Impulsfonds) was changed into the Cities and (the previously existing) Municipalities Fund. (Steden- en (reeds bestaande) Gemeentefonds). Both, the change into the Municipalities Fund and the creation of the Cities Fund, aim to give a more important budgetary autonomy to the cities and the municipalities.

The Social Impulse Fund obviously focused on the fight against poverty in the deprived city districts, and in that way local social policy was somewhat "earmarked". It is to be feared that more autonomy will entail different spending patterns of the slightly increased means, which will actually lead to a decrease of the budget for local poverty policy. We are eager to know in what way the Flemish Parliament will finally shape the Decree on Local Social Policy (Decreet Lokaal Sociaal Beleid) and whether this, from 2003 onwards, will lead to a good and structural embedment of the poverty and welfare policy of the municipalities. There will always remain the real danger that budgets will be reoriented towards middle-class-focused spending.

The Flemish policymakers aim high when they want to realize an inclusive poverty policy and to assess their policy while taking basic social rights into account. Such poverty policy is a long-term concern. Things that have been going wrong for many years cannot be put right in a short period of time, when the intentions are o.k. but the means are restricted. The policy measures to be found in the second edition of the Flemish Action Plan for the Struggle against Poverty (Vlaams Actieplan Armoedebestrijding) do not give evidence of a determined choice to fight poverty vigorously, neither regarding the budget, nor regarding the integration of initiatives. The long awaited decree on the struggle against poverty was eventually adopted at the beginning of 2003. It offers a series of guarantees concerning poverty related policy, but a further increase of the budget is needed to recognize and support the "associations where the poor have their say" (verenigingen waar armen het woord nemen), which must result in the development and reinforcement of the basic activities. A series of initiatives, such as the Conferences on Poverty and the Permanent Consultation regarding Poverty (Permanent Overleg Armoede) are ways to keep the policymakers' minds on the subject.

Two important policy tools

• Point of Support for the struggle against poverty, social insecurity and expulsion

In 1992, the Federal Government decided to make inquiries among the poor themselves, in order to find more accurate ways of fighting poverty. The associations cooperating closely with the poor and the local OCMWs were asked to write a General Report Concerning Poverty (Algemeen Verslag over de Armoede). It was published in 1994.

It led, among other things, to the following conclusions:

– It is necessary to increase the coherence of the poverty policy of the different relevant authorities.

– It is necessary to give a permanent structure to the dialogue between policymakers and the poor, and at the same time to extend its radius to other partners in the field.

In 1995, at the start of a new legislature period, the Federal Government announced that the recommendations of the General Report Concerning Poverty would be the subject of intense discussions within the Interdepartmental Conference Social Integration, founded as had been suggested by the authors of the Report. That Conference entered into a dialogue with the organizations concerned with the cause of the most deprived and with the Center For Equal Opportunities and the Fight against Racism (Centrum voor Gelijkheid van Kansen en Racismebestrijding), an autonomous public service.

In 1999, this partnership was given a legal basis, through a cooperative agreement regarding the continuation of the poverty policy, consolidated by the Federal State, the Communities and the Regions. This permanent structure is called: "Point of Support for the Struggle against Poverty, Social Insecurity and Exclusion" (Steunpunt tot Bestrijding van Armoede, Bestaansonzekerheid en Sociale Uitsluiting).

The recent coalition agreement announces a reinforcement as well as a larger autonomy of this Point of Support, and again a broad debate will be organized.

Http://www.armoedebestrijding.be

• Flemish Network of Associations where the poor can have their say
The Flemish Network was founded on 9 May 2003, according to the Decree on the struggle against poverty, adopted by the Flemish Parliament on 12 March 2003. In this Flemish Network, the associations cooperate in order to eliminate poverty and social exclusion completely. The associations are helped and the mutual cooperation is promoted with the intention of dealing with concrete situations of poverty and social exclusion, to improve poor people's living conditions.

Based on the everyday experience of the deprived, the associations and the Network make proposals for changes, together with other partners in the field and with policymakers.

Http://www.vlaams-netwerk-armoede.org

Struggle against poverty in word and deed

A look at recent evolutions regarding the fight against poverty within the Belgian and Flemish religious community.

Fight against poverty ... in WORD

Recent attention paid by the Episcopal Conference
The bishops of Belgium proclaimed the Christian Year 2002-2003, the year of helpfulness, to be seen as the first in a cycle of three years, preceding a year of preaching and one of liturgy.

Under the title "Sent to serve", a year full of dynamic initiatives was launched. The bishops described their purpose as follows:

"In the course of the next three years, we intend to focus on three tasks the Lord has asked his church to fulfill: serve, preach, pray and celebrate. During this first year we want the Church of our country to reflect on our mission to be ready to help and to cooperate. 'I haven't come to be served, but to serve' (Mt 20, 28), Jesus says. A Christian is willing to follow the Lord, and so is the Christian community: we are sent to serve! Are we a serving church and do we act the way the Lord wants us to?"

Statement by the bishops
In September 2002, the Statement of the Belgian bishops was published: "Sent to serve. The year of the church social welfare work."

The notion of readiness to serve is given a rather broad definition. For example: the family is presented as the first "workshop" of the parish and the bishops also pay attention to the service of faith, to the proclamation/preaching of the gospel, to prayer and hope. Yet they focus on the willingness to help society and on the evangelical choice for the weakest.

It is said as follows:

"We bear responsibility for the search of solutions to the problems of our society."

At the close of the Holy Year, the bishops had already mentioned faith/religion as a service to the world. They expressed their concern regarding four items: decent use of the fruits of the earth, environmental protection, relief of the unbearable burdens of the poor countries through debt acquittal, hospitality given to foreign people and coexistence with other cultures and religions, pursuit of peace and democracy (The Mission of Christians in the World, January 2001). It's obvious that Christians can contribute by doing something about those questions, in their direct surroundings or in a broader context, depending on their social and proSfessional situation.

"As bishops we appeal to you – parishes, Christian communities and associations – to examine the following: How can we be helpful in a concrete way? And to ask ourselves: What is our specific motivation of our commitment as Christians? What inspires us and what is the spiritual background of our Christian commitment?"

A service to the weak and the hurt

First of all, we have got to open our eyes. Do we indeed see where help is needed? Do we know if and where there are poor people in our neighbourhood?

Nowadays a lot of people sympathize with the weak and Christians also have a long tradition of organizing care for people in need. Nevertheless, we cannot stop asking what God may exactly expect from us today. Do we see the new needs, do we detect them all?

Activities in several dioceses

As a result of the year of the church social welfare work, in several dioceses, attention was asked to be paid to the challenges regarding concrete service in favour of people in need. There were meetings with speakers who reported on their experience in the field, there were articles in several publications. Worth mentioning is the pastoral project of the Vicariate Vlaams Brabant – Mechelen. It emphasized some aspects under the heading: "Recht – Op" (Straight-Up or the Right-To).

We quote from the policy text:

"The heart of the matter is that someone who is excluded or hurt will be made strong enough to take his/her fate in his/her own hands, and in that way manages to be or to become the person he/she really is. This is a concern inside the church community itself: there may be somebody who doesn't get enough room inside. But of course it also depends on the neighbourhood, the village, the whole society where someone lives. Attention to and service for the deprived do not imply they need to be a member of 'the club', but such attitudes are explicitly meant to be present in a society where there is room for everybody. This policy aims at a

society and a church for and with everybody. If we put it this way, we avoid having to give names to particular groups and so risk isolating them. Since an ideal situation is hard to realize, a radical priority must be given to all people who are not yet able to or allowed to belong to the more privileged. That is why we have to speak prophetic words, we should have the courage to protest, to take part in the social debate and in the ethical discussions and underline our points of view. Indeed, to give people the strength to stand up for themselves, we must at the same time fight against adverse powers and structures.

This concern can never be a matter of pity. We want to be at those people's side, carefully listen to their stories, be their allies, and so become aware that we need them. Nobody is perfect and consequently we need each other. Being there where people are hurt or vulnerable, in our neighbourhood or anywhere in the world, that is a central characteristic of a living Christian community."

IPB draws the guidelines

The Interdiocesan Pastoral Council (Interdiocesaan Pastoraal Beraad), the counselling and participation body of the Flemish bishops, drew some chalk-lines within the context of the year of the church social welfare work. Those guidelines can be found in the brochure: "Uw naam is hartstocht voor gerechtigheid. Krijtlijnen voor een kerkelijke diaconie, vandaag en morgen." (Your name is passion for justice. Orientations for ecclesiastical welfare work, today and tomorrow.)

In this concise brochure, we find some biblical-theological bases and a survey of different forms of church social welfare work, as well as a description of some paths to follow. Finally, there are some useful ideas regarding how those themes can be discussed.

The brochure focuses on the Christian organizations and institutes at work in the modern pluralistic cultural field.

... and DEED

Different players in the field

Here we focus on the church-related organizations at work in Flanders and Brussels. We did not intend to make an exhaustive survey, but we wanted to make clear how rich and diverse those initiatives are. And we made a far from subtle choice to divide them into two major categories: social services and solidarity-work.

Social services

It would be impossible to give a complete list and a decent description of the social services. For one thing, there are so many such initiatives, for another, several of them are quite small and more or less unknown. However different, they all have some characteristics in common.

First, there is the strong commitment of volunteers. Then, the service they offer is quite concrete, for example: food aid is given, second-hand goods are provided. And there is the link with the parish, mostly a link that is more loose or stronger, depending on the situation: Who is the initiator? Where precisely does the project take place? What role do the partners play in the parish context? The initiative itself does not generally belong to the parish as such. Only when there are some specific activities or on special occasions can the parish be clearly distinguished. And finally, those projects target on native as well as on immigrant people.

Some examples

• Kras (Kerk in de rand van de stad) Gent – Church on the fringes of the city Ghent

Kras is a cooperation of small-scale aid initiatives at work in the city of Ghent. Each service operates in a particular area in the city. Through communication and cooperation within Kras, all the partners aim to optimize their service. The monthly meeting is a forum of discussion, exchange of experience, information, as well as training, study and debate regarding a variety of themes and trends.

Guest speakers are asked to come and inform the partners on a specific item (debt mediation, asylum policy, health insurance ...) or to present an organization (legal aid centers, social housing companies, community work ...). It is of permanent concern to support the 350 volunteers. The central Kras-services do so by participating actively in the projects and in the local network.

At the town and regional level, Kras is ready to take part in the discussion regarding the struggle against poverty. Thanks to its experience, Kras can signal where and when particular needs are to be met.

Last but not least, it is Kras' purpose to play an important role in the sensitization of our society, via information-sessions in schools, parishes, organizations ...

http://home2.pi.be/kv928288/

● Sint-Vincentiusvereniging – Saint-Vincent-Society

This widespread international organization is represented in Belgium as well, mostly in the province of Limburg, where, based on a rich tradition, some active groups are at work, especially with food aid and second-hand clothes.

● Sint-Egidius

The community of Sant' Egidio is a Christian lay community with 40,000 members in more than 60 countries all over the world. The Dutch and Flemish centre of Sant' Egidio is to be found in the city of Antwerp.

The Association for Solidarity VZW (Vereniging voor Solidariteit VZW) coordinates the social services of the Sint-Egidius community in the Dutch-speaking part of Belgium.

Among those services:

– Kamiano, a restaurant for homeless people.
– A second-hand shop.
– Primary Schools for Peace.
– Old Age groups.
– Friends and Youngsters for Peace.
– Language courses for adult immigrants.

Http://www.sint-egidius.org/nl/index.html

- Poverello

Poverello was founded by a famous gynecologist who changed his way of life drastically. After his conversion, he decided to put himself at the disposal of homeless people in Brussels. Today this organization has 6 relief centers in Belgium. The house in the Brussels district of the Marollen is well known. Homeless people can have lunch there and there are some beds for the night ...

http://www.poverello.be

Solidarity work

It is typical for this kind of work that the approach is much broader than it used to be in social service work, which particularly focuses on fighting the consequences of poverty. Solidarity work fights against structural poverty and deals with the causes of poverty. Through sensitization of our society and through signals given to policymakers, solidarity work contributes to the prevention of poverty.

In Belgium, Caritas co-ordinates the wide spectrum of welfare and health institutions. Since 1999, organizations of solidarity with the weakest have had a seat in the general assembly and in the study group on national matters of Netwerk Caritas Solidariteit (NCS). The following have seats in this assembly: an episcopal official, Broederlijk Delen, Welzijnszorg, Caritas Internationaal Hulpbetoon and Caritas Gemeenschapsdienst Caritas Hulpbetoon, Missio, Commissie Rechtvaardigheid en Vrede, Pax Christi and Kerkwerk Multicultureel Sameleven.

It is Welzijnszorg in particular, that is active in the area of combating poverty. That is why we will give a more detailed report on the goals and the activities of this "movement".

Welzijnszorg is a non-profit association, founded in 1969, it grew out of Caritas Hulpbetoon. A team of professionals and many volunteers are at work in Flanders and Brussels. Welzijnszorg works on poverty: how to prevent it, how to fight it, how to ban it.

Basically the movement tries to promote a global and coordinated policy.

As a Christian organization, Welzijnszorg aims at cooperation with people who have no or different religious beliefs, on the basis of universal common values, such as equality, justice, solidarity. Consequently the annual Lent campaigns and cooperative initiatives go beyond the contours of the church community.

The action is mainly dependent on private contributions and, to a lesser extent, on government subsidy. Welzijnszorg considers its mission to ban poverty. In order to realize this ambitious goal, the following strategies have been developed:

• Sensitization

By means of information and animation, Welzijnszorg tries to make as many people as possible aware of the fact that poverty is a social problem. In that way people who are aware turn into partners who, in collaboration with the poor, are ready to look for ways to improve everybody's well-being, but first and foremost to improve the well-being of the deprived. Every year during Lent, Welzijnszorg organizes an extensive campaign, focusing on one particular poverty item.

The campaign is run around a central theme with a striking title so that sensitization, political action and fund raising go hand in hand. One specific poverty-related theme or group is focused on every year. Recent years' campaigns were run around: the lack of knowledge and information gap, debts problems, old age and poverty, health and poverty, poverty becoming more female, refugees ... The 2003 has been former prisoners.

• Supporting well-being initiatives

Through selective financial support, Welzijnszorg gives opportunities to local initiatives, and the movement tries, by lobbying, to have those projects subsidized by the authorities. Welzijnszorg supports more than 200 projects concerning poverty and exclusion annually. On the one hand, interesting long-term projects with limited financial means are taken care of, on the other hand, Welzijnszorg intends to stimulate new initiatives focusing on new needs. This network of projects succeeds in getting both the public and the authorities in touch with sensible options to fight poverty. Regional project committees – composed of specialists – select the applications, on the basis of clear criteria. Every year the prize called "Armoede Uitsluiten" (Ban Poverty) is awarded. The amount of 12,555 Euros is given to a particularly deserving organization working on poverty and social exclusion. This award is not meant to be just a financial help, at the same time it is a signal of national recognition of competent and courageous commitment.

• Political action

During the campaigns, a broad social basis is created regarding specific demands. It all results in a solid dossier, Welzijnszorg seeks and gets the support of co-operators, the citizens are asked to take part in a petition, press meetings are organized, political and social authorities are invited to listen to the demands. This all is done to gain more influence in favour of the deprived.

• Promoting solidarity

Voluntary work is considered a surplus value in our Welzijnszorg "movement". We believe that voluntary work is a vital link in a society willing to assume its social responsibilities. That's why Welzijnszorg recognizes and promotes it. Both during the campaigns and on a permanent basis in the Welzijnsschakels (Well-being Links), the volunteers are the keystones of the action. Most of the volunteers – yet not exclusively – are church-related people.

Well-being Links (Welzijnsschakels) – there are more than 80 of them – are local groups of volunteers who take part in the struggle against poverty and exclusion in their neighbourhood. Such a group is a varied alliance of people who suffer or don't suffer from poverty. All Links work on the same basis, ideas and principles, yet no two groups are the same, since each group adapts its actions to the local situation. What are the local needs? What is already done by other services? What are we able to do? It's considered quite important to cooperate with other local social workers and institutes.

Http://www.welzijnszorg.be

Hans Raun Iversen

Denmark

> *"Far more of metal, so red and so white*
> *Others got from mountains and plunder.*
> *Danes, anyway, have daily bread,*
> *Even in the hut of the poor man.*
> *That's when in richness we have gone far,*
> *When few have too much and fewer too little."*

A Christian vision of social equality?

Thousands of social and political gatherings in Denmark are opened by one of the famous national songs, "Langt højere bjerge" (Far higher mountains), which concludes as quoted above. It was composed by the Danish national bard and modern father of the Danish church and nation, N. F. S. Grundtvig (1783-1872) on the occasion of a Danish expedition to West India in 1820. Grundtvig was a liberal in his own way. Especially from around 1830, when he made his first trip to England, he advocated religious, political and economic freedom. The idea of a social welfare state, where each individual citizen has the right to economic help from the common basket of state and municipality, was far from his mind. Even so, as a Christian he wanted there to be food for the poor Lazarus – and he surely wanted there to be as few poor people as possible in our small country. Presumably, Grundtvig here is drawing on the story of how God nurtured the Israelites by sending manna to them in the desert: The people were instructed to gather as much as they needed, two quarts for each member of a household; as a result "those who gathered much did not have too much, and those who gathered less did not have too little. Each had gathered just what he needed" (Exodus 26:18). It is a similar vision of divine distribution of God's own gifts that is behind the words of Grundtvig in this famous Danish national song.

Obviously, Grundtvig's words are open to interpretation. One interpretation could be that it is all right to have, for example, ten percent of people who are very rich if only we have fewer who are very poor. However, the general understanding is that there should be social and economic equality among the Danes, at least in as far as this demand does not hurt the freedom of the individual to engage in investment, trade and industry. As unclear as it is, it is probably this theological statement that, for almost 200 years, has been and still is a common norm for social politics in Denmark. No one would ever run for office or seek any other high position in Denmark without swearing to Grundtvig's statement. On the one hand, the statement is open to manipulation, not least of all in today's world, where – in a global context – the majority of the Danes surely have far too much! On the other hand, it seems to have been guiding our society – preventing us from having very many extremely rich people and also from having many Danish citizens poor enough to die from hunger over the past 200 years. Denmark has no high mountains, nor does it have any deep valleys. We are, in all respects, mentally as well as socially, the plain Danes living on the plains (Iversen 1997:140-143).

Although today in Demark, as in most parts of Europe, we have social-political slogans such as "rights always go with duties" and "to eat you must work" (or at least have compulsory job training while on social benefits!), these are far from being Biblical allusions or theologically reflective social-political statements, even though 2 Thessalonians 3:10 says something very similar. This new politics of the 1990s is simply a product of economic calculations pointing to the imbalance between the size of the labour force and the expenditures for social benefits in the welfare society of today and, in fact, of any foreseeable future. One statement by Jesus, however, seems to be true everywhere, including Denmark: "You will for always have poor people with you" (John 12:8). In Copenhagen as in all major European cities, one cannot use the Underground without meeting them. In the countryside, one might escape meeting them, but there may be even more of them, hiding themselves from the busy eyes of the rest of us.

Poverty in Denmark

Generally speaking, living conditions still seem to be improving in Denmark. From 1989 to 1998, the proportion of households with an automatic dishwasher increased from 23 to 46 percent, and the proportion of families with a personal computer increased from 12 to 60 percent during the same period. Even though Denmark has a high rate of death due to cancer (connected with high numbers of smokers), the average lifespan has increased to 75 years for a man and 80 for a woman. Regarding the income available for individual consumption, equality improved slightly during the 1980s, whereas the tendency towards inequality grew during the 1990s, when Denmark had a social-democratic government (Bonke and Munk: 2002:7f.)!

In comparison with the other social welfare societies of Scandinavia, Denmark ranks rather low in Eurostat's statistics on poverty. In 1999 among the EU countries, only Sweden, Germany and France used a higher percentage of the BNP than Denmark for social expenditure (Danish Statistical Yearbook 2002:163). We are now approaching a situation where half of the population receives some form of income transfer from state or municipality.

The percentage of relatively poor households, i.e., those having less than half of the median income, is 9.2 in Denmark and thus a little higher than in Germany, France, Holland and Belgium (Bonke and Munk 2002:13). The percentage of those who consider themselves to be poor is only 7.5 – and thus considerably lower than the average for Europe (Bonke and Munk 2002:13). Thus, generally speaking the number of poor people in Denmark is relatively low – at least according to conventional calculations. Poverty has two main causes. The first is social heritage. For people who have been poor for a long time, or who come from poor families, it is hard to climb the social ladder towards better economic conditions. There is a considerable tendency for children of poor parents to follow the path of their parents and thus remain among the poorer parts of society (Bonke and Munk 2002: 21f.). The other main cause of poverty is psychological diseases and social de route due to personal disasters or abuse, which make people unable to administer the few resources they have so that they become poor, perhaps even homeless and begging in the streets.

We have no precise figure for the number of homeless people, since they may, for example, be registered as living in a home, where they are not able to stay for psychological or other personal reasons. Dr. Preben Brandt, who for many years has worked with and researched the social-medical and social-psychological situation in the poorest areas of Copenhagen, has suggested the following definition of the group of poor and homeless people in Copenhagen: "They are people who are 'wrong' in relation to what we others consider to be 'right'; they behave differently. They do not live in a way that we find right and cannot utilise society's institutions in the term's broadest sense. From the point of view of ordinary citizens, the homeless are different in a negative sense, and we exclude them from our ordinary social life. We do not like them" (Koch-Nielsen 2002:3).

We also tend to place immigrants and refugees in Denmark among the "outsiders" and "wrongdoers". Over the past few years, the economic and mental conditions that Danish society has created for its immigrants have turned from bad to very bad. Strict discrimination takes place as refugees and immigrants are far from having the same civil rights and access to social benefits as ordinary Danish citizens. In addition, it has been suggested that the right to vote at local elections should be taken away from immigrants. When the social rights of the twentieth century and even the political rights of the nineteenth century are not respected in the case of immigrants in Denmark, it seems to be connected primarily to the fact that the Danes tend to behave as a tribal people. To be a proper Dane one had better look and work like us! Although we have many immigrants who look very different from us (the number of Muslims in 2002 was estimated to be 195,000), Islam and other immigrant religions have no official recognition in Denmark. This is a major reason why the Muslims, for example, have not yet been able to build mosques or establish their own funeral places in Denmark. Denmark does not really want its immigrants to feel at home in our country. The lack of civil, cultural and social recognition of the immigrants is most likely to contribute to segregation of major parts of this new group in Danish society – perhaps causing poverty for many generations among major parts of the immigrant population (cf. Ploug 2002: 5f.).

Today, the economy of the nation (i.e., the growth of GNP) is always more important than social equality among the people of Europe. In Denmark as well, social politics are determined by the capitalist market. We first seek growth and competition, and only as we succeed in gaining a higher GNP do we consider the possibility of doing more for the poor. This is true for a social- democratic government as well as for the present right-wing (liberal-conservative) government. Only in special cases, such as the case of the immigrants, are there differences between the political parties in terms of social politics. In spite of positive political statements from the minister of social affairs and a great deal of goodwill from many individual politicians in major parts of parliament, we should not expect better social politics. In fact, we should expect more cutbacks in the income of poor people in the future. These are the conditions if one wants to compete in the world market and to encourage and please the majority of the working and voting population, which thinks it is only fair to have good (i.e. better and better) standards of living in return for the hard work required in most places of work today.

Social ethics of the churches in Denmark

The Evangelical Lutheran Church in Denmark is the only church in the world that is labelled a Folk Church in the national constitution, dating back to 1849. Practically speaking, this church is "the weakest monopoly church in the world" (Iversen 1997). It is comparatively weaker than any other church (or major religion) anywhere in the world in terms of attendance, conformity of the population with its teachings, and expectations of the church from its members. On the other hand, for the great majority of the Danes the church is a monopoly church without any competing alternatives. Due to some hesitation among young parents regarding the practice of infant baptism over the past three decades and to immigration of non-Christians, the rate of membership in the Folk Church had fallen to 84 percent of the population in 2002. However, the rate of church funerals, for example, is very stable at around 92 percent, as most people see no alternative at the time of the death of a relative. Even though since 1849 the constitution has foreseen that the Folk Church should have its own legal leadership, for a number of reasons the state still serves as legislator, administrator and legal subject for the Folk Church. As a result, the Folk Church has no official teaching, except for what can be found in the Bible and the Lutheran Creeds (Confessio Augustana and The Small Catechism by Luther). Thus, there are no official statements from the Folk Church concerning modern ethical and social questions.

The non-Lutheran churches are few and small in Denmark, making up a little more than one percent of the population in terms of their membership. The largest among them today, due to immigration, is the Roman Catholic Church, which of course has strong social-ethical teachings – and also undertakes social activities such as relief work in poor countries (Caritas). The same is true for some of the protestant "free" churches in Denmark, such as the Methodist church, which – in spite of having less than 2000 members – carries a good load of social projects. Most well known among poor people, and even among the general public, is the Salvation Army (also with less than 2000 members). The Salvation Army is extremely active in distributing "the sacrament of helping" in poor parts of major cities in Denmark.

During major parts of the twentieth century, especially from 1950 to 1990, the secular welfare state ideology was very strong, not least among members and pastors of the Folk Church in Denmark. This trend, to which the majority of the pastors belonged up to 1990, had a number of causes and background factors: 1) As in many Western European countries, the social welfare state was successful in making people believe that social progress would continue within the framework of the social welfare state, and thus private, not to mention religious, initiatives looked conservative or nostalgically misplaced. 2) Due to this understanding of social politics and probably even more to the position of the church as a legal part of the state, with the state as its legal subject and the pastors as civil servants of the state, the pastors have been very keen on developing a theology where preaching and listening to sermons are the only legal activities of the church. Karl Barth, Martin Luther, Søren Kierkegaard and even Grundtvig have been interpreted in a way that legitimised the absolute detachment of the church from any sort of social responsibility. As politics should be separated from Christianity, so should social responsibility, as it was seen as a political matter resting with state and municipality – and, of course, to a limited extent with the individual Christian in his or her daily life in the family or place of work (Iversen in Nissen (ed.) 2001: 35-39).

Since 1990, it has been recognised in growing areas of the Folk Church that this secular-oriented, individualistic, kerygmatic theology is very one-sided, if not heretical, when seen from the perspective of Bible and church history. There are many reasons behind this change in theology, including the following: 1) There is no need to strive for a social welfare state that is better than the communist states, when there are no communist states left. Instead, we can try to find a new balance between state, market and civil society as agents in cooperation, including social politics. 2) At the same time, the state is being reduced as many parts of its work are being "delegated" to agents at the market level or in civil society. This also is beginning to challenge the church: It is not safe any longer to swear to the state only, as the state is no longer a sovereign state but rather a responsive, negotiating and coordinating agent in our society (Bundesen et al. 2001). This means that the church is again taking up local social responsibilities, especially at the parish level where it has 100 years of tradition of parish boards taking responsibility for local church work together with the pastors. 3) Alongside these political and social developments, theology is also developing strongly, discovering and rediscovering social dimensions and ethical challenges in Christian theological traditions as well as in contextual theologies from other parts of the world.

This provides some of the background for the unanimous decision in 1999 by the bishops of the Folk Church to form a committee to review and give recommendations about the diaconal work of the Folk Church. Because of the state-church organisation of the Folk Church, there is no board or synod at the national level to receive, discuss and officially approve the analysis and recommendations in the committee's report, "Diacony – an integrated dimension in the life of the Folk Church" (Nissen (ed.) 2001). Nevertheless, the report points towards a new trend in the Folk Church in terms of social responsibility. The social work that has always existed in different forms in the Folk Church is being recognised, legitimised and encouraged in the report. In short, the report argues that Sunday services, Christian teaching, mission work and diaconal work are equal as areas of work for any church, even though the actual priority given to different forms of church work in the Folk Church must always depend on the decisions of parish boards and volunteer church organisations, which carry the practical burden of the work.

Church work among poor people

Social work in the Folk Church is basically organised in two ways: at the parish level and at the national level in free diaconal organisations – in line with the two traditions which developed in diaconal work in Germany in the wave of pietism (Nissen (ed.) 2001: 7-15).

At the parish level, the parish boards became responsible in 1903 for collections in the church for the poor people in the parish. Regular collections for poor people are still required in the church legislation, but in practice most congregations collect money for many purposes other than aid to the poor – and some collect very little and very rarely. Especially in Copenhagen and other cities, it is common to have a parish-based Congregational Care Organisation (based on the German concept of "Gemeindepflege"). Thirty-five percent of the congregations organise aid to poor people at Christmas especially; in major cities, 88 percent of the congregations are involved in this (Nissen (ed.) 2001:239). However, more parishes are involved in various forms of work for elderly people (74 percent), often social gatherings. In some parishes, there are other social activities such as visitation teams, and meeting and eating places for lonely and poor people. Today, work at the parish level is being strengthened by the introduction of catechetical and diaconal parish workers, who are now leading the social work in about 200 of the biggest parishes of around 2000 parishes in the Folk Church.

The most comprehensive and intensive church work among poor people is organised by volunteer (so-called free) diaconal organisations, with little or no formal links to the Folk Church as it is organised within the legal framework of the state. We can distinguish between four types of diaconal work carried out by diaconal organisations in Denmark.

Perhaps the most important type can be called *extreme diacony*, where the organisations provide food, shelter, medical care, human contact and ultimately the possibility for help to change the life situation for the most poor and downtrodden among us: homeless people, those suffering from abuse (often combined with prostitution), mentally disturbed people who cannot be placed in institutions, etc. The Church Army (founded in 1912 with English inspiration) is especially active here – with more than 5000 volunteers led by full-time employed social workers and pastors placed in most of the major towns in Denmark. For almost 100 years, the experience of The Church Army has been that there are always new groups of people who need attention at "the country roads and lanes" (Luke 14:23), where The Church Army considers its calling to be at work. This work has placed the pastor leading The Church Army as the most respected ad-vocate for the weakest placed among the poor.

The classic form of diaconal work may be called *pioneering diacony*. Historically, most forms of social and health work known in our society today have been pioneered by the volunteer church organisations. This is still taking place, for example, in the introduction of hospices, which are decisive not only for the terminal patients admitted to them, but also for the possibility of resistance to suggestions about new legislation allowing doctors to give active death assistance to dying people. Both of the two major old deaconess houses in Copenhagen spent considerable resources pioneering hospice work during the 1990s.

A third form of diaconal work is *alternative social work*, where volunteer organisations attempt to provide better procedures and standards than those provided by state and municipality. This is especially the case in preventive work, for example, among alcoholics and drug abusers, who are always at risk of ending up among the poor and outsiders. Parish churches and diaconal organisations are also involved in creating places for different types of job training and protective jobs.

A fourth type that some diaconal organisations also undertake today is what could be called *competitive diacony*. This is especially the case where state and municipalities want to privatise social work – for example, home care among disabled and elderly people who cannot care for themselves. Wherever volunteer organisations, including those in the church, can set better standards than those found in public or private organisations, it is very worthwhile to do so.

The best parts of the work among poor people are often organised as "welfare mix", having input and participants from various agents such as state, municipality, parishes, church organisations, humanitarian organisations and others. This is a great challenge and, at the same time, a great opportunity for the Folk Church especially, which to a large degree is still an integrated part of the Danish society (Nissen (ed.) 2001:149-164).

It is estimated that 1.2 million people are involved in some form of volunteer work in Denmark. Of these, 300,000 are active in social work, 50,000 of the volunteers being active in social work organised by churches and diaconal organisations. In spite of fears to the contrary, there seems to be a growing number of people who will let themselves be recruited to volunteer social work in church and society, provided that there are leaders who organise good structures for the work and call upon volunteers to join it. Whether we like it or not, voluntary giving of money (and not least of all, time) seems to be a necessary way forward if there is any hope for a better future for the poor among us (cf. Habermann 2001 and Nissen (ed.) 2001:240f.).

Conclusion

At the time of the Reformation in 1536, the conquering King Christian III, and thus the state, expropriated the church and all its belongings in Denmark. The state took the property, the right to tithe, the solid infrastructure, the pastors, and thus the ideological apparatus from the church. This may be the most important historical precondition of the modern Danish social welfare society. It is arguable that the state also took over the social project of the church, even though it was 400 years later before the state was economically and politically in a position to realise the "Christian" vision of social equality in the form of the social welfare state (Knudsen ed. 2001). Today it seems obvious that state and municipality will never be able to realise the full vision by caring properly for those poor people who are most vulnerable. Even if the state gives them enough bread and money to survive from day to day, they cannot live from that alone. In order for the poor to have a life with the experience of love and at least some hope for changes to the better someday, others must step in. The churches in Denmark, including the Folk Church, are challenged to be among these others – teaching their members social responsibility and organising work among the poor.

Finally, it must be mentioned here that there is a strong connection between experiences from volunteer social work, the general attitudes towards the poor in the population, and the actual social politics of state and municipality (cf. Nissen (ed.) 2001:230). Only those who give their time and have the courage to be close to the poor and outsiders can argue convincingly that the poor are at least as human as the rest of us. If we do not care for the poor, we destroy the human standards of our society! Only if the experience from work among the poor is kept alive among ordinary people will those people have the strength to demand social justice and ethical standards in our society. And the politicians, who after all are people from the people, depending on the goodwill of the people, will adjust the social politics accordingly. Thus, diaconal practice among the poor is a cornerstone in the fight against the many forms of Social Darwinism that are infiltrating society. Only those who attend to the poor can be proper advocates for the poor.

References

Bach Iversen, J. C. et al. (2000): Kirken og det civile samfund (Church and Civil Society), Det Økumeniske Center, Århus.

Bonke, Jens / Munk, Martin D.(2002): Fordeling af velfærd I Danmark. Resultater og perspektiver fra Socialforskningsinstituttets forskning om velfærdsfordeling (Distribution of Welfare in Denmark. Results and Perspectives from The Danish Social Research Institute's Research on Distribution of Welfare), Copenhagen.

Bundesen, Peter / Henriksen, Lars Skov / Jørgensen, Anja (2001): Finaltropi, Selvhjælp og Interesseorganisering. Frivillige organisationer i dansk socialpolitik 1849-1990'erne (Philanthropy, Self-help and Organization of Interests. Volunteer Organization in Danish Social Politics 1949-1990'ies), Odense.

Good News Bible. The Bible in Today's English Version.

Habermann, Ulla (2001): En postmoderne helgen? – om motiver til frivillighed (A post-modern Saint? – on Motives in Volunteer Work), Lund Dissertations in Social Work 3, Lund.

Iversen, Hans Raun (1997): Leaving the Distant Church: The Danish Experience, In: Bar-Lex, Mordechai / Shaffir, William (eds.): Leaving Religion and Religious Life, London.

Knudsen, Tim (ed.) (2002): Den nordiske protestantisme og velfærdsstaten (The Nordic Protestantism and the Welfare State), Århus.

Koch-Nielsen, Inger (2002): Danish literature review on research in access to housing and homelessness. Unpublished Paper, Danish National Institute of Social Research, Copenhagen.

Nissen, Karsten (red.) (2001): Diakoni – en integreret dimension i folkekirkens liv (Diaconia – an integrated Dimension in the life of the folk church), Copenhagen.

Ploug, Niels (red.) (2002): Velfærd I Europa. Resultater og perspektiver fra Socialforskningsinstituttets komparative velfærdsforskning (Welfare in Europe. Results and Perspectives from The Danish Social Research Institute' comparative Research in Welfare), Copenhagen.

Statistical Yearbook, Danmarks Statistik, Copenhagen 2002.

Mikko Malkavaara

Finland

When Finland became independent in 1917, it was a poor and peripheral country whose main source of livelihood was agriculture. During the time of early independence, Finland was in Europe's backyard as regards development as well.

Now the situation is different. Finland is among the front-row welfare societies and is repeatedly ranked top in areas such as: education, environment, security, use of technology, competitive ability, lack of corruption etc.

However, this success story has another side. It is undeniable that there are poor and marginalized people in Finland. Researchers have pointed out that it is possible to give a two-fold description of the situation of poverty in Finland. The process of social exclusion takes place rapidly in Finland. On the other hand, the welfare state does quite a good job. In spite of deteriorating circumstances, it has succeeded in preventing too many individuals from dropping through the safety net. Therefore, even though there is a poverty problem in Finland, the proportion of poor people is one of the lowest in Europe.

In this article, my aim is to give an overview of the role and actions of churches in Finland in regard to the problem of poverty during recent decades. Because the Evangelical Lutheran Church of Finland is a majority church with a membership of about 85 % of the population (the second largest church is the Orthodox Church with a membership of 1 % of the population), this article deals mainly with the Lutheran majority church.

Between the two World Wars

Before the Second World War, Finland was a one-horse town with regard to social policy. Finland was among the slowest in Europe in developing social insurance and living allowances, and this was not only a result of slow industrialisation and urbanization. The reason was more a lack of political will.

Soon after the Russian Revolution and Finland's declaration of independence (1917), an unfortunate civil war took place in 1918, in which the right-wing "white" troops (supporters of a bourgeois model of society) beat the rebellious red army led by the labour movement. After the civil war, the political left and the trade union movement were powerless. Those who had won the war were slow to improve the economical circumstances of those who had lost the war. It was a punishment or even revenge against the rebellious ones who had dared to shake the peace and harmony and status quo of society. The general line of social policy was public assistance that was directed only at the margins of the society.

The Church supported the white army, and after the civil war, the clergy adopted a right wing, Finnish-national and patriotic worldview. It did not show any notable interest in the weaker sections of the population or measures of social policy. At the same time, there was some development in the Church's diaconal work, but its main interests were directed towards the mentally disabled, orphaned children, handicapped people etc.

In the field of social policy, different NGOs were more important than the government, even until as late as the 1930's. The majority of the population lived in the countryside where there was no public assistance, and there were no hospitals or active NGOs. Little by little, the attitude in society developed more positively towards reforms in social policy. Worries concerning an aging population produced new thoughts about pensions, and fears of a reduction in the population produced ideas of developing family policy. The main reasons for Finnish social policy, the national integration of all groups within the population, became possible again during and especially after the Second World War.

Understanding the development of Finnish social policy also presupposes consideration of the religious background of the country. Lutheranism accepted the role and tasks of the State and did not argue about the justification of the state-run social and health services as the Catholic Church did. A common religion strengthened national cohesion and a sense of belonging to one nation, people and culture. The Finnish-national movement, the fact that the majority of the population were peasants or at least lived in the countryside and the lack of wealth and capital influenced development in the same direction. Unlike other Nordic countries, local municipal administration was separated from the parish administration in Finland by the 1860s. Finland acquired a separate Church law that guaranteed independence from the Church as early as 1869. Because the joint parish administration had taken care of the poor, in the beginning the separation process diminished the resources destined for poverty relief, but in the long run, the State and the local municipalities, motivated by the State, formed the basis for Finnish social policy.

Towards the welfare state

The general atmosphere in the country after the Second World War was contradictory. The preserved independence was a source of joy, but on the other hand, cessions of territory in the eastern part of the country, material destruction and human losses created sorrow and bitterness. About 420,000 Finns who escaped from the ceded territories had to be repatriated. The situation with regard to nutrition, clothing, health and housing were difficult for a long time. Political life was insecure and confused. The Control Commission of the Allies in the hands of Soviet officers exercised power and authority until the Paris Peace Treaty in 1947. The Communist Party, which had been illegal before the war, was already one of the major parties in the government in 1945. The influence of the Communists was especially strong in internal policy. There were constant fights between Communists and Social Democrats in work-places, strikes were commonplace, and a revolution was generally feared. The war crimes trial, in which Finland's wartime political leaders were convicted and sentenced to prison, cast a dark shadow on social and political life.

The lost war ruined the former national idealism in Finland. The focus of the new foreign policy was to maintain good relations with the Soviet Union. Because the Communist movement and its hostile ideological stance towards religion was seen to be a severe threat to the Church, for many church leaders and church members, it was difficult to give up their fear of the former enemy. In practise, the Communists did not cause any harm to the Church, nor did the period of transition directly affect the position of the Church. The Church was seen to be a protective factor in keeping national identity, and it was able to continue its activities as a folk church as before. Thus, the war even led to a strengthening of the role of the Church. In 1946, the Social Democrat Party gave up its traditional claims concerning the separation of State and Church and abolition of religious instruction in schools. This was seen to consolidate ideas that were born during the pressure of the war and aimed to reinforce the role of the Church as a Church for all layers and parts of the population. In public political life, there were no more pastors from the extreme right, and the first pastors were elected to parliament from the lists of the Social Democrats in 1948. Opening up towards society meant a slight transition to the left for the Church.

The Second World War was also a turning point for Finnish social policy. The era of local municipal poverty relief was over. The responsibility of the State was emphasized right after the war. According to the models from England and Sweden, the goal was to guarantee protection in the cases of illness, incapacity for work, old age and the rising cost of living. Furthermore, social policy was made into a tool of national integration. However, a welfare system did not exist at all yet, and there were no special means to cope with the shortages of the most basic necessities.

During wartime, the synod of the Evangelical Lutheran Church of Finland proposed an important amendment to the Church Law. From 1944, it became compulsory for every parish to have a post for diaconal work. There had been deaconesses earlier in the parishes, but without any regulations relating to that. The years of reconstruction after the war were also years of building the new diaconal organization inside the Church.

Generous gifts from churches abroad – Sweden, Denmark, the World Council of Churches and especially from the American Lutherans – meant notable support for humanitarian aid and for how the deaconesses tried to confront and to relieve poverty. Because of the political pressure from the Soviet Union, Finland was not able to receive Marshall Aid which was so important for many West European countries that had suffered during the war. With help of donations from the American Lutheran churches, the

Evangelical Lutheran Church of Finland was able to rebuild 18 church buildings, 26 parish houses, 32 folk high schools or other educational centres. In addition, a similar sum of money was given to humanitarian aid programs delivered mostly through the new diaconal organization.

In the 1940s, the aims of the diaconate were deeply social, even political by nature. The Church nominated a board for diaconal work, and there were representatives present from all important political groups. The idea was to influence as directly as possible the social structures of the country. It did not last long, however, and the diaconal board had to be discontinued because of political disagreements. There was also another reason for this kind of development inside the Church. Pietism had been a very important factor in Finnish church life. The pietistic circles could not understand the new interpretation of the Gospel, in which the Church was seen as a servant of the people. The old pietistic movements and the new evangelistic movements joined with this critical attitude against the new folk church ideology. The diaconal work in the parishes was now defined as charitable by nature, taking place on a personal level because of Christian love.

In spite of the discussions at the national church level, the deaconesses in the parishes were able to work with and for the weak and poor. They sent out nurses who were well known even in the most remote villages. Cooperation with the local municipalities, local doctors etc. was easy and natural. In the 1950s, the ministry of the diaconate was opened to men, too. Deacons were not nurses but social workers that had been educated to work with different age groups, with those with drug and mental problems and with other socially marginalized people.

In the welfare state Finland

Building the welfare system did not mean anything special to the Church. At least the Church did not react much towards any plans, and it was not asked to participate actively in creating new service structures for society.

A great change for the Church took place in 1972 with the new National Health Act, which no longer recognized the work of the deaconesses.

"The golden age of the welfare state" in Finland did not last longer than two decades, the 1970s and 1980s. The ideology behind the welfare state saw that society was capable of solving all the problems with legislation and different social institutions and services. There was also a very rapid growth in the health and social services. Administration systems were centralized, local municipalities had an important role, but the Church and the third sector with different NGOs were left with very limited and supplementary tasks. Because positive economic development also meant more possibilities for the Church, parishes were able to continue their diaconal work and even create new ways of confronting and helping those who were most in need and marginalized. Public sector social care and the work of the Church were almost totally separated and there was not much cooperation. Even though the Church emphasized help to the poorest and weakest as a slogan of the diaconate, in fact the focus of diaconal work in most parishes was on spiritual activities with the elderly.

Ironically, for the Lutheran Church, the golden age of the welfare state meant a period of new understanding of the Church itself, its ecclesiastic essence, its diaconal and missionary dimension and its role in ethical discussions in society. The most important reasons for this theological change were the development and discussions in the ecumenical movement and ecumenical research both in Finland and abroad. The first echoes from the politically-oriented liberation theology were heard. The general atmosphere in the late 1960s and 1970s was socially and politically loaded. The international diaconate had the leading role as mouthpiece and advocate of the poor. The new interpretation of Luther's theology no longer prevented the Church from taking a critical stand towards the state authorities. When the Church raised its critical voice, it was not always taken that seriously. President Mauno Koivisto (1982-1994) especially regarded the Church as being for religion and spiritual life, not for interference in politics.

The depression

During the first half of the 1990s, the Finnish economy was struggling with a serious depression, which led to an increase in unemployment, decrease in the household unit income level, and increased taxation. However, despite the major changes that took place in the national economy of Finland in the 1990s, the number of people classified as poor and the average poverty rate remained constant and relatively low by international comparison. When the difficult times with deep and serious unemployment finally came to an end, property income and especially higher income salaries increased and tax progression decreased. Consequently, the differences between people's income levels became steeper, and in 1998, the number of low income workers started to increase in Finland.

The positive impacts on employment of economic growth after the depression could mostly be seen in and around the capital, i.e. in Helsinki and its surroundings, and in the biggest centres of growth. An exceptionally intensive migration has been and still is going on in these areas. Economic differences between the wealthy and the poor Finland have thus increased after the depression of the 1990s. Unemployment and the threat of unemployment are still a burden in many areas, and the problem of inequality between regions has not been solved. It has even been said that Finland has been split into two parts. A survey from the summer of 2003 claims that differences between areas in Finland have grown faster than in any other country in Europe.

A household is defined as a low-income household if the available income per consumption unit is less than 60% of the median income of the whole population. In low-income households, the person responsible for the income is usually a student or an unemployed person. It is notable, however, that in Finland the number of people working in a profession and belonging to the low-income group increased at the turn of the last decade. To give some figures: the last available reliable data about poverty show that, in 2001, 10.8% of the population was poor. In August 2003, the unemployment rate in Finland was 7.7% (in August 2002 it was 8.1%). Among the youngest, the unemployment rate was 16.1% (in 2002 it was

14.9%). Unemployment in the province of South Finland was the lowest, 6.5%. In the province of East Finland it was the highest, 11.7%.

In the 1980s, during the golden age of the Finnish welfare state, poverty in Finland could be called a privilege of homeless alcoholics with little exaggeration. Income disparity was the smallest of all industrial countries, and proportional poverty was in some years even lower than in Sweden. Social transfers of income lifted people above the poverty line, and poverty diminished steadily until 1990. Thus, social policy was a successful tool against poverty.

Depression in the 1990s brought poverty to the streets and gave it a new face. When the figures of unemployed increased to over 20 % of the whole population, the number of customers at the social welfare offices increased as well. As new groups, there were families with children, elderly people and students.

Reasons for the depression were international recession, the collapse of the Soviet Union, which meant the loss of one fifth of Finnish foreign trade, and a domestic bank crisis after years of overheating in the capital markets. Problems were so severe that the government had to cut many public health and social care services. Some of the most visible changes were reductions in the mental health care services. Thousands of patients that had earlier received care in the hospitals were now sent away without sufficient treatment. Many of the reductions were so slight and invisible that researchers have called this development that weakened the Finnish welfare system in 1990s as sneaking or insidious change.

The bread queue

As the situation worsened, the NGOs and churches started to work actively for the unemployed and other disadvantaged groups. The Salvation Army organized delivery of free bread for everyone who wanted to queue for it. "The bread queue" became a symbol of the 1990s in Finland. It became widely known for the first time when a Finnish television channel presented a report on the poverty situation in Finland in 1993, using photographic material from the bread queue in the Kallio quarters in Helsinki, where hundreds of needy people stood waiting for their daily bread as they did every day. This was crushing for the public image of the welfare state. When the international media became curious, the then social minister tried to minimize the problem, but with little success. The churches and the most prominent NGOs were challenged, together with government experts, to try to solve the problem.

The poverty problem became directly visible to the Church during those years. The clients of the deacons and deaconesses simply changed. Taking care of and providing recreation for the aged had to be more or less set aside when two new groups of clients crowded their consulting hours. The first group was those with mental health problems. The second group consisted of people of working age experiencing problems in earning a living. Many of them were unemployed, many were in debt or former private entrepreneurs who had lost their enterprise in bankruptcy. New skills were now required of the deacons and deaconesses. They were needed not only for pastoral care, but also as consultants for those in personal debt crisis, to solve their clients' economic situation, and to negotiate about their unpaid rents or loan securities. As an emergency measure, the diaconal workers gave their customers a coupon for a grocer's store or a cafeteria; in other words, very often it was a question of hunger.

Food banks

The provision of material aid, food aid, too, had always been the role of the diaconate. During the golden age of the welfare state, it was not much needed. Statistics of the Lutheran Church of Finland show how sharply the situation changed during the first year of the depression in 1991. At first, the parishes organized meal services for the unemployed. The intention was also to offer a meeting place where they could gather and discuss their own situation. The number of different requests for aid gradually grew so much that no appropriations were sufficient. Something had to be done when there were so many in desperate need. In the diaconiate centre of Tampere parishes, the second largest city of the country, they created the idea of a food bank system according to some models of food banks in Central Europe. Finland had become a member of the European Union in 1995. Now it was possible for the churches and NGOs in Finland to apply for special assistance from the EU for intervention supplies to be delivered on social grounds. It meant something new in the Finnish social security system, when private NGOs and churches organized a large-scale delivery of free food for those in need. Everyone had thought that the era of soup kitchens was over. The diaconate centre also expected donations from the food industry and commercial firms. Because there were many other aid organizations feeding the poor, the Lutheran Church wanted to register the word "food bank" for their purposes only to guarantee the reliability of the activities.

The main difference between the food bank system of the Lutheran Church and many other aid programs was that the Church diaconate could offer the assistance of the well-educated diaconal workers, deacons and deaconesses. People came to "the bread line" of the Salvation Army in-cognito, but in the Lutheran Church, the idea was the opposite. The Church workers wanted to know their customers and their situation thoroughly; thus, it was not only the lack of food that was to be addressed. Other principles were that nobody should become dependent on that aid, so it was always temporary by nature. Quite soon, it had to be admitted that, even in the food banks, the ways of distributing aid were too mechanical and many times very humiliating for the clients. It was also not easy to prevent customers from coming over and over again to the food bank.

The first food bank started in Tampere in November 1995. Within a couple of months, there were many food bank units working in bigger cities throughout the country. On the national church level, there was already a steering group for the growing food bank program in February 1996. Diaconal workers from different parishes frequently visited Tampere and some of the other first food banks. The most meaningful event leading to the growth of food bank activities was when the Church's annual fund-raising campaign, Common Responsibility, took supporting of the food banks into its program. The Common Responsibility

Campaign is organized by the Church and takes place in every parish. Always with the President of the Republic as its patron, it is the largest and best-known fund-raising operation in the whole country.

Common Responsibility saw this topic as a chance to speak about poverty in Finland strikingly and movingly. As a means of social policy, it was not seen as important, indeed quite the opposite. In the leadership of the Common Responsibility, it was seen as a low-standard, contemporary form of quick aid, but an interesting way to create a general discussion on hunger and poverty and thus to influence public opinion. Therefore, the diaconal leaders of the Church exceptionally but carefully informed beforehand the then social minister Terttu Huttu-Juntunen about their plans. The Minister expressed her fear about the possibility that people would get used to the food banks and regard them as a useful and good form of social aid, after which public opinion would accept more reductions in the social sector of society. The representatives of the Church assured her that they empathised with her unease and stated that their aim was not to establish a new poor relief system. They wanted to show people what dramatic changes there had been in the basis of the values of society and, as a consequence of a new nonchalance, there was a great danger of creating a new poverty culture and a poverty spiral that would extend over generations. Therefore, the food banks were more or less to be seen as a demonstration for strengthening the welfare state and the social ethos of society.

Those involved in the Church diaconate were well aware that in the social security system of society there was a crush that continued to grow. The Church saw it as its responsibility to react and try to represent those in need and to encourage the local parishes to help them. Therefore, the Common Responsibility fund-raising campaign and the national steering group for the food banks asked Helsinki Bishop Eero Huovinen to call a broadly-based group of influential politicians and the best experts in the field of social policy. There were representatives of the six biggest groups of Finland's parliament, of the most important labour market organizations, of local municipalities, of the biggest NGOs, of the Church and of the universities. The group called itself the Hunger Group. In November 1998 the Hunger Group published a statement and, in addition to that a broad survey about the situation of poverty in Finland. The statement was formed to be a part of the program of the new government that was to be formed after the general elections in spring 1999. The Hunger Group proposed that the next government would focus on such measures "with which it will prevent and diminish severe poverty problems, marginalization and accumulation of the badly off". Naturally, the statement got a lot of publicity. More importantly, it had a direct political influence. The new government led by Prime Minister Paavo Lipponen adopted the statement of intent into its program as it stood. Thus, the Hunger Group, set up by the Church, was able to raise the prevention of poverty to the agenda of daily politics. The result was remarkable and important to the Church even though it was only a short step towards reaching the primary goal of solving the poverty problem.

The food bank was a temporary phenomenon. In 2001, there were still about 60 parishes operating food bank activities and about 200 parishes of the total 580 were delivering EU aid packages. In 2003, those figures are lower. Still the Lutheran Church and its parishes deliver more food aid than any NGO in the country. Close cooperation with different NGOs is more and more important.

Taking up the poverty problem and serving people's genuine need brought the Church a lot of positive publicity and more respect. On the other hand, it was self-evident that the argument of protest or demonstration was no longer valid when the activities went on and on. Rather, there were many who asked whether the food banks had had a negative effect: maybe it had calmed down and dulled the minds of the well-to-do majority and led it to accept this kind of poverty relief by the Church because it was so advantageous from the point of view of the tax burden. If that was true, the Church's criticism against neo-liberalism and results of the new market economy for the poor had not been so successful. Direct material aid led the diaconia to multiply and to increase cooperation with the social work of the local municipalities. In some cases, it caused problems when the social workers directed their customers to the Church, going against the principles of the welfare state and the law.

The most important thing is that the Church has raised its voice to defend the opinion that basic security always belongs to the responsibility of society. Archbishop John Vikström (1982-1999) in particular became famous for his well-argumented defence of the welfare society. What is more interesting is that when the foundations for the welfare state were laid, the Lutheran majority Church was quite passive and not particularly interested. In the new situation, it was essential to show that the foundations for the welfare society were founded in Lutheran theology. When Finland became a member of the EU, it was quite popular to analyze differences in social policy between different parts of Europe because of different religious backgrounds (Lutheran, Reformed, Catholic). Of course, it has also been important that the Church has responded to the needs of the poor and it has kept the poverty problem in the public eye. Now the Church repeatedly reminds us that the basis of the welfare state lies in the Lutheran ethical background and that the discussion about poverty is always involved with the morale of the whole of society.

The government of Paavo Lipponen was not so successful in preventing the poverty problem. Even though it had that special poverty program, only some parts of it were implemented. At the same time, the diaconal leaders of the Church understood that the Hunger Group had been used once but that kind of operation could not be repeated. The advisers of the Hunger Group still continued to work with the diaconal leaders, and they expressed very clearly the opinion of the Church: the minimum support for the unemployed must be higher. Without a clear improvement in that, the Church would continue its activities. However, the Church wanted to say that no-one should be left to live on charity. Therefore, the Church wanted the poverty issue to be included in political programs. Problems of marginalization should and could be solved only by means of national politics. The Church wanted to challenge the politicians to make social policy but also wanted to give information about its work among the poorest and tell them about ideas developed by the diaconal workers on how to solve the problems.

All the time, there has been an audible voice expressing the view that special poverty programs do not belong to the Nordic view of social policy, but that the problems should be solved by universal solutions that concern everybody. The Church has not commented on this. Its opinion has been that the details belong to the politicians, but the first thing to be done is to raise the minimum support for the unemployed.

The socio-ethical line of the Church

The food banks and political work linked with it brought the Church into the midst of the "political diaconate". Some seeds of that had been seen already right after the Second World War, but compromises between different diaconal views and traditional Finnish theology had faded into invisibility. In the 1960s, there was a new wave of political diaconal or political theology. It was a reaction to a much broader wave of liberalism and radicalism which were typical for that time. The most important channel and interpreter for that was the ecumenical movement. Even though there were some circles in the Church where these critical socio-ethical ideas remained influential and important, it was not until the 1990s that the diaconate's criticism against society became more powerful and united with the more radical socio-ethical views. It has also been said that new research on Luther and Lutheranism had liberated the Church from its old theological thinking. The result was that diaconates had to face the poverty problem and start to work very genuinely with the poorest and openly argue their case in political life.

The change in the Church's thinking can be very clearly noticed in the socio-ethical report entitled "Towards the Common Good", which was published by the bishops of the Lutheran Church of Finland just before the Finnish parliamentary elections in 1999. The bishops defended the Nordic model of the welfare state. The statement aroused widespread discussion in the Finnish media. It was praised in the editorials of many newspapers, but the economists' opinions were conflicting. Some considered that it was undesirable for the bishops as representatives of the Church to take a stand on social or economic issues. As the debate progressed, some criticized the bishops' report for not placing enough emphasis on the cause of entrepreneurs and the self-employed.

The report was a joint statement by the nine bishops of the Lutheran Church of Finland. It stated that Nordic society with its acceptance of social responsibility is an achievement which should not be given up. It is a task of the State to protect the weak and defend justice. Basic social security must be extended to subsistence, education and health care to such a degree that it serves all citizens regardless of wealth, place of residence or social status. "In order to limit the deleterious effects of market forces, we need both morality and political strength which transcends the frontiers of national states and cultural circles." The Finnish bishops called for mechanisms and structures to regulate the global economy. In their opinion, it was irresponsible to build a society that is dependent solely on economic growth.

"Towards the Common Good" is an important document. Perhaps its most interesting feature is that, for the first time, the Church appeared to be worried and even more, it expressed that it had lost its trust in the value basis of society and the State's ability to solve common problems in changed circumstances. The Church was no longer faithful to State authority but wanted to express its own opinion.

The Church has changed its old role and renewed its social profile. It can be said that the Church is nearer the political left than ever before. It is also interesting to note that the Church's doctrines have changed, mostly because of ecumenical research and international contacts. The Church is now more independent from the State. It is not only a loyal partner of the State as earlier but also much more conscious of its own essence. This has caused more space and freedom for the Church to take up its stands on moral and political issues.

References

Anttonen, Anneli & Sipilä, Jorma, Suomalaista sosiaalipolitiikkaa (Social Policy in Finland). Vastapaino. Tampere 2000.

Heikkilä, Matti & Vähätalo, Kati (editors), Huono-osaisuus ja hyvinvointivaltion muutos (To be disadvantaged and the Changes of the Welfare State). Gaudeamus. Tampere 1994.

Heikkilä, Matti & Karjalainen, Jouko (editors), Köyhyys ja hyvinvointivaltion murros (Poverty and the Rupture of the Welfare State). Gaudeamus. Tampere 2000.

Heikkilä, Matti, Karjalainen, Jouko & Malkavaara Mikko (editors), Kirkonkirjat köyhyydestä (Poverty and the Church). Kirkkopalvelujen julkaisuja 5. Pieksämäki 2000.

Julkunen, Raija, Suunnanmuutos. 1990-luvun sosiaalipoliittinen reformi Suomessa (Change of Course. The Reform of the Finnish Social Policy in the 1990s). Vastapaino. Tampere 2001.

Kangas, Olli & Ritakallio, Veli-Matti (editors), Kuka on köyhä? Köyhyys 1990-luvun puolivälin Suomessa (Who is poor? Poverty in Finland in mid-1990s). Stakes tutkimuksia 65. Helsinki 1996.

Kantola, Anu & Kautto, Mikko, Hyvinvoinnin valinnat. Suomen malli 2000-luvulla (The Choices of the Welfare. The Model of Finland in the 2000s). Edita. Helsinki 2002.

Malkavaara, Mikko (editor), Ei etsi omaansa. Tutkimuksia altruismista ja yhteisvastuusta ("It does not insist on its own way." Researches of altruism and joint responsibility). Kirkkopalvelujen julkaisuja 4. Pieksämäki 2000.

Mäkinen, Virpi (editor), Lasaruksesta leipäjonoihin. Köyhyys kirkon kysymyksenä (From Lazarus to the Bread Queues. Poverty as a Question of the Church). Atena Kustannus. Jyväskylä 2002.

Peter Bartmann and Saskia Jung

Germany

Poverty and social inequality

Since the first Government report on Poverty and Wealth in 2001, what the general public and the scientific community were aware of before has also been officially recognised: namely that Germany has no significantly high poverty rate in general, but there are special groups that experience very high risks of poverty. The present tax and social systems do not abolish poverty linked to children. The high risk groups include single parents and families with three or more children. They are three times as likely to be poor in comparison with the general mean, and four to six times more likely to suffer poverty compared to households without children (for detailed figures cf. Nationaler Armuts- und Reichtumsbericht, 2001, Vol. 2, especially table I.24). A second risk of poverty in this welfare state, which is mainly based on social insurance and income-related benefits, exists in unemployment, especially long-term unemployment. Germany holds rank 12 out of 15 European nations according to ILO-standards of long-term unemployment exceeding 12 and exceeding 24 months (Eurostat, Statistics in Focus 9/2003, Theme 3, p.2.).

Poverty has slightly increased: The general poverty rate between 1992 and 2000 rose from 10.5 to 13 percent (cf. DIW Wochenbericht 4/03, Armut in West- und Ostdeutschland). However, taking (natural) fluctuation into consideration, it is advisable to be cautious and not describe this as a general trend. But the poverty gap has clearly increased since 1992. That means that the gap between poor and better-off people in society is deepening.

All poverty rates are lower in the Eastern "Länder" (federal states) of Germany, but only if you use regional poverty thresholds (cf. DIW Wochenbericht 4/03, Armut in West- und Ostdeutschland, Nationaler Armuts- und Reichtumsbericht, Vol. 2., table I.15 to 24). Poverty thresholds for the whole of Germany show that poverty in the East ranges from 50 to 80 percent – depending on the definition of poverty used – higher than in the Western German states, mainly due to economic structural causes.

Hidden poverty is estimated to top the official rates by about 50 to 100 percent, with a probable growing tendency because of increasing conditions for the rewarding of benefits being enforced (pre-conditions to get unemployment benefits, and reluctance in the granting of social assistance for people in precarious situations ("Hilfe in besonderen Lebenslagen"). Hidden poverty has not yet been recognised as a genuine policy issue, though in 2001, there was brief recognition of that problem. At that time, the government introduced a special minimum income for elderly and incapacitated people without taking into account the income of relatives ("Rückgriff"). At the same time, the first report on Poverty and Wealth and the first Action Plan on Social Inclusion were published. The result was an increase in awareness but consequences as regards political actions are yet to be seen.

Contrary to the general understanding of the Bismarckian Welfare State's impact, income in Germany is rather equally distributed and social transfers have a great impact. Laeken indicators show the Gini coefficient of inequality (80/20) to be one of the lowest in the EU, just ranking behind the traditionally equal Nordic countries (Eurostat, Statistics in Focus 8/2003, S. 6).

Discussions of social exclusion mainly revolve around participation in the labour market. Questions of social participation (social contacts) and political involvement in the areas of exclusion, of standards in housing and health care only arise as a secondary issue. However, there is a strong correlation between income poverty and low social and political participation.

Different living conditions are generally accepted and seen as a result of labour market effects. The German social model based on social security that redistributes primarily between people of the same social strata and less between different strata is being strengthened. Redistributive parts of social security – so called "versicherungsfremde Leistungen" because no contributions are paid for them – are being cancelled, like sickness benefit. Private insurance for example in pension politics is morally supported and subsidised. Social justice is currently being discussed with emphasis on the balance of "supporting and demanding" ("Fördern und Fordern"). That means that the recipient's duties have to emphasised, the reasoning being that spending money without satisfying efforts on the part of the recipient is no longer "affordable". The main actors in this debate are politicians and big company employers. The debate on the justice issue of redistribution ("Verteilungsgerechtigkeit") is losing ground. Even the churches do not really fight considerable cutbacks in social benefits for people with low income. Exemptions from taxes for high incomes and companies continue to exist and resist efforts to reduce them (legislation aiming at abolishing tax exemptions just failed, having the intended volume cut back from 3.5 to 1.5 billion Euro). The principle in the German Constitution "property obliges" still exists, but is not attributed to all kinds of property equally.

Regarding unemployment, the problem is that Germany neither follows the Scandinavian example with high social contributions and high taxes that finance a considerable number of public employees in the social sector, nor does it follow the Anglo-Saxon model: It does not provide for high private purchasing power with very low taxes that thus creates jobs in the private service sector. Unemployment is therefore stuck in the middle way (Manfred G. Schmidt, West Germany: The Policy of the Middle Way, in: Journal of Public Policy, 1987, H. 2, S. 139-177).

Today the German welfare mix is changing in several ways: The state is reviewing its responsibilities, privatising and cutting spending in the social sector. Meanwhile, market mechanisms are growing, but companies seldom play an active role in the area of corporate social responsibility, and faced with mass unemployment, unions are not able to uphold their influence. Hopes are thus based on families and social networks to fill in the gap. Whether these protagonists are able to take over this burden has yet to be seen. Families are already experiencing a limitation of their resources and have come under pressure; high poverty gaps are clearly an indication.

Poverty as a theological challenge for the churches

In 1997, the Protestant Church in Germany and the Roman-Catholic Bishops' Conference issued a joint declaration with the title "Für eine Zukunft in Solidarität und Gerechtigkeit" (Towards a Future in Solidarity and Justice), 1997. This document is quoted with paragraph numbers.). This document which is often quoted as the "Gemeinsames Wort" or "Joint Memorandum" is the milestone in recent ecclesial reflections on poverty, unemployment and the crisis of the German Welfare State: It is a milestone not only because the two major churches speak with one voice on an issue controversial in society but also because the churches' declaration was prepared in a public dialogue with a broad range of individuals, groups and institutions in society and, of course, within the churches (cf. for the dialogue with the unions: Frank von Auer / Franz Segbers, Markt und Menschlichkeit. Kirchliche und gewerkschaftliche Beiträge zur Erneuerung der Sozialen Marktwirtschaft, Hamburg 1995). As a milestone, it marks the departure from the post-war years of the "economic miracle" – a period of extraordinary economic growth, which seemed to provide continuous full employment and the economic resources to overcome all forms of poverty and disadvantages. This period came to an end in the mid-1980s when it became clear that full employment could not be re-established so that a growing minority would not participate in the growing wealth of the country. At that time, theological reflections on poverty were newly influenced by the "option for the poor" that was initiated by the Latin-American Bishops' Conference in Puebla in 1979 (cf. Heinrich Bedford-Strohm, Vorrang für die Armen. Auf dem Weg zu einer theologischen Theorie der Gerechtigkeit, Öffentliche Theologie, ed. by Wolfgang Huber, vol. 4, Gütersloh 1993, 150 pp.). The "option for the poor" was first seen as an option concerning the *global* economy (cf. Ulrich Duchrow, Weltwirtschaft heute – ein Feld für Bekennende Kirche? 1. ed. Munich 1986). However, in the mid-1990s, the "preferential option for the poor, weak and disadvantaged" has become an issue of German social policy (cf. Towards a Future..., § 105).

According to the Joint Memorandum, it is the "Christian love of neighbour" that turns "preferentially towards the poor, weak and disadvantaged". But there are also arguments taken from the Old Testament traditions such as the experience of Israel's liberation from Egypt as an obligation to act in favour of the poor. Solidarity with the poor is called a precondition of the final and ultimate communion of God and man (following Matth 25) and is described as a proper place for the encounter with God (cf. Towards a Future..., §§ 105-6). The basis of the theological reasoning is the biblical tradition, which is more important for the Protestant side, and major achievements of Scholastic Theology (definitions of justice) and Roman-Catholic "Social Teaching" (the principle of subsidiarity, concept of the people of God [Vaticanum II]).

The preferential option for the poor is not only seen as an obligation for the churches and their members, but also as the benchmark Christian ethics set for all decisions and actions in society, economy, and politics (cf. Towards a Future..., § 107). In order to understand the idea that the church sets the rules, not only for believers, but for society in general, it is helpful to take into consideration the concept of the "public church" that is, on the Protestant side, behind the church memoranda. According to Wolfgang Huber, formerly professor for social ethics in Heidelberg, now bishop in Berlin and President of the Protestant Church of Germany, the Protestant church has a specific role in an open society which is particularly reflected in the memoranda of the Protestant Church in Germany (EKD). The term "Denkschrift" already announces that these papers do not represent definitive teachings or (what after the Declaration of Barmen (1934) in the German discussion would be called) questions of the *status confessionis*. Rather they are specific contributions to public debates on crucial social or political issues. From an ecclesiological point of view, the memoranda are part of the proclamation of the Gospel in a specific situation. Unlike Sunday sermons, they do not speak to practising believers, but rather to a society which has been formed by Christian tradition indirectly and is now an open, democratic society in which the church cannot address ethical questions in an authoritarian manner. Thus the memoranda are based on the premise that the ethical Good in modernity will be revealed in an open process of communication (cf. Wolfgang Huber, Kirche und Öffentlichkeit, Stuttgart 1973, 579-607. Huber has taken up the issue of the "public church" recently in his: Kirche in der Zeitenwende. Gesellschaftlicher Wandel und Erneuerung der Kirche, Gütersloh 1998, 97 pp.). The Joint Memorandum has certainly received much attention in society (In 2003 the two spokesmen of the churches, Präses Manfred Kock and Cardinal Karl Lehmann were awarded the Hans-Ehrenberg-Preis acknowledging the importance of the Joint Memorandum.).

In addition to the theological reflections mentioned above, additional reasons are given, aiming at a general consensus in society with reference to human rights (including the economic, social, and cultural rights), the German ideas of a "liberal" and "social" democracy and a market economy with social and, most recently, ecological ramifications (cf. Towards a Future..., §§ 126-143). The churches demand a human right to work and a new social culture nurturing new forms of solidarity (cf. Towards a Future...).

The "option for the poor" is primarily seen as an "obligation for the strong to opt and act for the rights of the poor" (cf. Towards a Future..., § 135.) rather than empowerment at the margins of society (From its beginnings in Latin-American theology of liberation the preferential "option for the poor" emphasizes the participation of the poor. In the German debate, the focus seems still to be on the obligation of the strong to act for the poor, with some important exceptions: cf. Gerhard K. Schäfer, Die Option für die Armen als Herausforderung für Diakonie und Sozialethik, in: Diakonie der Versöhnung. Ethische Reflexion und soziale Arbeit in ökumenischer Verantwortung. Festschrift für Theodor Strohm, hg. v. Arnd Götzelmann / Volker Hermann / Jürgen Stein, Stuttgart 1998, 204-15.). So the churches' plea is for a description and analysis of wealth in society in order to identify abundance which can be re-distributed in favour of the poor (cf. Towards a Future...§ 135. A definition of *poverty* is more or less rejected by the Joint Memorandum, cf. Towards a Future..., §§ 68-9). Since 1997, this has often been emphasised in church documents (cf. e. g. Reichtum und Armut als Herausforderung für kirchliches Handeln. Ein deutscher Beitrag des APRODEV-Projektes "Christianity, Poverty and Wealth in the 21st Century", ed. by Werkstatt Ökonomie in the name of the centres for social responsibility and ecumenical issues and the Diakonisches Werk of Evangelische Kirche in Hessen und Nassau: Heidelberg: Werkstatt Ökonomie 2002. A regional body of the Evangelische Kirche im Rheinland has initiated a regional analysis of poverty and wealth, cf. Rainer Volz, Armut und Reichtum an Nahe und Glan, http://www.ekd.de/swi/Volz_Armutsbericht.pdf). From an ecclesial perspective, wealth is not only seen as a resource of welfare, but also as the subject of "religious" hopes and longings which are criticised from a Christian point of view (cf. Uwe Gerber's and Franz Segbers' s contributions to Reichtum und Armut..., 245-279). So the churches are called upon to start a dialogue on poverty, wealth and social justice within the church in order to influence public debates both on the national and global levels (cf. Was Kirchen tun sollten und könnten, in: Reichtum und Armut, 291-294). Such a dialogue in Germany can benefit from the fact that the two major churches support nation-wide welfare organisations: the Protestant "Diakonisches Werk" and its Roman-Catholic sister organisation "Caritas". Diakonie and Caritas are, on the one hand, parts of their mother churches and on the other hand welfare organisations and thereby part of the German social system. They could provide the necessary expertise on the living conditions of the poor and on adequate strategies and practices to cope with, or rather, to prevent poverty. Unfortunately, these professional debates and practices do not receive much attention in general church life so one could get the impression that the churches delegate their solidarity with the poor to their welfare organisations. These however work in permanent tension between the execution of state policies and advocacy for and empowerment of the poor (cf. Johannes Degen, Diakonie im Schatten des Wohlstandes – eine biblische Option für die Armen, in: Diakonie der Versöhnung. Ethische Reflexion und soziale Arbeit in ökumenischer Verantwortung. Festschrift für Theodor Strohm, hg. v. Arnd Götzelmann / Volker Hermann / Jürgen Stein, Stuttgart 1998, 71-77). This conflict has been growing since there is no consensus on social policy, its main objectives and financial basis any more.

The churches are strongly engaged in the current debate about the future of the social system in Germany, but they also represent an *oikumene* perspective striving for global solidarity against poverty. In its mission statement "Justice for the Poor – 2000" the Protestant development agency "Brot für die Welt" ("Bread for the World") emphasises the necessity of "activities that are apt to bring about change here in the North and on a global scale" (Justice for the Poor – 2000. A Statement by Bread for the World, published by Diakonisches Werk der EKD e. V. for Brot für die Welt/Bread for the World, P.O. Box 10 11 42, D-70010 Stuttgart.).

The churches' social services and political strategies to combat poverty

Both the Protestant and the Catholic churches play an important role, in policies and in practice, to combat poverty in Germany. An important role is played in social practice by both churches and their social service agencies Caritas and Diakonisches Werk. Diakonie is first and foremost based on the principle of subsidiarity. This means that social services provided by five major welfare organisations – of which Caritas and Diakonie are the most important – have legal priority over public and private services. The priority policy includes tax exemptions and a ban on establishing public services where these charitable services are available. The subsidiarity principle is still in force, even if recent policies have restricted it, by trying to foster competition in social policy. But the weakening of the principle is more important in health policy and less in policies combating poverty.

Diakonie with 450,000 employees (in January 2002) is among the most important players in the field of social policy and supporting of poor people. The 5,000 services for "people in precarious social situations" represent the biggest part of diaconal services apart from the facilities for young people. However, only two percent of all employees work in this field, while the predominant part work on assistance for sick, young or handicapped people. (For more information cf. www.diakonie.de, Publications, Statistical Information.)

In order to understand the political influence and behaviour of the churches and their social service agencies, it is crucial to assess the relationship between these and state institutions: Being an integral part of the social system, they are not as critical towards public policy as they could be. Their general strategy is less concerned with rabble-rousing and more concerned with influencing matters. Often their arguments match arguments of professional social work.

In the following, it will be discussed am now going to discuss in more detail the influence of the Protestant church and its agency on the raising of consciousness and attentiveness towards the situation of poor people; lobbying / influencing public policy and providing practical aid to combat poverty.

The raising of consciousness and attentiveness towards the situation of poor people

The raising of consciousness towards the situation of poor people among church members and more generally towards social culture in Germany used to be one major issue but has diminished since the beginning of the 21st century. Even if the general public still trusts in the churches as moral guards of social justice, in current debates on social reforms, the churches have become more reticent: "The churches would rather concentrate on spiritual welfare and preaching" (Ulrike Herrmann, taz Nr. 7066, 30.5.2003, p. 3). The general expectations that the churches protect basic values is even emphasised by the highest political representative, the Federal President Johannes Rau (Interview in Rheinischer Merkur, Nr. 21, 22.5.2003): "Of course, the churches should get actively involved [in politics and policy], because Christian faith has to do with changing the world." This is a response to a question about areas where clerical influence could be salutary: "For example in the field of social justice – churches can contribute a lot. The law of markets must not simply be transferred nilly-willy to areas like education or social affairs. It is also a question of justice to help those who are not able to or are no longer able to work."

The Protestant church, very much like its Catholic sister, uses diverse means to influence public opinion and to raise consciousness. On the national level, there are institutions like the Head Office of the Protestant Church in Germany, the Social Service Agency Diakonisches Werk der EKD, the Sozialwissenschaftliches Institut der EKD (Institute of Social Sciences and Social Ethics of the EKD) and others, which publish papers, statements and discussion papers for the broader public or special target groups. Among these papers are: the memoranda mentioned above, church newspapers distributed widely ("Sonntagszeitungen"), journals (p.ex. Diakonie Report), and press releases and documentation on the multi-faceted church activities. The Protestant press agency "epd – Evangelischer Pressedienst" publishes a weekly newsletter on social issues ("epd sozial") in addition to its usual activities.

Countless numbers of events to discuss poverty and social exclusion issues are organised by local, regional or national church activists. The 18 Protestant colleges (Evangelische Akademien) and diaconal colleges offer courses on a variety of issues, amongst others poverty and integration issues (p.ex. Bad Boll on refugees). The German Catholic, Protestant or ecumenical church convention "Kirchentag", organised every two years, mobilises several hundred thousand people to celebrate and discuss matters of faith and social justice during a period of three days. (In 2003, 200,000 to 400,000 people participated in the first ecumenical "Kirchentag".) On the local level, some parishes organise discussion groups to mobilise people. They are often linked to direct aid like public meals cooked by volunteers or free / low-price clothing.

The generally accepted authority of church positions in public debates is also shown by the fact that public radio stations run religious editorial offices.

While the Protestant church tries actively to divert the attention of the broad masses towards poverty issues, Diakonie's task is rather to deliver direct aid and to influence policy (see below). But its former name "internal mission" ("Innere Mission") shows part of the philosophy that is connected with the word "mission" – if you consider the 450,000 employees in a country with 80 million inhabitants the raising of poverty- and diaconal-related questions is almost natural. Moreover, a huge number of volunteers are mobilised to spend their time actively combating isolation and social exclusion. Estimates range around 400,000 volunteers. But there are also some diaconal activities aimed purposefully at the general public like a leaflet "Arguments against prejudices toward social assistance recipients" distributed in 2002.

Lobbying and Influencing public policy
The Diakonisches Werk of the Protestant Church in Germany puts the main emphasis on influencing public policy. This is done by statements on current legal drafts like social assistance law or the law on aiding children and youngsters as well as discussions with politicians and relevant civil servants. In 2003, the main issue was the future design or system of social assistance and of unemployment benefits. Diakonisches Werk is invited to public hearings of the Parliament or the relevant ministries when legislation on poverty is under discussion. Similar procedures are usually followed on a regional and, where sufficient, on a local level. On a local level, the Committees on aid for young people (Jugendhilfeausschüsse) are a good example of the concerted action of welfare organisations and public authorities.

Furthermore, Diakonisches Werk and Caritas, in combination with the other major welfare organisations, have been running a national organisation called "Deutscher Verein für öffentliche und private Fürsorge" with the major players in the field of social assistance, community associations ("kommunale Spitzenverbände") since 1880. Within this organisation, the institutions financing social assistance and the organisations delivering most of the social assistance services are united and can solve problems or develop proposals for reforms.

Practical aid to combat poverty
Direct aid to people experiencing poverty and other forms of need is the main task of Diakonie's 450,000 employees. The objective is to satisfy individual needs and to overcome poverty in a sustainable way.

Other activities are directly linked to parishes. Mostly, these activities are brought together in the basic social work offices called KASA ("Kirchliche Allgemeine Soziale Arbeit"). In addition, counselling plays a major role, e.g. counselling offered to families, couples or individuals and psychological-social counselling. There is also some aid for homeless people, mostly in the form of food handouts, and the organisation of visits to prisoners. Discussions about challenges for these activities mainly promote the idea that the approach is not sufficiently resource-oriented but rather concentrates on compensating deficits. A second critical aspect says that there is the risk of professional and bureaucratic paternalism. Most parishes would rather attract people of the middle strata. Projects organised by poor people themselves or based on their strong participation remain exceptions. There are some activities with drug addicts and unemployed people themselves: e.g. unemployed training other unemployed people or organising internet cafés. The aim is to create space for self-help initiatives facilitated by communities and religious beliefs.

But support for actions by poor people themselves is generally carried out by professional staff, as social work is done professionally; while volunteers do play an important role in the delivery of some services, this is not the case in the organising process. An important exception is drug addiction: 2,000 self-help groups are part of Diakonie.

Direct aid to poor or excluded people mostly consists of providing (interim) homes for homeless people or drug addicts, refugees and other migrants as well as specialised counselling for these people. There are 430 homes for people in precarious social situations, 260 day centres (Tageseinrichtungen) and 1500 counselling centres for these people. The day services mainly consist of employment and vocational qualification initiatives, some with special focus on pedagogical care. The counselling centres are numerous: 25 percent of the work with drug addicts, the remaining three quarters for indebted people, migrants including refugees, homeless people and comprehensive counselling and service centres at railway stations or anonymous counselling by phone.

There are some formal co-operations with self-help initiatives of poor people, e.g. "BAG Sozialhilfeinitiativen", but they mainly exist at the national or occasionally regional level (German Anti-poverty network) for joint political lobbying.

Gender aspects play a limited role in the provision of social services, but they are not a substantial part of the diaconal profile and political reputation. There are special services for women: In addition to counselling during pregnancy and women's refugee homes there is, for example, separate counselling for homeless women whose needs are very different from those of homeless men.

A more prominent role in diaconal work is in combating a different form of discrimination: that against migrants. Work with refugees in particular is a task that is widely recognised among church members and even the whole population as being important. The task ranges from spiritual welfare / spiritual help offered (Seelsorge) to new immigrants at the airports to the organisation of "multi-cultural weeks" in cities, including language schools and assistance for migrant children in doing school homework of. Some parishes grant "church asylum" to migrants who are threatened with expulsion from Germany in their church buildings. This is much appreciated in society and even sometimes recognised by the state. Practical aid for migrants in the parishes is often combined with working groups on the "third world", on refugees or related issues.

To conclude, the main objectives of diaconal and church activities is individual support for people living in poverty or threatened by poverty, with the intention of re-integrating these people into the socio-economic system. This practical aid is backed by political initiatives to create an inclusive society and to achieve a satisfactory framework for social work. However, neither the Churches nor their social service agencies have a strong commitment to a transformative perspective to change the prevailing socio-economic system.

References

Data on poverty

Eurostat, Statistics in Focus 8+9/2003, Theme 3 (http://europa.eu.int/comm/eurostat)

DIW Wochenbericht 4/2003, Armut in West- und Ostdeutschland – Ein differenzierter Vergleich. [Poverty in West- and East-Germany – a differentiated comparison]

German Ministry for Labour and Social Affairs, "Lebenslagen in Deutschland. Der erste Armuts- und Reichtumsbericht der Bundesregierung", First Report on Poverty and Wealth by the German Federal Government, 2001, Vol. 2 ("Daten und Fakten"). [("Data and Facts")] (www.bmgs.bund.de/downloads/arm_reich_daten_fakten.pdf)

Sell, Stefan (ed.) (2002): Armut als Herausforderung, Bestandsaufnahme und Perspektiven der Armutsforschung und Armutsberichterstattung, Berlin. [Poverty as a Challenge, Review and Perspectives of Poverty Research and Reporting]

Publications on the theological and diaconical discussion on poverty and combating poverty

Concerned institutions

EKD-Memoranda, a. o. Kirchenamt der Evangelischen Kirche in Deutschland & Sekretariat der Deutschen Bischofskonferenz (ed.), Für eine Zukunft in Solidarität und Gerechtigkeit. Wort des Rates der Evangelischen Kirche in Deutschland und der Deutschen Bischofskonferenz zur wirtschaftlichen und sozialen Lage in Deutschland, Hannover/Bonn 1997. [Protestant Church in Germany & the Roman-Catholic Bishops' Conference (Eds.), Towards a Future in Solidarity and Justice, Joint Memorandum publ. by the Council of the Protestant Church in Germany and the Roman-Catholic Bishops' Conference on the Economical and Social Situation in Germany, Hannover/Bonn 1997]

Publications by the Institute for Social Sciences of the EKD, a.o. Przybylski, Hartmut, Zur Zukunft sozialer Gerechtigkeit.

http://www.ekd.de/swi/zurzukunftsozialergerechtigkeit.pdf [About the Future of Social Justice]

Publications by the Institute for Diaconal Research (Institut für Diakoniewissenschaft) of the Faculty for Theology at Heidelberg University, a.o. Strohm, Theodor, Reform und Konsolidierung des Sozialstaats. Zum Stand der Willensbildung innerhalb der EKD, in: Zeitschrift für Evangelische Ethik, Vol. 40, no. 3, 1996, p. 186–204.

http://www.dwi.uni-hd.de/publikationen/publikationen.htm. [Reform and Consolidation of the Welfare State. About the Formation of Opinions inside the Protestant Church in Germany]

Werkstatt Ökonomie (ed.) (2002): Reichtum und Armut als Herausforderung für kirchliches Handeln, Oktober 2002. [Wealth and Poverty as a Challenges for the Church]

Position Papers by Diakonisches Werk der EKD, http://www.diakonie.de/de/html/fachforum/publikationen/Stellungnahmen/177_1297.htm, a.o. Anforderungen an Arbeitsmarktintegration und Existenzsicherung: Eckpunkte des Diakonischen Werkes der EKD August 2003, [Requirements concerning the Integration into the Labour Market and the Subsistence Level Protection] Position paper on the Draft of the National Action Plan "Social Inclusion" 2003-2005, May 2003.

Series of publications of Diakonisches Werk der EKD "Diakonie-Korrespondenzen", http://www.diakonie.de/de/html/fachforum/publikationen/Korrespondenz/653_1295.htm, a.o. Nachhaltig solidarisch leben – Bericht des Präsidenten des Diakonischen Werkes der EKD auf der Diakonischen Konferenz 2002. [Practising Sustainable Solidarity – Report of the President of Diakonisches Werk der EKD at the Diaconical Conference]

Journals „Diakonie Report" and „Diakonie Impulse", a.o. A Totally Different Employment Initiative: Usable and Good, Diakonie Report 3/2003 (May), p. 26-27.

Justice for the Poor – 2000. A Statement by Bread for the World, published by Diakonisches Werk der EKD e. V. for Brot für die Welt/Bread for the World, P.O. Box 10 11 42, D-70010 Stuttgart

epd sozial, http://www.epd.de/sozial/sozial_index.html

Yearbooks of Diakonisches Werk der EKD, a.o. Jürgen Gohde (ed.), Diakonie-Jahrbuch 2002: Die Zukunft der sozialen Dienste, Stuttgart. [The Future of Social Services]

Authors

von Auer, Frank / Segbers, Franz (1995): Markt und Menschlichkeit. Kirchliche und gewerkschaftliche Beiträge zur Erneuerung der Sozialen Marktwirtschaft, Hamburg [Market and Humanity. Church-based and Union-based Contributions to the Renewal of Social Market Economy]

Bedford-Strohm, Heinrich (1993): Vorrang für die Armen. Auf dem Weg zu einer theologischen Theorie der Gerechtigkeit, Öffentliche Theologie, ed. by Wolfgang Huber, vol. 4, Gütersloh. [A Preference for the Poor. Towards a Theological Theory of Justice]

Degen, Johannes (1998): Diakonie im Schatten des Wohlstandes – eine biblische Option für die Armen, in: Diakonie der Versöhnung. Ethische Reflexion und soziale Arbeit in ökumenischer Verantwortung. Festschrift für Theodor Strohm, hg. v. Götzelmann, Arnd / Hermann, Volker / Stein, Jürgen, Stuttgart, 71-77.

Duchrow, Ulrich ([1]1986): Weltwirtschaft heute – ein Feld für Bekennende Kirche? Munich. [Word Markets Today – An Issue for a Confessing Church]

Huber, Wolfgang (1973): Kirche und Öffentlichkeit, Stuttgart, 579-607.

Huber, Wolfgang (1998): Kirche in der Zeitenwende. Gesellschaftlicher Wandel und Erneuerung der Kirche, Gütersloh, 97 pp.

Reichtum und Armut als Herausforderung für kirchliches Handeln. Ein deutscher Beitrag des APRODEV-Projektes "Christianity, Poverty and Wealth in the 21st Century", ed. by Werkstatt Ökonomie in the name of the centers for social responsibility and ecumenical issues and the Diakonisches Werk of Evangelische Kirche in Hessen und Nassau: Heidelberg: Werkstatt Ökonomie 2002.

Schäfer, Gerhard K. (1998): Die Option für die Armen als Herausforderung für Diakonie und Sozialethik, in: Diakonie der Versöhnung. Ethische Reflexion und soziale Arbeit in ökumenischer Verantwortung. Festschrift für Theodor Strohm, hg. v. Götzelmann, Arnd / Hermann, Volker / Stein, Jürgen, Stuttgart, 204-215.

Schmidt, Manfred G. (1987): West Germany: The Policy of the Middle Way; in: Journal of Public Policy, 2/1987, 139-177.

Volz, Rainer (2001): Armut an Nahe und Glan. Ein Bericht zur sozialen Lage im Landkreis Bad Kreuznach, Bochum. (http://www.ekd.de/swi/volz_armutsbericht.pdf)

Niall Cooper

Great Britain

Church Action on Poverty (CAP) is a national membership-based educational charity founded in 1982 as an ecumenical response to poverty in Britain. It is an independent, non-denominational organisation, working across all sectors to tackle the root causes of poverty in the UK.

CAP is one of a handful of national organisations committed to working in an empowering and participatory way with people in poverty. CAP creates opportunities for people in poverty to bring their unique insights, knowledge and expertise gained from living with poverty to bear in reforming policy, challenging bad practices that sustain poverty and to be their own advocates for change. To find solutions to poverty, it is vital that Church and Government policies and other initiatives are rooted in and tested against their experiences.

The growth of poverty and inequality

The UK has become a tremendously more divided and unequal society over the past two decades. For the vast majority of UK citizens, our own material circumstances and life chances are incomparably greater than that of our parent's generation. Yet this is a far from universal experience. For all too many, life in twenty-first century Britain remains harsh and soul destroying.

In 2001/02, twelve and a half million people were living on incomes of less than 60 percent of median household income, nearly 20 percent of the population. Women are 14 percent more likely than males to live in households with incomes below 60 percent of the median. But the real number of women living in poverty is likely to be far higher: Government figures reveal that almost half of all women have total individual incomes of less than £100 per week, compared with less than a fifth of men.[1] Poverty also disproportionately affects members of black and ethnic minority communities; disabled people; older people and those living in London and other major urban centres.[2]

Inequality in the UK increased rapidly from the late 1970s, with the advent of mass unemployment and neo-liberal policies pursued by the Thatcher government from 1979-1992. Mrs Thatcher was famously quoted as saying "there is no such things as society" and pursued aggressive policies in relation to privatisation of public services, large scale cuts in direct taxation and the welfare state and punitive policies in relation to trades unions, unemployed people, lone parents and those generally considered "undeserving" of public support. Whilst these policies were moderated to some extent during the mid-90s, by 1997 Britain was one of the most unequal of the modern "developed" economies. Child poverty had more than doubled between 1979 and 1997, rising from 13.7% to 34% of all children.[3]

The last twenty years has also seen a massive shift in the structure of the labour market in the UK. Both the nature of work and the types of jobs have changed as the importance of the male dominated manufacturing sector and heavy industry declines and the numbers in the female dominant service sector increase. The number of full time permanent jobs has decreased while the number of part-time and short-term contracts grew as the labour market moves towards ever greater flexibility. Women's increasing involvement in the labour market has meant that wage rates fall as women are consistently paid less than men and work for shorter hours. The greatest single group of poor people are now in work. Three and a half million poor people live in working households. There are more working poor than there are unemployed or poor pensioners. People work hard for long hours, and in the absence of a living wage, still fall below the poverty line.[4]

At the same time, wealth inequality has increased substantially. Between 1988 and 1999 the top one per cent of the population has increased their share of personal wealth from 17 to 23 per cent. The top 2,4 million households own wealth to the tune of £1,300bn, while the bottom 12 million households own only £150m.[5]

These levels of poverty put untold pressures on family life. Poorer parents have frequently been shown to try to protect their child from poverty

– often by going without themselves. Nila is an articulate Asian woman, married with three young children, who spoke at Church Action on Poverty's National Poverty Hearing in 1996. For her – *and thousands of families like hers* – the consequences have been devastating: Redundancy; poverty; debt; mortgage arrears; homelessness.

"Eventually the building society repossessed the house, and we found ourselves at the mercy of the housing department. On the morning we were due to move I sent my son to school as normal. He asked me where we would be sleeping that night and I had no answer to give. We had been through rough times before. I had always had an answer, and explanation. I had never lied to him. The look in his eyes as he refused to look into mine haunts me still."[6]

Government responses

The advent of the New Labour Government in 1997 saw a new – and more positive – approach being taken to tackling poverty and social exclusion. Since 1997, the Government has made a series of policy commitments in relation to tackling child poverty, social exclusion and promoting work as the best route out of poverty.

In 1997, the Government embarked on a major "Welfare to Work" programme and established a new "Social Exclusion Unit." Most strikingly however, in March 1999 Tony Blair committed the Government to "abolish child poverty within a generation."

The "Welfare to work" programme has, in many ways, been the central plank of the Government's anti-poverty strategy. In contrast to more traditional Labour welfare based approaches, its central tenet is that "work is the best route out of poverty" and has therefore focussed resources on increasing the skills and employability of individuals, and financial and other incentives to work. This has included large scale employment and training programmes for under 25 year olds, lone parents, disabled people and the over 50s under the overall heading of the "New Deal." Government has also sought to increase work incentives by introducing a National Minimum Wage (£4.50 an hour from October 2003) and Tax

Credits to boost the wages of low to middle income earners. In addition, the "Surestart" programme has directed substantial resources at providing early interventions and support to families with children under five.

Responses to social exclusion

The establishment of the Social Exclusion Unit was a significant sign of the Government's commitment to address a number of deep-seated social issues, foremost of which has been the situation facing people living on many of Britain's deprived urban neighbourhoods. In most of the more disadvantaged estates in Britain, community resources are very poor. Many shops have withdrawn from poor areas and banks do not exist. Levels of crime and violence are very high and public spaces are often run-down and degraded.

The Government has sought to address these issues through a ten year "National Strategy for Neighbourhood Renewal." Although coordinated by a national "Neighbourhood Renewal Unit" and in part, funded centrally, the programme is intended to be delivered by 88 "Local Strategic Partnerships" that seek to coordinate the efforts of central and local government, private, voluntary, faith and community sector organisations. Alongside the commitment to partnership, there is also a growing interest in the ideas of "social capital" and "community empowerment":

"Investing in the human and social capital of marginalized individuals and groups enables them to develop the capacities needed to thrive, and to play an autonomous role in developing and renewing their communities."[7]

The emergence of debt and financial exclusion

A further emerging issue of concern in relation to poverty in Britain is the growth in household debt amongst low-income families. This is especially problematic for families with children, with limited or no access to credit at reasonable rates. People have very few, or no savings and are vulnerable to any kind of crisis or shock.

Citizens Advice Bureaux reported a 47% growth in debt problems over a five year period to May 2003, whilst almost eight million people are systematically refused access to mainstream credit. This has lead to a growth in legal, but largely unregulated, money lending businesses. Over three million people regularly borrow money from doorstep lenders, frequently at rates of interest in excess of 170% apr.[8] The impact of high levels of debt at extortionate rates of interest on families already struggling on inadequate incomes can be particularly severe.

In spite of this, the Government has to date failed to develop a coherent and joined up anti-debt strategy. Church Action on Poverty has identified at least six Government departments that have some responsibility in relation to debt and financial exclusion, but none with an overall coordination brief, nor a brief to promote access to alternative forms of affordable credit.[9]

The idea of the "underclass" and the invisibility of the poor

The establishment of the Social Exclusion Unit was also significant as it was effectively the first time that the term "social exclusion" had been used within public debate in the UK. However, the manner in which the idea was interpreted has had a particularly British interpretation. According to the Unit's own definition:

"Social exclusion is a shorthand label for what can happen when individuals or areas suffer from a combination of linked problems such as unemployment, poor skills, low incomes, poor housing, high crime environments, bad health and family breakdown. It means being cut off from the things that most of us take for granted: a job, qualifications, a home and a safe environment."[10]

This has similarities to the more traditional British idea of *multiple deprivation* – that people are frequently trapped in poverty as the result of suffering from a number of problems at the same time. At worst – although it would not be appropriate to accuse the Social Exclusion Unit of this – the line of argument can be extended to say that social exclusion (or poverty) is the fault of the individuals concerned. There are a great many such myths in popular circulation. Poor people are ignorant and lazy; poor people only have themselves to blame; there are jobs out there if you can be bothered to look for them. Underlying all of these myths is an attitude that poor people are in some way different from the rest of us – and that there is nothing wrong with us making sweeping moral generalisations about the character of "the poor".

This kind of thinking is most clearly expressed in the idea of the "underclass" which frequently surfaces in public debate about poverty in the UK, although the roots of the concept are to be found in the United States.[11] Such attitudes continue to inform public attitudes to poverty – and certainly are keenly felt by the people who experience poverty at first hand.

But poverty doesn't simply sap peoples' confidence in themselves. In the work that Church Action on Poverty has done with people in poverty over recent years, one theme which consistently crops up is the way in which poor people in today's society feel "invisible". Peoples' own direct experiences of poverty, and their own attitudes and ideas about what can be done to tackle it are held to be of no value whatsoever.

In the words of Wayne Green, another speaker at CAP's "National Poverty Hearing" in 1996: *"What is poverty? Poverty is a battle of invisibility, a lack of resources, exclusion, powerlessness ... being blamed for society's problems."*[12]

The Churches and the "re-discovery" of poverty

The past twenty years has seen a steady growth in awareness amongst the churches of the persistence of poverty in the UK. In 1982, Church Action on Poverty was established as an ecumenical response; the following year the Methodist Church launched a national "Mission Alongside the Poor" programme and the then Archbishop of Canterbury launched the "Archbishops' Commission on Urban Priority Areas". After two years deliberation and visits to neighbourhoods across the UK, the Commission's report "Faith in the City" detailed the decline of Britain's cities, the growth of mass unemployment and poverty and outlined a series of policy recommendations to church and nation. It concluded that: *"Poverty is not only about shortage of money. It is about rights and relationships; about how people are treated and how they regard themselves; about powerlessness, exclusion and loss of dignity. Yet the lack of an adequate income is at its heart."*[13]

The fact that the report was immediately dismissed as "marxist" by a prominent member of the Thatcher government only served to increase its impact, ensuring that it received major coverage in the national media for several weeks. It is now looked back on as a key moment when the Church of England, previously viewed by many as the "Tory party at prayer" took a clear political stand against the growth of poverty and inequality, and the predominant values of the Government of the time.

The Churches and the Common Good

The mid 1990s saw two further official church reports which deliberately sought to engage with and alter the terms of political debate on poverty and unemployment in the UK, and which had a significant impact both within and beyond churches.

In 1996, the Catholic Bishops' Conference of England and Wales published an official statement on "The Common Good and the Catholic Church's Social Teaching." This very accessible document, accompanied by study and reflection material, explicitly sought to apply Catholic Social Teaching to the contemporary political context, immediately in advance of the 1997 General Election. In his foreword, Cardinal Basil Hume was clear that *"Church does not present a political programme, still less a party political one"*.[14] Nevertheless, it was clear in its condemnation of inequality and unfettered wealth: *"there must come a point at which the scale of the gap between the very wealthy and those at the bottom of the range of income begins to undermine the common good. This is the point at which society starts to be run for the benefit of the rich, not for all its members."*[15]

The Common Good focussed much of its attention on the deficiencies of the market. Although the market is clearly strong on wealth creation, its appeal to self-interest had to be set against wider social goals represented by the notion of the "Common Good". *"A wealthy society, if it is a greedy society, is not a good society. (...) Unlimited free markets tend to produce what is in effect an option against the poor."*[16]

In the light of this, the Catholic Bishops urged not only the introduction of a statutory minimum wage, but that employers had an obligation to pay a "just" wage. *"Employers have a duty to pay a just wage, the level of which should take account of the needs of the individual and not just his or her value on the so-called labour market. State welfare provision is not a desirable substitute for a just wage."*[17]

Unemployment and the Future of Work

In parallel with the "Common Good", the Council of Churches for Britain and Ireland published its own report on "Unemployment and the Future of Work". This ecumenical report was carried out by an independent working group, with an eminent economist, Andrew Britton, as its Secretary. The report challenged the fatalism that viewed mass unemployment as a permanent feature of modern economic and social life. It regarded this not simply to be a matter of social justice, but a "spiritual issue": *"Underneath the subjects of Unemployment and the Future of Work lie despair, waste of God-given talents, contempt, hiding the eyes from the pain of brothers and sisters."*[18]

It therefore called for a re-ordering of fundamental policy priorities, much greater levels of labour market intervention, a national minimum wage and was in favour of a return to the idea of full employment: *"Enough good work for everyone has to become an explicit national aim in its own right."*[19]

It was notable that, in spite of its publication in the middle of the General Election campaign, the report was welcomed by all the major political parties, and many if its key policy recommendations subsequently featured within the programme of the New Labour Government.

The Paradox of Prosperity

The late 1990s have seen a further shift in the churches' thinking on matters of inequality, wealth and poverty. By the end of the decade, Britain had experienced almost ten years of economic growth, bringing unparalleled levels of prosperity for some, alongside persistent and high levels of poverty affecting others. In response to this, and its own decline as a denomination, the Salvation Army commissioned the Henley Centre for Economic Forecasting to analyse current social trends in Britain, and predict changes over the next ten years. Its report *The Paradox of Prosperity* identified a range of challenging issues, many inter-linked, which were predicted to impact strongly on people's lives by 2010. It painted a bleak picture of a society in the grip of social upheaval and rife with family breakdown, drug dependency, workplace stress and an ageing population. The report argued that in spite of increasing levels of wealth and prosperity for some, with a predicted 35% increase in living standards by 2010, people will feel considerably less content with their lives.

"We expect the wealth gap to become even more pronounced by 2010, with The Henley Centre forecasting that the top ten percent of people will be ten times richer than the bottom ten percent. Other divisions will contribute to a 'poverty cycle' for some sections of society. Those born into poverty are statistically more likely to suffer ill-health, to receive a substandard education and to obtain poorly paid jobs (or no job at all). Their children are therefore likely to suffer in a similar way."[20]

Devolution and the churches in Scotland and Wales

Since 1997, the creation of a Scottish Parliament and Welsh Assembly – admittedly with limited powers – has begun to alter the British political landscape. In response, the Scottish and Welsh Churches have begun to develop distinctive approaches, reflecting subtle differences in theological and cultural outlooks from the English-dominated "mainstream". Both Cytun (Churches Together in Wales) and ACTS (the Scottish ecumenical instrument) have established separate Parliamentary/Assembly Offices, and actively sought to engage with their respective policies.

The Scottish Ecumenical Assembly, held in 2001, was an attempt by ACTS to establish a specifically Scottish churches' public policy agenda. As part of the overall process, the Assembly adopted a statement on the theme of "Breaking out of Poverty". Whilst its starting point was that churches' need to repent and put their own house in order, it moved beyond this, to make a clear statement in favour of greater equality and redistribution, funded through direct progressive taxation; reform of benefits system and the empowerment of communities in areas of urban and rural deprivation. Although some of these themes had been implicit in earlier UK-wide church reports, the strength of language represented a clear and distinctive Scottish perspective on the issues.

Poverty, prosperity and globalisation

At the same time as the churches are seeking to come to terms with an increasingly diverse range of perspectives, as a result of Welsh and Scottish devolution and English regionalisation, they are also being forced to respond to the "meta-phenomena" of globalisation. It is noticeable that even in the 1997 report "Unemployment and the Future of Work", globalisation hardly warranted a mention. However, by 2003, globalisation had become a central focus within Churches Together in Britain and Ireland's latest attempt to shape a theological and ethical response to poverty and wealth:

"Growing prosperity in the UK is inseparable from the facts of globalisation, as the UK is a key global location. The positive features of greater prosperity are evident. But the disparities must also be emphasised (...) It is also possible for Christians to be sharply critical of the ideology of development, especially in its contemporary form. Christians have reason to be scandalised at the shallow hedonism of current society. Even worse, the traditional virtues are encroached on by spreading consumerism, to the destruction of community bonds and of public life."[21]

The outcome of CTBI's "Poverty, prosperity and globalisation" project is not expected until late 2004 at the earliest. It remains to be seen how churches and their members are able to square their evident enjoyment of the fruits of prosperity with their theological and ethical concerns for the "victims" of globalisation.

When Church Action on Poverty was formed in 1982, the churches' concerns for poverty at home were at a low ebb. But no longer: there is now a broad consensus that poverty, inequality and the pursuit of social justice is a legitimate and indeed, an essential concern of the Churches.

Faith based organisations come of age?

On all sides of the political spectrum, from Prime Minister Tony Blair to the leader of the Conservative party, politicians have been seeking to extol the virtues of faith-based welfare projects, and seek partnership with the faith communities. In March 2001, Tony Blair gave a speech at a Christian Socialist Movement conference, in which he remarked that, *"I sense a new and vital energy within the churches and other faith groups about engagement in the communities within which you work and have your being. And a new appreciation of the valuable work done by countless ministers of religion and their congregations, day in day out."*

Politicians are increasingly realising that, in a deeply fractured and post-modern society, faith communities are in many cases, the strongest community organisations in any given area. A 1999 Home Office report observed, *"black majority churches, mosques, temples, gurudwaras are particularly strong in identifying and responding to unmet needs in black and minority ethnic communities"*.

Charity, welfare and philanthropy: the Victorian inheritance

Churches in the UK have a long tradition of serving on the frontline, binding up the broken hearted, often where the open sores most irritate and offend. Pioneers of so many responses from medieval almshouses, through the nineteenth century housing developments of Octavia Hill, and the work of the Salvation Army, to the establishment of myriad local housing associations, day centres, night shelters, soup runs and credit unions in the past twenty five years. According to one survey, up to a third of all voluntary housing projects have their roots in the church, or the endeavours of individual Christians[22]. Government support just for the larger Christian development agencies, children's charities, housing associations alone already runs into millions of pounds. The story is one of which, in many ways, the church should be rightly proud.

The impulse behind many soup runs, night shelters, hostels and day centres is to be found in the Christian concepts of hospitality and sanctuary. A national survey of day centres for homeless people concluded in 1992: *"The philosophy of many day centres is rooted in Victorian Christian values, and a wide range of denominations are involved in providing services to single homeless people."*[23]

The Churches' commitment to engaging in local action to tackle poverty and the "urban question" has been reinforced since the 1980s by a number of national denominational funding programmes, including most notably the Church of England's Church Urban Fund, which has raised over twenty million pounds to fund local church-linked urban regeneration projects since 1988.

Whilst churches can rightly be proud of their long-standing commitment to addressing the needs of people suffering from poverty and social exclusion of all kinds, their track-record is nevertheless mixed. The national day centres survey also found that many church projects continue to offer very basic services, to a predominantly white and male clientele, rooted in a passive and philanthropic attitude that *"homeless people were the passive recipients of hand-outs from urban missionaries."* And in an interesting reversal of the usual direction of "exchange visits", two homeless activists from Sao Paulo (Brazil) spent a fortnight visiting church homelessness projects in London during the summer of 1996. What they found was that, unlike in Sao Paulo, the churches in London, with a few notable exceptions, were using a social work model, in which homeless people tended to be seen as recipients rather than as partners.[24]

In the task of developing practical response to poverty at a local level, churches do have a theoretical advantage, in the form of its local neighbourhood base. This is not so much to be found in the increasingly weak Anglican claim that the Parish church, by definition, in some way "services" the whole community, but in the existence of church congregations and workers (clergy and lay, paid and voluntary) within virtually every community, neighbourhood and estate across the country. No other social institution or movement can make such a claim. However, it is important not to overstate this:

"The church is in an ideal position to be an agent of change because of its independent nature, because it has access to resources that other organisations do not and because the very nature of its witness demands it to be a fellowship of people who sit with others, hear their stories and support them in their struggles. However, this is a difficult message to get across both to the church which sees itself as respectable and not wanting to taint itself with politics on a local level, and to people in the community who see the churches a patronising agency, ready to play lady bountiful but not ready to enter into their real situations."[25]

Faithworks: Christian social action re-invigorated?

On the other side, many within the UK churches are looking for churches, Christian charities and agencies to adopt a much higher profile, and to "put faith back in the heart of the community."

Rev Steve Chalke, a high profile broadcaster and founder of the Oasis Trust, launched the "Faithworks" campaign in 2001, bringing together a broad alliance of church groups from the Catholic Agency for Social Concern through to the Evangelical Alliance. Faithworks' founding statement asserts that *"poverty is a spiritual issue as well as a material problem and the biggest problem facing our society is that many people don't have any hope that their situation can change. That's why Christian faith is so important. Put simply: faith transforms both individuals and communities."*[26]

A two year research project on the role of faith communities in urban regeneration confirmed the significant contribution that churches and other faith groups play: *"Faith communities can bring to regeneration activity distinctive and strong motivations for social action, their long-term presence, the provision of informal settings and activities, and a commitment to listening to local people."*[27]

A second survey of a range of church based social action projects across England and Scotland confirmed that religious belief clearly adds an urgency to social commitment across a wide spectrum of theological and faith perspectives. However, in his conclusion, Jim Sweeney observed that, *"Church-based social action projects make a significant contribution to the well-being of the community at large, and it would certainly be worthwhile to seek to expand them. But this is a major challenge. The churches still have only a poor grasp of their potential role in networking with other agencies to tackle social exclusion and promote social justice. The work of their social action agencies often goes unrecognised and under-valued, even within the Church, and certainly in the wider community."*[28]

Prophesy or collusion?

At another level, the UK churches are sometimes open to the accusation of being more concerned with philanthropic first aid work than being agents of long term change. Ken Bartlett, an Anglican priest with thirty years experience of Christian social activism has asked serious questions about whether the churches are guilty of colluding with injustice. *"The danger for the church's work in society is that we accept pagan agendas and try to make them less oppressive, rather than challenging those agendas and trying to replace them with the vision and values of Christ. (...) As a result, the church offers people not hope, but survival; it ceases to be a prophetic body and becomes the fifth emergency service – after fire, police, ambulance and the AA."* [29]

And yet, when the church does get itself organised to address issues of "structural injustice", it continues to reveal its potency as a lobbying force. In 1992, the Churches National Housing Coalition organised the first ever churches lobby of parliament on housing and homelessness. In little over six months, and with minimal resources, 3.000 people were mobilised to travel to Westminster, and something over half of all members of parliament were lobbied by organised delegations of local church members, project workers and homeless people. The potency of the lobby was not so much in the numbers involved, but in the fact that it was rooted so clearly and directly in the churches' direct involvement in meeting hous-ing need. As one MP commented after the event, *"I had no idea the church was doing so much in the field of housing. It's been a well-kept secret!"*[30]

Political engagement

Within the sphere of international development, the churches engagement in political action to tackle poverty and debt has been decisive. The Jubilee 2000 campaign, spearheaded by the Churches' development agencies, lead to a major shift in the international debate and understanding about debt relief. Will Hutton reflected in the Observer newspaper: *"At the end of an increasingly secular century, it has been the biblical proof and moral imagination of religion that have torched the principles of the hitherto unassailable citadels of international finance."*[31]

Yet the churches have been far less successful in mobilising their still considerable resources to shift the debate about how to tackle poverty closer to home. It is interesting to note that several denominations now employ their own Parliamentary liaison officers in Westminster, in addition to the newly established offices at the Welsh Assembly and Scottish Parliament. Up to a dozen Church of England Bishops continue to sit in the partially-reformed House of Lords, as befitting their status as an established church, but their influence on political debate is increasingly muted, if not to say marginalized.

Initially founded to encourage the church to speak out on behalf of the poor, Church Action on Poverty took a strategic and theological principled decision in the mid 1990s, that this approach was insufficient. For campaigns and statements to have authenticity, it was important not so much to speak on behalf of the poor, but to create space for people in poverty to speak for themselves. Instead of relying on the moral authority of the Bishops, CAP now seeks to mobilise churches to campaign in support of policy changes identified by people in poverty themselves.

A key event in this process was the National Poverty Hearing held in March 1996, attended by over 500 people: Archbishops; Bishops; Members of Parliament; leading trades unionists and business leaders... The Hearing was a profoundly moving experience both for speakers and listeners. In the words of one Bishop:

"I was impressed with the capacity of people who have experienced deep poverty to articulate their concerns. It deepened my sense that communities of the poor have the resources but lack the opportunity to control their own lives."[32]

At the end of her comprehensive account of Poverty Close to Home, Hilary Russell – long time Chairperson of Church Action on Poverty – posed what, for the churches in the UK remains the central question: *"Whose story are we living? (...) 'The real story of a people is not written by the manipulations and coercions of those in power, ready to sacrifice people to economic theory and national security. It is written by the emerging hope and involvement of the poor.' Which is our story? There is an option, but for Christians there is simply no choice."*[33]

Annotations

1 Equal Opportunities Commission, Gender and Poverty in Britain, 2003.
2 For up to date statistics on poverty in the UK see: www.poverty.org.uk/
3 Mike Brewer, Tom Clark and Alissa Goodman, What really happened to child poverty in the UK under Labour's first term? The Economic Journal, 113 (June), F240–F257.

4. Polly Toynbee, Hard Work, 2003.
5. Will Paxton and Matthew Taylor, Bridging The Wealth Gap, in New Statesman, 12 July 2002.
6. Church Action on Poverty, Speaking from Experience, Voices at the National Poverty Hearing, 1996, page 25.
7. Inside Out, Rethinking Inclusive Communities, Demos 2003.
8. New Economics Foundation, 2002.
9. Stephen Matthews, Forgive us our debts, Church Action on Poverty, 2002.
10. Social Exclusion Unit, information pack, Cabinet Office, 1997.
11. Paul Spicker, Poverty and the Welfare State: Dispelling the myths, Catalyst working paper. September 2002. See also the article of Beaumont on US situation in this publication.
12. Church Action on Poverty, Speaking from Experience, Voices at the National Poverty Hearing, 1996, page 30.
13. The Archbishop's Commission on Urban Priority Areas, Faith in the City, Church House Publishing, 1985.
14. The Catholic Bishops' Conference of England and Wales, The Common Good and the Catholic Church's Social Teaching, 1996, page 1.
15. ibid, page 17.
16. ibid, page 19.
17. ibid, page 22.
18. Council of Churches in Britain and Ireland, The Churches Inquiry into unemployment and the future of work, CCBI, 1997, page v.
19. ibid, page 8.
20. The Salvation Army/The Henley Centre, The Paradox of Prosperity, 1999, page 6.
21. Prosperity and Poverty in the Context of Globalisation, unpublished working paper, 29 April 2003.
22. Unpublished research, Jubilee Centre, Cambridge, 1992.
23. Jacqui Waters, Community or ghetto? An analysis of day centre for single homeless people, CHAR, 1992.
24. London Churches Group, From Sympathy to Solidarity, 1996.
25. Bethan Galliers, in Building for Community, Churches National Housing Coalition, 1997.
26. Steve Chalke, Faithworks: actions speak louder than words, Oasis Trust, 2002.
27. Richard Farnell, Robert Furbey, Stephen Sharns al Haqq Hills, Marie Macey and Greg Smith, Engaging faith communities in urban regeneration, Joseph Rowntree Foundation, 2003.

28 James Sweeney, From story to policy, social exclusion, empowerment and the churches, Von Hugel Institute, 2001, page 80.
29 Ken Barlett, Is the Church colluding with injustice?, in Not Just Houses, Christian Action Journal, spring 1995.
30 Niall Cooper, Just Homes for All, it's not too much to ask, Churches National Housing Coalition, 1993.
31 Quoted by Stephen Timms, Tawney Lecture 2000, Christian Socialist Movement, 2000.
32 Speaking from experience, report of the National Poverty Hearing, Church Action on Poverty, 1996.
33 Hilary Russell, Poverty close to home, a christian understanding, Mowbray, 1995, p.270.

Herman Noordegraaf

The Netherlands

Crisis in the welfare state

The welfare state, as developed in the Netherlands after the Second World War, aimed to provide basic security for citizens by eradicating poverty and want, as well as the fear of falling into poverty due to unemployment, disability, illness, old-age, widowhood or orphanhood. For that purpose a comprehensive system of social services and social security was developed. The Dutch welfare state represented a unique variant within the whole group of welfare states. In the typology of Esping-Andersen, one could designate the Dutch welfare state a blend of the social-democratic and corporatist variants (Esping-Andersen 1990,1999; Van Kersbergen 1995): relatively generous benefits when viewed internationally (social democratic regime), but also a large role for social partners in social security, and much stress on the breadwinner principle in the areas of taxation and social security. With the economy growing strongly, the living standards of the population were raised significantly, and poverty was reduced during the years of reconstruction (1945 to mid-1960's). However, this should be qualified with the observation that, even during the heyday of the welfare state, there always remained a "substratum" of people who were by-passed by the emancipation towards full citizenship. They belong to what is called "the fourth world". The solidarity movement which connects itself with the poorest people in rich and poor countries and which started in France is also active in the Netherlands.

Ever since the 1970's, the welfare state, to the realisation of which all political groupings (social democrats, Christian democrats, and conservatives) had contributed, has been coming under fire. The background to this tendency is both socio-economic and cultural. The economic recession that occurred in the seventies led to company restructuring and closures. The older business sectors like shipbuilding and textiles were especially hard-hit. Shifts in employment opportunities have a partly structural component. The so-called newly industrialised countries like South Korea and Taiwan entered the economic world stage. Transfers to Third World Countries also occurred. The resulting mass retrenchments led to a rising demand for welfare. This rise was further stimulated by demographic developments such as ageing population, and an increase in the number of divorces. All this raised the question of the affordability of the welfare state. The pressure on the labour market was, moreover, increasing due to the larger number of youths from the post-war baby boom, and the growing number of women seeking paid employment (this number was always low because of traditional family roles: the man is the breadwinner and his wife runs the household).

Furthermore, in the flood of literature dealing with "the crisis of the welfare state", a fundamental criticism emerges, which is aimed at the unintended and undesirable side effects of this form of society. It is claimed that the citizens' sense of responsibility is violated, that their personal initiative is stifled, and that the function and significance of all sorts of in-between' social structures, like associations, churches and so on (the so-called "social midfield"; compare with the discussion about civil society), are undermined. Briefly: it is claimed that the welfare state has promoted the rise of passive, dependent and amoral, if not hedonistic, citizens, who bank all their desires on the government's account.

Under this socio-economic and cultural constellation, a new policy was pursued from the end of the seventies onwards, which was aimed at reducing collective expenditure, including spending on social security. The economic restoration policy led to the fundamental restructuring of social security. Welfare payments were frozen or decreased. Transfer- and subsidy expenses for housing – rent subsidies –, healthcare, education, legal assistance, welfare and culture also underwent notable interventions. Moreover, access to social security was impeded by, among other things, making the requirements relating to employment biografy, age, acceptance of employment (broadening of the concept of "appropriate employment") more stringent.

This policy with its neo-liberal features, which replaced the Keynesian approach to crisis management, took place within the specific Dutch context with its so-called "polder model": a strong consultative structure between government and the social partners (employers and trade unions). An "exchange" took place with an eye to, on the one hand, the creation of more employment opportunities, and, on the other, strengthening the position of enterprise. The instruments used for this purpose were control of wages, tax reduction, reduction of state deficits, reduction of government intervention in favour of the market, and less regulation of the labour market.

Thanks partly to this policy (in connection with a favourable international economic conjuncture), a significant increase in employment opportunities was realised in the nineties: whereas officially registered unemployment stood at 12% in 1984, it was down to 5% in 1999. Many of these jobs are part-time. This growth in employment benefited especially those who entered the labour-market after ending their education, as well as women. Traditionally, as already mentioned, the Netherlands had low participation of women in paid labour. In 1977, only one third of Dutch households had two sources of income; by 1996 the number had increased to more than two thirds.

The striking fact, however, is that poverty levels showed only a relatively small decline in the boom years in the 1990's. The economic boom had some positive influence and there were tax exemptions for the elderly. The number varies, depending on which definition is used as a criterion. However, it is estimated that 12.3% of all households (801,000) had a low income. There were 370,000 households (5.4%) which were in a long-term position of low income (four years or longer). A specific point of attention with regard to poverty is the "fixed costs": expenditures which are more or less "unavoidable" and difficult to influence, such as rent, water, energy, insurance. The proportion of fixed costs is about 40% of the income.

The development towards a post-industrial society, in which service provision plays a greater role, is linked to persistent poverty, albeit among a minority of the population. It affects especially un- and low-skilled people and people with bad health and/or disabilities. In addition to the stimulating effect of changes in job structure on this "mismatch", there is also a certain displacement effect in that more highly trained persons simply by-pass the less highly trained unemployed. Immigrants of non-western descent are overrepresented among poor people. This is also the case with single (older) women (with little accumulated pension) and single mothers (whether widowed or divorced). Here we still see the influence of the fact that women's participation in paid labour was low over along period. Another point is that mainly non-paid working people (re-entrants to the labour market and school-leavers) benefited from the growth in employment: age, health, education level and ethnic origin (this last one mostly combined with the other factors mentioned) are important selection criteria on the labour market, though the economic boom led to some betterment of the position of low-skilled workers and members of ethnic minorities. Physical and mental disability and chronic illness are a major obstacle to participation in paid labour. For instance, only 38% of people with disabilities have a paid job, compared with 61% of the general population aged 15-64 years. On average, 18-64 years-olds with severe physical disabilities have an average income which is more than EUR 3,000 lower than that of those without physical disabilities. People with disabilities or people who are chronically ill mostly have health-related expenses.

The character of the Dutch welfare state changed in these years: it was a "compensating welfare state": people who were unemployed or disabled received financial assistance, but there was not a very active policy to get them back into paid labour. Now, the Dutch welfare state gained more the character of an "activating welfare state": people became more obliged to look for a new job, to accept jobs, more assistance to get people into jobs was provided by public services, such as more training schemes and so on. Also, it was made more unfavourable to stay in the position of benefit-entitlement by reducing the duration and the level of benefits and by making it more attractive in a financial sense to work. Most benefits are now at a minimum level.

At the end of 2001, the number of people in receipt of disability, unemployment or national assistance benefit stood at just under 1.5 million. It is estimated that in practice the number of people eligible for reintegration is about a quarter of this. During the last few years, an economic downturn led to a reduced growth in employment and rising unemployment.

Churches confronting (new) poverty

This preliminary sketch was necessary in order to clarify the background to the activities of the churches as expressed in the church campaign "The poor side of the Netherlands".

Since the end of the seventies, the churches have also been encountering the phenomenon of what has come to be called "new poverty". Questions regarding poverty came from at least three quarters. First, the industrial mission which – via its contacts inside the companies – were faced with issues of unemployment, disability and other forms of welfare dependence. Moreover, organisations representing welfare dependents and labour unions appealed to the churches to take the side of those who were resisting what was called the one-sided devolution of the effects of the economic crisis onto welfare dependents. In addition, local ecclesiastical bodies like deaconates[1] and charitable institutions received requests for financial assistance, or took their own initiative to help ease the distress somewhat. This, in turn, led to – sometimes heated – discussions over whether the churches were not being turned into institutes of philanthropy. To give just one typical example from the early 1980's: When one deaconate gave Christmas parcels to those church members who were known to be dependent on welfare, an organisation of welfare dependents wrote an open letter stating that this was only acceptable if, at the same time, the churches also protested against the cost-cutting policy. The subsequent controversy, which also reached the press, came to be dubbed the "bowl of soup controversy", an allusion to the older kind of care for the poor, which took the form of favours and begging.

The national profile of the church effort was shaped especially through the Council of Churches in the Netherlands[2], DISK ("Dienst in de industriële samenleving vanwege de kerken" i.e. "Church Service in Industrial Society": the national body for labour ministry), and the national diaconal bodies. It included, for example, informing the local churches about the situation of people who were entitled to benefit and about the systematic revision of social security, correspondence and discussions with the Cabinet and participation in demonstrations. The efforts of the churches mainly involved drawing attention to the difficult situation of those who were on welfare, and standing up for the principle that "the strongest shoulders ought to carry the heaviest burden", as an expression of the biblical demand for justice.

When in 1987 it became clear that the systematic review of social security would nevertheless be carried through, so that dependency became pervasive among those entitled to welfare, the Council of Churches and DISK took the initiative of organising a conference on "The poor side of the Netherlands", which took place in a church in Amsterdam on 29 September 1987. The conference was prepared together with people entitled to benefit and their organisations. The aim was to send a clear signal to the churches' own support base as well as to politicians and society in general that the problem of poverty in society should be taken seriously, and to give a sign of hope to those who were affected. The term "poor side" was deliberately chosen in order to hint at the situation of those who live at or under the social minimum over a long period of time, and to formulate an indictment against a society in the process of growing increasingly wealthy, and which seems to tolerate the exclusion of some of its members from full social participation. The poverty spoken of here, it was repeatedly stressed, is not the kind of poverty encountered in the Third World, where physical survival is at stake, but rather poverty in the context of the situation in the Netherlands. The keyword in this kind of poverty is exclusion, which translates into isolation, the development of financial "survival strategies", one-sided dependencies (on both welfare institutions and political decision-making) and a limited perspective that the situation will improve in the future.

Theologically, a link was made with the growing consensus, both in the ecumenical movement and in Roman-Catholic social teaching, regarding the interpretation of the biblical concept of justice (tsedeka), which implies a preferential option for the poor. As the American (Roman Catholic) bishops put it in their pastoral message of 1986, *Economic Justice for All*: "Policies should be judged according to what they do for the poor, what they do to the poor, and what they enable the poor to do for themselves. The basic moral criterion for all economic decisions, policies and institutions is this: they should be in the service of all people, especially the poor."

The campaign

The conference was followed up by a campaign based in a lot of regional and local "poor side groups", and in a national working group, which operated by order of the Council of Churches and DISK. The guiding principle was that activities were to be launched involving the affected parties themselves. The point of departure was to do things "together with" rather than "doing for". These groups often include ecclesiastical functionaries in the field of church and society, but emphatically also (church) volunteers and those entitled to welfare themselves.

A second guiding principle was the determination that churches should not turn into institutions of philanthropy and favours. That would mean regressing to the situation pertaining before the introduction of the General Welfare Act (1965), when help for the "needy" took the form of favours, with all humiliations associated with such an approach.[3] The issue at stake was and still is that social security should clearly remain a right. Therefore the formula "helping under protest" was coined. If financial assistance had to be given to people in crisis situations, who could not claim their rights anywhere else, the local churches should inform politicians and society that they had to give help where this ought not to have been necessary. Thus some deaconates wrote to the government, to Parliament and to the city council about their provision of financial assistance. Nevertheless – this is the experience – in churches the temptation to regress to favours is still there.

The campaign yielded a whole array of activities, in which, however, a pattern can nevertheless be discerned. It can be schematically represented as follows, if we cluster the many hundreds of activities under four aims:

1. stimulating encounters;
2. forging alliances;
3. supporting organisations established by those affected;
4. promoting changes in society and politics through political-social discussions and by lobbying.

1) Stimulating encounters

By the stimulation of encounters, we mean the stimulation of intensive communication between church people and those entitled to social security. Naturally these categories might also overlap, but that is often not the case. A commonly used model in this regard is the encounter model, where those entitled to welfare are given the opportunity to tell their stories. It should be said that this method makes its own specific demands. It can easily lead to a one-sided conversation, also (especially) if well-intentioned individual advice is offered to those on welfare. The discussion can acquire a confrontational character so that communication is smothered. Another common experience is that those entitled to welfare get tired of telling their stories ("Don't they know it by now?").

Yet such efforts to give visibility to the world of experience of those entitled to welfare are very important – first of all in order to provide insight into their situation. Also, however, because they are so rarely given a hearing in the political and social debates, which, moreover, are often carried on in macro terms without being translated into the terms of the world of those entitled to welfare.

Thus this model, if handled well, can help to break through prejudices such as the belief that people on welfare do not seek hard enough for a job, or do not handle their money well.

2) Forging alliances

The next phase is often the forging of an "alliance" between churches and people entitled to welfare, with an eye to activities aimed at improving the position of the latter. Such alliances are important because those entitled to welfare constitute a minority in our society, and have very little political or economic influence. Thus their interests are easily disregarded. Therefore other people and organisations have to take up their cause if an improvement of their situation is to be made possible. On base of these alliances, also material help and social support can be given and is given to individuals and their households.

3) Supporting organizations established by those affected

It is important that churches do not take over the initiatives of poor people themselves. Therefore, churches should work together with organizations of poor people and support them, if needed, material and in a non-material sense. It should be pointed out, however, that the organizations of those entitled to welfare are mostly on a rather small scale and, moreover, very diverse. This last fact reflects the heterogeneous constitution of the group entitled to welfare: women/men, allochthonous/autochthonous people, the youth/the aged. Differences with regard to the grounds on which welfare is claimed and so on.

4) Promoting changes in society and politics

The important thing here is to put an end to poverty being hidden. The first precondition for solving a problem is the recognition that it exists. The recognition that poverty is a reality, and that there are groups of people who face structural exclusion, is not a matter of course. Thus there were some heated debates between the churches and the minister and secretary of state of Social Affairs and Employment about whether poverty actually occurred in the Netherlands.

The stimulation of social and political discussions concerning the possibility of promoting an adequate anti-poverty policy, and the realisation of such a policy is important.

At a national level, a second large conference was organised on October 4th 1988, and on May 19th, 1990, the rally "Holland against pauperisation" was held. A number of study conferences was also organised to address specific themes like poverty and children, youth, women, immigrants and so on. According to the formula which was consistently followed, both those entitled to welfare and experts were given a hearing, and reports with recommendations were brought out on the basis of their contributions.

Experiences and insights gained during the local and national campaign were collected and described in the report *Armoede opgelost? Vergeet het maar!* (Poverty solved? Forget it! – 1991), which was handed over to the government. However, the position of the Cabinet, which was revealed shortly afterwards, breathed the spirit of the hardening welfare state, and included an activating labour market policy, stricter legislation and sanctions, and an emphasis on those entitled to welfare.

The national working group "The poor side of the Netherlands" saw in the reaction of the Cabinet to the campaign report, a decline in the recognition of the incidence of poverty. In a lengthy reaction, the working group expressed its disappointment about this denial of poverty, which was seen in the use of the mystifying term "backlog" instead of "poverty" or "exclusion", and about the one-sided emphasis on paid labour. The working group felt, moreover, that society's responsibility had been insufficiently emphasised; instead the burden of the social security problems was laid one-sidedly on the shoulders of those entitled to welfare (blaming the victim).

In opposition to government policy, the working group decided to start a "campaign for justice and solidarity" under the motto: "You are touched by poverty".

The aims of this new campaign were to place and keep the problem of poverty on the political and social agenda; to encourage those involved, those entitled to welfare and their alliance partners; and to maintain and expand the involvement of the church. In a widely distributed "solidarity magazine" a plea was made to restore solidarity to a place of honour, illustrated with experiences from various areas of social life. By means of leaflets with various practical examples of concrete solidarity from the daily life of child rearing, education, work, sport etc., people were called upon to make already existing or new "solidarity commitments".

An important part of this campaign was the "adoption" of members of parliament and other important politicians. Local and regional working groups made appointments with politicians for more than just a passing contact. A well-prepared working visit, including a discussion, usually formed the start of this. In many cases, this contact also continued after such first encounters; mutual agreements could be reached and new themes for discussion and action could be introduced.

Churches and poverty – the years 1995 and after

In 1995 the Council of Churches published a report that was to serve as the point of departure for reflection on the future of social security: *Deelnemen en Medelen: sociale zekerheid van uitsluiting naar participatie* ("Participating and sharing: social security from exclusion to participation"). The report pleaded for a broad concept of participation: along the way of paid labour also in the field of unpaid labour (at home and volunteering work). The importance of this last type of work is under evaluated in society. So, especially the unpaid care labour and all the work at home of women is insufficiently seen. Every citizen should have the possibilities to participate in paid and unpaid labour.

Also in this year, a new campaign, "Poverty is injustice", was launched, to give an impulse to consciousness, attention and action in the churches. Ongoing campaigns have problems to motivate people.

That year, 1995, was also an important year, because the government acknowledged for the first time that there was poverty in the Netherlands. Also, some recommendations of the Social Summit of the United Nations in Copenhagen in 1995 were taken up. The minister of social affairs and employment published a policy report about "The other side of the Netherlands". From 1996 till 2000 a yearly report – "Poverty in the Netherlands" – on poverty and social exclusion was published and national conferences on these reports were organized, A "Poverty Monitor" is also published. The possibility was created for local authorities to develop an anti-poverty policy and to give special social assistance. However, the government refused to increase the minimum benefit level by a substantial amount. This is a big difference in opinion between the government and the anti-poverty movement: the government is saying that in principle the minimum level is sufficient. If there are specific circumstances where this is not the case, then there is special social assistance, which is mostly on an individual basis. However, reports by the anti-poverty movement show clearly that this is too low especially when people live at a minimum level for long periods. Another objection against this certain decentralization to the local level is that big differences arose between local authorities policies which led to legal inequality.

The churches had to reckon with these developments. So, more attention was paid to the question of what church groups could do on a local level, especially to influence local policies.

From 1995 onwards, more attention was also paid to the question of enrichment. The campaign against poverty was explicitly connected with that against enrichment to make clear that there was a growing rich side of the Netherlands. Up until 1983, there was a tendency towards more equality. After this year the differences in income grew. An important factor is the difference in properties (houses, shares and so on). In the 1990ties, there was a booming economy which worked in favour of big parts of the population. Spectacular increases of income could be seen especially at the top of companies. Between 1993-1999, the real value of properties increased with by 45%, between 1999-2001 by 13%. Because most poor people do not have properties they did not take part in these developments. After these years there was an erosion of properties and of shares, so the situation has changed.

The working group "The poor side of the Netherlands" organized several conferences about "The rich part of the Netherlands", published a book about this theme and produced material for discussion in local parishes. As a spin off of these activities, a particular initiative group "investors for taxes" was established which protested against these changes in tax legislation which were in their eyes too favourable for shareholders. This group was not successful on this point. The money which they thought had to be taxed, they gave to a fund which supported initiatives of poor people.

The working group also stimulated attention on questions which got too little attention. So, research was done on the effects of poverty on children, which resulted in a report with recommendations for national and local politics, schools, churches and so on. The effect of this was that other research centres were paying more attention to the position of children and at the local level initiatives were taken to reckon more with them in schools, in clubs and so on.

In 1996, the roman catholic bishop of Breda, Muskens created a lot of commotion because of his opinion about poverty in the Netherlands, as he expressed in interviews, in which he strongly criticized politics for their lack of willingness to take the problem of poverty seriously.

This led to a lot of discussion in the media and an invitation from the prime minister to speak about the problems of poverty.

Another important development is that in 1997 the churches, the humanistic movement and the trade unions (both the general and the confessional) decided to connect their struggle against poverty in the "Platform Struggle Against Poverty". The construction of this network led to a range of common activities such as the organizing of debates with politicians, of collecting autographs for actions, comments on government intentions and so on. In 1999, the network was broadened with all kinds of organizations of benefit entitled people, of migrants, of handicapped and chronically ill people (about forty organizations). They found they had a common manifesto, which contains a vision on poverty as a structural problem and proposals to improve the income status, to recognize the value of unpaid care labour (mostly done by women), the accessibility of health care, education, housing and so on and more specific measures for different groups. This "Alliance for Social Justice" is recognized by the government as representing the poor side of the Netherlands and is consulted about developments and policies, though the Alliance is sceptical about the results.

Looking backwards and forwards

Looking back on all this, it may be stated that the four aims mentioned earlier are still relevant: communication between churches and the poor, building alliances to improve their position, supporting their organizations, making poverty and exclusion visible, lobbying and stimulating the social and political discussions. The effects of the campaigns are hard to gauge, since they have never been systematically researched. Yet I would like to convey some impressions:

The church campaign has made a real contribution to an acknowledgement of the existence of poverty in Dutch society and a growing awareness inside and outside churches of these problems. However, it is essential to repeatedly attract attention to these matters, because attention is very superficial and can quickly be replaced by other things.

Awareness in politics has also grown and some measures have been taken to improve the position of the poor. But it has not proved possible to bring about a change of direction in politics and society of a kind that would realise an effective anti-poverty policy. The position of those who stay at a minimum level for years has hardened in particular.

We should realise that even in a rich society there are structural tendencies which produce poverty and wealth unless countervailing power is built up. So, the prospects for churches in a welfare society are such that the struggle against poverty is also an ongoing one.

Annotations

1. In the Protestant churches with a calvinistic orientation, the diaconate is part of the church structure, with deacons who are members of the church councils on the local, regional and national level. Besides they have their own collegues. They do their work as volunteers, but have an official position within the churches. For a long time the diaconate bore the responsibility for work among the poor, until social legislation increasingly eroded that function.
2. Council of Churches is the ecumenical body for inter-church cooperation in the Netherland, with at that time eleven participating churches, among them the Roman Catholic Church and the main protestant churches.
3. The General Welfare Act replaced the Poverty Act. The latter had laid the main responsibility for the care of the poor at the door of (especially ecclesial) initiative, whereas the General Welfare Act gave the main responsibility to the government. Since then the poor could stake a legal claim with society in the form of the government.

References

Albeda, W. et al., De rijke kant van Nederland. Armoede staat zelden op zich zelf (The rich side of the Netherlands. Poverty rarely exists in itself), Amsterdam 1998

Alliantie voor Sociale Rechtvaardigheid (Alliance for social justice), Om sociale rechtvaardigheid. De strijd tegen armoede en sociale uitsluiting (For social justice. The struggle against poverty and social exclusion), Utrecht 2000

Centraal Bureau voor de Statistiek / Sociaal en Cultureel Planbureau, Armoedebericht 2002 (Message about poverty 2002), Voorburg 2002

Engbersen, G. et al. (ed.), Arm Nederland. Jaarrapporten 1996 – 2000 (The poor side of the Netherlands. Yearly reports 1996-2000) , 's Gravenhage, Amsterdam

Esping-Andersen, G., The Three Worlds of Welfare Capitalism, Cambridge 1995 (1990)

Esping-Andersen, G., Social Foundations of Postindustrial Economies, Oxford 1999

Hoff, S. / G. Jehoel-Gijsbers, De uitkering van de baan. Reïntegratie van uitkeringsontvangers: ontwikkelingen in de periode 1992-2002 (Benefits not longer necessary. Reintegration in paid labour of benefit entitled people: developments in the period 1992-2002), Den Haag 2003

Nistelrooij, R., "Dan had mijn moeder een som in haar hoofd". Project: Kinderen arm in arm ("My mother was always thinking about how to make both ends meet". Project: Children and poverty), 's Hertogenbosch 1998

Pommer, E. et al., Inkomen verdeeld. Trends in ongelijkheid, herverdeling en dynamiek (Incomes distributed. Tendencies in inequality, redistribution and dynamics), Den Haag 2003

Raad van Kerken / Werkgroep De Arme Kant van Nederland (Council of Churches/Working Group the Poor Side of the Netherlands), Deelnemen en meedelen. Sociale zekerheid van uitsluiting naar participatie (Participating and sharing. Social security from exclusion to participation), Amersfoort/Leidschendam 1995

Sociaal en Cultureel Planbureau, Armoedemonitor (Poverty Monitor), 1997-2001, Den Haag 2003

Sociaal en Cultureel Planbureau, Rapportage gehandicapten 2002. Maatschappelijke positie van mensen met lichamelijke beperkingen of verstandelijke handicaps (Report about handicapped people 2002.

The position in society of people with bodily limitations and intellectual disabilities), Den Haag 2002

Valk, L. van der, Van pauperzorg tot bestaanszekerheid. Armenzorg in Nederland 1912-1965 (From care for paupers to social security. Poor relief in the Netherlands 1912-1965), Amsterdam 1986

Van Kersbergen, K., Social Capitalism. A study of Christian democracy and the welfare state, London/New York 1995

Vlek, R., Inactieven in actie. Belangenstrijd en belangenbehartiging van uitkeringsgerechtigden in de Nederlandse politiek (People, who are not active, in action. The struggle for interests and promotion of interests of benefit entitled people in Dutch politics), Amsterdam 1997

Werkgroep De Arme Kant van Nederland (Working Group the Poor Side of the Netherlands), Armoede opgelost ...? Vergeet het maar! (Poverty solved? Forget it!), Leidschendam 1991

Werkgroep De Arme Kant van Nederland/EVA (Economie, Vrouwen en Armoede) (Working Group The Poor Side of the Netherlands/Economy, Women and Poverty):
E-mail: info@armekant-eva.nl;
Internet: www.armekant-eva.nl

Ninni Smedberg

Sweden

The Swedish welfare state: background and characteristics[1]

When Sweden is studied, it is important to remember that (the Lutheran) church and state were firmly joined together at the time of the reformation (16th century). Especially at the local level, the Swedish system of geographical parishes became the areas of religious and social control. It was the task of the local church, through its pastor, to take care of the poor.

In the 19th century, this firm relationship started to loosen (dissolve) and from about the 1850s up until today, there has been a differentiation process between church and state, which is very strong and obvious. The 19th century was the time of industrialisation in Sweden. At the end of the century, new areas with dense population appeared close to saw mills, factories and mines. The poverty of that time appeared in relation to the urbanization process. The pattern is basically the same as in other Western countries. The interesting part of Swedish development is that the traditional folk movements of that time (revival movements, temperist movements and workers' movements) became very strong and forceful entities. They did, in many ways, recruit their members out of these lower strata in society. That explains partly their nearly explosive growth up to their peak in the 1920s.

As a result of the misery in new cities and working places, revival movements and new associations were also formed to provide individual help or create hospitals and diaconal institutions. The Swedish diaconal movement, which relatively quickly became institutionalised, has its roots both in the revival movements in the 1850s and in the social situation of that time. Their appearance can be seen as an answer to problems created by industrialisation for a large part of the population.

This explains why the workers' movement in Sweden, through the Social Democratic Party and the Workers Union, gained strong influence in society. As a matter of fact, the Social Democratic Party was in power from the 1930s up until the mid 1970s and still is, although in a significantly altered manner.

The building up of the Swedish welfare state ("folkhemmet"/"folk home") started in the thirties of the last century, when, in 1932, the Swedish Labour Party came to power. In this period, a welfare state was built up in which the capitalist system was combined with social rights and participation of the labour movement (trade unions) in the decision making of the economy. This was possible by institutionalising a number of compromises between labour, capital, the agricultural sector and consumers (Sweden has a strong cooperative movement). The state had an important role in this, especially in setting the aims of a system of planning in a lot of sectors of society (economy, social housing, population, education etc.). The concept of the welfare state became deeply rooted – also on the ideological level – in Swedish society. Discussions between political parties and in society took place within the framework of this concept. There was a spirit of responsibility for society as a whole. This idea of a basic responsibility in relation to every citizen in the country became the basis of the "folk hemmet" concept. This all made possible a high level of taxation and a mastering of the development of incomes, which are conditions for a high level of employment, also in the collective sector, and a highly developed system of social security and social services. The concept underlying social security was that it should not be based on charity, but should be a fundamental right that is universal and has income-related benefits rather than a system of minimum benefit levels. The guiding principle is that people should be guaranteed an adequate income in the event of temporary interruptions in their working careers due to illness or unemployment and when they no longer work due to invalidity or age. A universal system also makes administration cheaper than a system of means-tested benefits. The view is that the most disadvantaged groups are better off with a universal social security system than a system that is based on means tests or a minimum income. A system which benefits many people is also supported by many people, which is essential for its legitimacy. It also ensures long-term distributive effects (Sweden's Action Plan Against Poverty and Social Exclusion 2001, p. 12/ idem 2003, p. 17).

The building up of the welfare state was connected with an active labour market policy with the aim of full employment. Everyone who was able to work should work. When there was an interruption, people got assistance (for instance by schooling) to come back to paid labour.

The Church as part of the "Folk home"

It is quite important to remember that the idea of the "Folk home" also included the national church. Although the bishops of the Church of Sweden published a memo in 1929 stating that they wanted the church to be regarded as part of the folk movement of Sweden, the government decided to include the church as one authority among others within the welfare state system. The new law introduced in the thirties gave the local church an organization similar to the local community. The task of the local religious community was to perform religious services alongside other services performed by official institutions in society. The strong state did not accept any diversities from the idea of an egalitarian society with solidarity for every citizen. The law stated that the church was not allowed to get involved in social issues in the local community, as these issues were the obligations of the state or municipality to carry out. This explains why the Church of Sweden has become, in many ways, a detached church concerned with buildings and rites and not very much with national social issues. This is, however, not true when international or global questions are raised. This is an interesting peculiarity of the Swedish situation today with strong involvement in ecumenical and social issues at an international level, but a much weaker involvement in national or local issues of this kind.

The economic crisis of the nineties

It was the deep economic crisis of the first half of the nineties which also disturbed the Swedish system. This crisis led to a manyfold increase in unemployment and substantial cuts had to be made in the budget in order to address the imbalances in central government finance. For the citizens, these cuts meant lower levels of compensation or other changes in the health, unemployment and parental insurance systems, lower pensions and increases in municipal rates and charges. A substantial increase in the cost of social welfare allowances and unemployment, in combination with shrinking tax revenues, forced local authorities to make cutbacks in health and care services and school education. This development coincided with a large influx of refugees and a decline in the number of births. The economic situation turned upwards in the mid-nineties, and the previous policy of austerity gave way to a policy of reform and increased resources for health and care services and school education, as well as higher social security benefits.

Poverty and social exclusion

One of the new items in the EU meeting in Gothenburg (2001) was that every country had to provide a National Action Plan against poverty and social exclusion. The process started and lead to an action plan in 2001. A revised version appeared in 2003, the Sweden's action plan against poverty and social exclusion 2003-2005. In this report, we can find a lot of data about poverty and social exclusion, from which we make use in the following.

The economy and the labour market
The years 1998-2000 were a period of strong economic growth in Sweden's economy. But ever since then, the international situation has been marked by uncertainty and recession. The war in Iraq only served to increase this uncertainty. The international downturn has also affected Sweden, and, as a result growth has declined and is expected to be no more than 1.4% in 2003 and 2.4% in 2004. The employment rate dropped in 2002 for the first time since 1995. The percentage of people in employment is highest in the age group 25-54 (84.2% in 2002) and lowest in the age group 16-24 (46.5% in 2002). The percentage of people at work fell in all age groups between 1990 and 1995, after which it increased once again.

The recovery made least impact on people between the ages of 16 and 24, which is largely due to the fact that nowadays more young people continue to study after leaving school.

Percentage of the population in regular employment, age group 20-64

	1990	1995	2000	2001	2002
Total	86	76	78	79	78
Men	89	78	80	81	80
Women	84	74	75	77	77

(Source: Welfare Data 2003, Ministry of Health and Social Affairs)

Open unemployment, which fell in the second half of the 1990s, and was down to 4% in 2001 and 2002, increased again in the autumn of 2002, and in February 2003 was 4.5% (men 5.2%, women 3.7%). The Government expects the average annual unemployment rate in 2003 to be 4.5%, but this figure should fall next year as the employment rate rises again. Most of this increase will be in the age group 25-54, in which unemployment has increased among both women and men. Unemployment among young people is especially sensitive to cyclical variations. Whenever unemployment increases, it increases most among young people. Youth unemployment in 2002 was 9.4%, which was an increase of 1.4 percentage points on 2000. As a result of the high rate of unemployment among young people and the expansion of the upper secondary school system in the last decade or two, young people enter the labour market and adult life in general later than before. One consequence of this is that they form a family and have children at a later age. In 2004, unemployment is expected to fall as the employment rate rises again. The regular employment rate for persons between the ages of 20 and 64 is expected to be 77.6% in 2004.

Persons born outside Sweden were hit especially hard by the decline in employment during the first half of the 1990s. Starting in 1997, employment among immigrants has increased every year. This applies both to men and women, but the increase has been larger among men. Despite this positive trend during the last few years, the differences between persons born in and outside Sweden are still large. The employment rate among those born in EU or EEA countries was 70% in the second half of 2001, while it was 61% among those born in the rest of Europe and 54% among those born outside Europe. The corresponding figure for persons with no foreign background was 77%.

The chances of finding work increase the longer a person has lived in Sweden. Immigrants have to build a new network of contacts and acquire a basic knowledge of the new language. Apart from this, the labour market is not ethnically neutral. Persons born outside Sweden usually have a suitable level of education and age structure for the labour market, but this does not give them the same advantages as it would for native-born Swedes. The rate of employment is not the only difference between immigrants and native Swedes in the labour market. There is a marked concentration of immigrants in certain labour market sectors and they often perform work that does not correspond to their qualifications. The National Integration Office has also pointed out that certain mechanisms in society unintentionally discriminate against persons with a foreign background. One example of this is that employers who lack adequate information about an individual's capacity and are unable to pick the best candidate on the basis of qualifications and job interviews tend to use group affiliation as a recruitment criterion. As a result, it is harder for some individuals to get a job simply because they are assigned to a certain group on account of external factors such as their name or appearance.

The percentage of disabled persons at work varies greatly between different groups, depending on the disability. While the employment rate among the hearing-impaired is similar to that of the population as a whole, the rate is much lower among persons with reduced mobility, the visually impaired and persons with a history of mental problems. The employment rate among disabled persons fell by over nine percentage points for both women and men between 1988/89 and 1998/99. The proportion of students is also lower among certain groups of disabled persons.

Income and economic vulnerability
The economic situation became precarious for more and more people during the economic crisis of the 1990s. This was especially the case among

young people, single parent providers and immigrants. There was, however, no fall in the disposable income of old-age pensioners (as a group) during the 1990s. The improvement in the financial position of households that started in the second half of the 1990s has continued in the last few years, and household income is now higher than at the start of the 1990s. This does not apply to the lowest-income households, however. Families with children were one of the groups that suffered most from the recession of the 1990s. It took many years for them to achieve the same levels as at the start of the 1990s. There has been a recovery in recent years, but the rate of increase in income is lower among single parents with children than married/cohabiting parents with children.

Various indicators may be used to describe economic vulnerability. One such indicator is the basic social assistance allowance[2], another is the proportion of the population whose income is lower than a certain percentage of median income (50 or 60%). In 1990, about 5% of the population had an income that was lower than the basic social assistance allowance. This percentage increased during the second half of the 1990s, and then fell again to 7% in 2000. The most vulnerable groups – new immigrants, single parents with children and young people – have improved their financial position considerably since 1996, but they have still not achieved 1991 levels. Although the cost of financial assistance and induction allowances[3] has continued to fall, there has been no reduction in the proportion of households that are dependent on social assistance for long periods of time[4]. On the contrary, long term dependence increased throughout the 1990s, until the trend was reversed in 2001. Just under one-third of recipients of social assistance were dependent on a subsistence allowance from the social services on a long-term basis. The costs for this group amounted to over 60% of total costs that year.

The family situation and the composition of the family play an important part when it comes to household income. Single parents with children are often financially disadvantaged. The percentage of persons with an income under the basic social assistance allowance in this group, 72% of whom are women, increased from 10% to almost 30% between 1991 and 1996, after which it dropped to 16% in 2000. The most vulnerable of all are those with three or more children. In 12% of families with children aged 0-6 disposable income was lower than the basic allowance in 2002. This is only just over half the figure for 1996.

The time factor must also be taken into account in the context of financial vulnerability. Estimates made by the Ministry of Health and Social Affairs show that 5% of the population lived in households whose income was less than half of the median income during the period 1994-1999. Just under half of these were in this situation for only a year, while for 70% of them the situation persisted for two years. Less than 1% of financially vulnerable persons remained vulnerable throughout the six-year period.

Not unexpectedly, new immigrants have the greatest difficulty in supporting themselves, since they are not available for the labour market during their first few months in this country. During the civil war in the former Yugoslavia in the first half of the 1990s, Sweden accepted a large number of refugees from that area at the same time as the country suffered its worst economic crisis since the 1930s. This made it extremely difficult for this group of refugees to get a foothold in the labour market. Starting in 1996, however, there has been a positive trend. The cost of maintaining a refugee during his/her first year and the three following years was, for the refugees accepted in 1997, the lowest recorded during the 1990s.

The social assistance needs of persons born outside Sweden correlate closely with the period of residence in this country. Among recipients of social assistance who arrived in Sweden before and during the 1970s and received such assistance in 2001, only about 20% were dependent on assistance for lengthy periods, while the figure for those who immigrated during the 1990s was almost 50%. Immigrants who have lived in Sweden for more than 21 years have generally seen their incomes rise at the same rate as those of native Swedes.

Financial problems (difficulty in paying day-to-day expenses and lack of financial buffer) are more common among disabled persons than others, which is mainly because they have extra expenses in the form of fees and charges and so on compared with the average citizen. Elderly disabled persons (65-84) have significantly lower incomes than non-disabled persons in the corresponding age group.

The most disadvantaged

Misuse of alcohol and drugs
Both alcohol consumption and the use of drugs increased in the 1990s. Per capita alcohol consumption in 2002 was 9,6 litres of pure alcohol for persons over the age of 15, which is an increase of 20% since 1996. The share of overall consumption accounted for by women has increased sharply over a long period of time. Up to 2000, this increase had not led to any visible increase in alcohol-related mortality, which was basically constant in the 1990s among both women and men. The percentage of young men reporting for national service (age 18) who stated that they had tried drugs tripled in the 1990s and was 18% in 2002. Experience of drugs among pupils in the 9th form also increased sharply during the 1990s from about 3-4% at the beginning of the period to almost 10% in 2001. In 2002 the figure had dropped to 8%. These levels are relatively low by international standards. The number of heavy[5] misusers increased between 1992 and 1998 from about 19,000 to about 26,000. About a quarter of these were women both in 1992 and 1998. The number of drug-related deaths increased by more than 100% during the 1990s from 143 in 1990 to 353 in 2000.

Crowded housing and homelessness
In 2001, there were 4,3 million housing units in Sweden. 42% of these were owner-occupied houses, 40% were rented apartments and 18% were tenant-owned apartments. According to "Statistics Sweden", the proportion of people living in crowded housing (more than two persons per room, not counting the kitchen and living-room) has, for the first time since the early 1980s, increased in recent years from just under 2% in 1998/99 to 2.7% in 2001. More blue-collar workers than white-collar workers live in crowded housing. Families with children live in crowded conditions more often than families without children.

Homelessness is a serious social problem with implications for both housing policy and social policy. It is extremely difficult to obtain reliable information about the extent of homelessness. Just under 10,000 homeless were reported in 1993. In a survey carried out in 1999 the National

Board of Health and Welfare estimated that there were about 8,400 homeless persons. In both these studies about one-fifth of the homeless were women. The fact that different methods were used for these two studies makes it difficult to compare them. However, the Board has concluded that the figures for 1999 broadly correspond to those for 1993. According to the 1999 survey, three-quarters of the homeless were born in Sweden. Among those born outside Sweden, there was a marked over-representation of Finns in relation to the percentage of the population that is of Finnish origin. According to the 1993 study, there were more than 100 homeless persons in 14 local authority areas. The corresponding figure for 1999 was 15.

Crime and vulnerability

The crime trend
Crime is unevenly distributed. Most crimes are committed in areas where social and financial resources are below of average. The risk of falling victim to a crime is therefore greater in these areas, which makes it especially important to take measures to reduce crime and increase security in such areas. There is no reliable documentation on the extent of crime in Sweden, but the trend is relatively clear. While crime increased sharply between 1950 and 1990, the crime level has now stabilized. The crime profile has changed in recent years. There is evidence to suggest that violent crime and criminal damage have continued to increase since 1990, while crimes against property, i.e. mainly theft of various kinds – a major category – have decreased slightly. About 1.2 million crimes are reported to the police every year. However, not all crimes come to the knowledge of the authorities. The majority of undetected crimes are ones that are not usually committed against an individual, e.g. drug, smuggling and traffic offences. Crimes against the person, e.g. assault and battery, sexual offences and unlawful threats are not always reported either. The real number of crimes and victims of crime is therefore larger than criminal statistics indicate.

Violence against women
About 18,000 cases of assault and battery against women were reported in the first half of the 1990s. This figure had risen to 21,400 in 2002. One reason for this increase is greater willingness to report such offences, but the actual number of cases has probably increased all the same. A recent study issued by the Department of Criminology at Stockholm University on vulnerability to threats and violence among young single mothers shows that women with welfare-related problems, such as unemployment, poor health and precarious finances, are much more vulnerable to threats and violence than women who do not have such problems.

Prostitution
In 1999, one year after the coming into force of the Prohibition Against Purchasing Sexual Services Act, the National Board of Health and Welfare carried out a survey of the incidence of prostitution in Sweden. The survey confirmed the findings of previous studies, i.e. that visible street prostitution is only the tip of the iceberg. It is generally assumed that about one-third of all prostitution consists of street prostitution, while two-thirds is invisible. Street prostitution did not undergo any radical changes between 1998 and 1999. The number of known prostitutes in the three largest cities, where outreach workers work with prostitutes, is much greater than in smaller towns without such activities. It is impossible to estimate the number of known female prostitutes since it is impossible to check that women are not counted more than once. The National Board of Health and Welfare plans to follow up its survey. According to a report on trafficking in women issued by the National Police Board in February 2003, there is a good deal of evidence that the legislation has made a positive impact on this form of trafficking. As a result of the Act, human traffickers and pimps no longer consider Sweden a profitable market for their activities.

Networking

This action plan, which we used extensively to give a picture of the situation in Sweden, is a political document and it contains statements from political decisions and visions. It is not always that the reality matches the pictures of political documents. When the process with the action plan in Sweden was starting, a network was formed. About 30 members in the network representing non-governmental organisations and voluntary organisations (The Church of Sweden as well as other ecumenical organisations participated actively). The network aimed towards a dialogue with the Government, but the first years, it was only information that was shared, no dialogue. In the first report from the Government, it was only indicated with one phrase that a network was active, that there had been contacts and that further contacts should be thought about. The result was that the network wrote its own report concerning poverty and social exclusion in Sweden in 2001. For the new plan 2003-2005, the Governments National Action Plan against poverty and social exclusion included three pages from the network as an appendix. This means that the network has marked out a few points for a further discussion and dialogue.

When the process started to work with the second action plan, there where instructions on the national levels. One of the points, the so-called fourth aim, says that it is necessary to mobilise all actors in our work against poverty and social exclusion. The network pointed out that the other aims in this action plan could not be achieved without a mobilisation of all actors. Some of the main issues from the networks document are: To co-ordinate work towards the most vulnerable, and that means both politically and between levels (national, regional and local) as well as between actors. It is necessary that the official decision-making people meet with the people in exposed situations for a direct dialogue. It is not enough that there is an action plan on the national level. More and more of our direct welfare work is moving from the national level to the local level, this level must also produce an action plan against poverty and social exclusion.

One of the most problematic areas right now is the care of mentally handicapped people. This care moved, about ten years ago, from the national level to local level without giving the receiving level the adequate resources. Today many NGOs (for example the city mission in Stockholm) give signals and reports in which it is shown that this group of people (mentally handicapped) are in most exposed and problematic life situations. They often end up homeless and drifting around in the bigger cities without proper care. This group is not only poor but also exposed in many ways. Local congregations have also seen the life situation for this group change radically over the last ten years. Some end up in the local congregation without money, home or social network.

One important demand from the network is a regular dialogue between and meeting space for the decision-making people, on all levels. This has to start at the level of the Government and to function as a signal to the local level as well. One of the Ministers from the Government has made this a promise. The focus in that coming dialogue has to be the bottom up dialogue rather then a top down. In July 2003, the Government decided that a kind of delegation should be formed that includes all levels (and different actors), also the so-called grassroots. The Minister of Social and Health affairs will be in charge of the delegation. The first meeting was held in December 2003. Among other things, a conference is planned to be held in 2004 with the focus of the users of the special efforts within the social welfare system.

Priorities and a new role for the Church of Sweden

In 1994, a study was made concerning prioritised target groups and diaconal working areas. Deacons and vicars were asked to answer a questionnaire. This resulted in the report "För att tjäna" (To serve) (Bäckström 1994). In 2002, a new questionnaire was sent out that to a certain extent asked the same question from 1994 (this questionnaire is still not published and I have taken the following numbers directly from the study). This time, the Church of Sweden office in Uppsala was responsible. Did deacons make the same priorities in 2002 as in 1994 and were the target groups the same? Just a few comments concerning the findings in connection with the focus of this article. The main priorities in 1994 as well as in 2002 are the home visits and counselling and the target group is still the elderly. But we also see some changes since 1994. Group activities focusing crisis and losses (dead husband or wife for example) are even more priorities now than in 1994 (1994: 50%, 2002: 70%) as well as families (1994: 30%, 2002: 55%). When you look at the areas of priorities inside the diaconal work, one finds a few changes. For example when it comes to co-operation with both social authorities (1994: 35%, 2002: 52%) and other NGO's (1994: 14%, 2002: 49%) there is a major change. This depends firstly on the change hat the Church of Sweden went through in the year 2000. From a State Church to a "free Church". Before the year 2000, the Church of Sweden had the tradition to "run its own spiritual business". Until that time, it was forbidden to run anything that was supposed to be run by the welfare state (different levels, more and more the local community). As we mentioned above, the Church was not allowed to use its tax money in the welfare sector (as schools, elderly care, hospitals etc.). All these areas were handed over from the Church to the State (and communities) at the beginning of 1862.

Secondly, there is a new need to co-operate among all NGOs and voluntary organisations as well as authorities because of the historical change of running the welfare as a purely state business towards more of a private market and towards the more catholic based welfare in which families have the first responsibility and not the State. This together with lack of money in this sector (or reduced money because of other priorities) makes it necessary to co-operate. For the Church of Sweden, this is rather new (from the year 2000), but one can also find a rising interest inside the welfare sector itself to work with alternatives. There is also a growing need because of the growing income gap and because people in marginalized situations are not taken care of any longer as they used to be. People who are not profitable (in any sense) are having difficulties to get the care that they are entitled to. Congregations, deacons, have now for some years worked with counselling for these people. Claiming their rights at the local social authorities for example. Almost all voluntary organisations working with these groups have seen a more cynical attitude and constant reducing of resources for these people. One organisation for single parents (Makalösa föräldrar, "Remarkable parents"), mostly single mothers, has seen this change drastically during the last years. In this group, 50% have no cash margin and over 60% have difficulties to manage regular payments every month. The children's organisation (Save the Children) have recently published a report where they seriously talk about child poverty in a so called welfare state such as Sweden.

This is also why one finds in the report that deacons are saying that they are more often now then before (1994) co-operating with other organisations. There is a small change when it comes to hand out money to the needy (1994: 17%, 2002: 19%) and it's probably mostly a big city problem (Congregations inside the community of Stockholm hand out 16 million Swedish Crowns in cash every year). When it comes to active lobbying etc. towards politicians and decision-making people, there is only a small change (1994: 3%, 2002: 9%).

Diaconal work and a new situation
This reflects a consequence from our diaconal history, the institutional side which was also connected with charity. During these years when the diaconal awareness was growing in Sweden, the Church was not allowed to conduct welfare service (as said before), but a municipal or state institution should do it. And they also carried out charity. This was how it came to start (also) inside the congregations, diaconal work as mostly charity and not service inside the welfare system. This was conducted by deaconesses, from the beginning mostly educated nurses or teachers.

Today, however, inside more areas then before, the capacity of the community is not enough. That means that some of this work is also done by other actors then the official community. The consequence is that there is a growing market concerning taking care of marginalized people. So, at present, congregations and religious groups are familiar with work like "openhouse activities for psychological weak people", activities for people addicted to drugs and alcohol, people without jobs, and with serving soup to homeless people. Some congregations have started to open homes for homeless people. This is not only the case in the bigger cities. A lot of this work is done in an ecumenical context and in the bigger cities city missions organizations are active (seven city missions and five diaconal institutions).

Today we are also talking about an understanding of diaconal work that also includes advocacy and being a voice for marginalized people that is being more and more silent and invisible. In a country like Sweden with a strong middleclass, it is a shame not to be able to support your children in the way you want, to go to the dentist when you need, to buy enough food to your family at the end of the month, pay for your medicine when you are old. One of the biggest unions in Sweden (LO) writes in a new report about the unacceptable growing gap between the small group in top positions (managing companies) and the ordinary worker (manager earns today about 47 times more then the ordinary worker). The income gap is getting bigger and people in vulnerable life situations are getting more exposed and poor then ever before. That is why it is of great importance that our definition concerning diaconal work includes not only charity but also advocacy.

As a first step inside diaconal work, there has to be the helping side, direct help with money, food, cloth, home and so on. The second step is to influence the situation for a person in difficult life situation, by being a voice, by accompanying a person to local authorities and to look at every human beings rights. Thirdly, there has to be a moment of political questions: how to change a system where people more often now than before fall apart, where gaps between the successful and not so successful are growing. Then it is not enough with charity and handing out money so that *one* day can be saved. All this is only a scratch on the surface and below this surface the causes lie. The *why* people are getting poorer, the *why* people are being more silent, the *why* children get poorer in a rich country. Deacons, congregations can not only work by scratching a surface, there must be diaconal work that reaches beyond. Beyond the first step.

Solidarity in a global world
The Christian council in Sweden has published a small booklet about the globalisation of solidarity – an active Swedish policy of globalisation (Sweden's Council of Churches 2001). One chapter in this booklet has the

headline "All peoples value the fight against poverty". From this chapter, I have chosen some parts:

All human beings exist because of the will of God and Gods purpose with the human being is that she takes care of creation. The human being was created with a responsibility for the rest of creation and for this reason holds a special role as God's partner when it comes to the care of the creation as God thinks good and in accordance with what he has decided (1 Mos. 1). The ongoing life of creation depends on how the human being fulfils her tasks and completes the responsible admission she has got. The future of creation lies mainly in the hands of human beings. All humans are equal. The same way that all humans have the same origins all share the same destiny. Humans live in a mutual partnership. Together with the task of caring for the animals and the earth, it also becomes the responsibility of the humans to show respect and to care for each other. In our shared heritage and our shared destiny, we as humans are mutually dependant on each other in spite of the fact that we are different and equipped with different resources and gifts. The earth is one, and it is the common home of all humans. The gifts of the earth, like air and water, are limited and the ones who live on earth must learn how to manage with the resources and share them in such a way that it comes to all humans' favour.

Even though all humans have the same value, it is a fact that the possibility to make something for the future of the earth and the welfare of the humans is different. We do not have the same starting point when it comes to doing something for the common good. Our ability to make a contribution is often dependant on which part of the world we were born and who our parents are. Those of us that are rich and have had the possibility to get an education have a special responsibility to offer material and spiritual resources to the other.

A letter from the Bishops

There is also a Letter from the Bishops' Conference 1993 with the title "Rich and poor, A letter from the Bishops of the Church of Sweden about justice and morality in the global economy". In that report, it is stated clearly that the tradition of the church warns against the accumulation of property and advocates a policy of minimization as sufficient for a worthy life. The biblical concepts of amassed richness and the ownership of property are mainly based on the idea that God is the true owner of all that has been created. Human claims, therefore, must always be conditioned by the concept of responsibility in stewardship. Traditionally there is an insight, running like a red thread, that wealth is something good but also dangerous. Creation itself offers an abundance of life and the means of subsistence, but all that can be abused, and the blessing slips out of our hands. In the tradition of the Christian faith, one of the leading principles is that the relationship between the poor and the rich must be considered from the point of view of the poor. The poor have the first option on interpretation. The rich are not competent to witness because they do not have the same insight into the truth of the matter. Secondly, the gifts of life, which are at hand in abundance, have to be shared generously in order to be a blessing. If not, nature will sooner or later kick back. In a life style of simplicity, there is a harmony with the given order of creation.

This letter as well as the booklet from the Christian council in Sweden thus mostly focus on the international situation and lift up a global perspective when it comes to poverty. This is not unusual when it comes to the discussion about poverty. We are not used to seeing poverty in our own society. Sweden has for many years come to stand as a model of welfare for everyone. The last twenty years have changed that scene radically: It was too expensive, it was too much one standard way of producing welfare, it was when a stronger middleclass wanted to have more options and be able to choose, it was when we become a part of EU and had to adjust our social system to fit in, it was when solidarity is no longer a common value, but rather something that is too expensive for me, it was ...

Of course, all these things are too easy explanations and can not bear the truth alone. But when you put it like a puzzle and look at it together with the massive individualism and privatisation that is seen all over Europe then ...

Inside the Church of Sweden, we have to learn how to be more outspoken and make unjust systems visible (not only the people being unjustly treated). That means including counselling in our conception and understanding of diaconal work. That means being as radical and fearless as we are when it comes to our international diaconal work.

Annotations

1 For this paragraph, we made extensively use of the publications of Anders Bäckström (Bäckström 2001 and 2003).
2 In 2002, this allowance was SEK 3,255 for a single adult. The allowance is for expenses for food, clothes and shoes, play and leisure activities, disposable items, health and hygiene, newspapers, telephone and TV fees. Expenses for housing, household electricity, journeys to work and householders insurance are assessed separately.
3 Since 1993, local authorities have been authorized to pay induction allowances instead of social assistance to refugees who have been granted a residence permit and are taking an induction programme.
4 Households that receive social assistance for at least 10-12 months.
5 Misuse is defined as heavy if a person has injected drugs any time during the past 12 months or used drugs daily or almost daily during the last 12 months, irrespective of the method of intake.

References

Bishopsmötet, Rich and Poor. A letter from the Bishops of the Church of Sweden about justice and morality in the global economy. The Bishops' Conference 1993.
Bäckström, Anders, För att tjäna. En studie av diakoniuppfattningar hos kyrkliga befattningshavare (To serve. Opinions about diaconia from professionals within the Church), Uppsala 1994.
Bäckström, Anders, Svenska kyrkan som välfärdsaktör i en global kultur. En studie av religion och omsorg (The Church of Sweden as a Welfare Provider in a Global Culture. A Study of Religion and Care), Stockholm 2001.
Bäckström, Anders, "Church Based Social Service in a Late Modern Welfare State" . Lecture in Oslo, 26 September 2003 (unpublished).

Sweden's Action Plan Against Poverty and Social Exclusion, Stockholm May 2003.

Sweden's action plan against poverty and social exclusion 2003-2005, Stockholm July 2003.

Sweden's Council of Churches, Solidaritetens globalisering. En aktiv svensk globaliseringspolitik (Globalisation of solidarity. An active Swedish policy of globalisation). Nr. 2, Stockholm 2001 (to be found on the homepage www.skr.org)

IV. Contrast

Justin Beaumont

Workfare, associationism and the "underclass" in the United States: contrasting faith-based action on urban poverty in a liberal welfare regime

Introduction

Since the mid to late 1990s politicians, journalists and other commentators in the US increasingly proclaim that faith-based organisations (FBOs) – such as churches, mosques and para-religious organizations of various types – are better placed to eradicate urban poverty than government and the welfare state more generally.[1] This chapter goes beyond the rhetoric to reveal the ideologically contrasting role of FBOs in their efforts since the 1960s to combat poverty and achieve social justice in US cities. The chapter claims that the shift from "roll-back" neoliberalism towards a reformulated "roll-out" version (Peck and Tickell 2002) facilitates the delegation of many welfare functions and services to FBOs that are governed through new governance arrangements. New forms of poverty in the US and continued welfare state retraction have opened spaces for greater involvement of FBOs in the treatment of poverty in cities. While some faith actors have become active partners in state-managed programmes, others have entered the fray as active partners in progressive antipoverty and social justice struggles. From a firm conceptual and empirical basis, the normative aim of the chapter is to trigger debate about possibilities for the radicalization of multi-agency efforts in cities in the US, The Netherlands and beyond.

There are at least three reasons why the US situation illuminates developments across the Atlantic and particularly in The Netherlands. First, a longstanding debate about inner city ghettoization, the situation of concentrated and extreme deprivation among African Americans in the US

(Wilson 1996; Wacquant 1993; 1996; Marcuse 1997), resonates with concerns about socio-spatial segregation in Europe (Rex 1988; Musterd and Ostendorf eds. 1998; Marcuse and van Kempen eds. 2002). Second, debates over the political economy of neoliberalism in the western world raise questions about the viability of generous state welfare that lead to pressures for welfare reform (Esping-Andersen ed. 1996) and points to the recasting of relations between state and civil society, both with consequences for urban governance arrangements (Brenner and Theodore 2002). The tightening of eligibility criteria for benefit claimants in hitherto staunchly social democratic and corporatist regimes like The Netherlands suggests a tentative convergence with the US where more liberal and residual forms of provision is the norm.[2] And third, many commentators observe the official Jeffersonian separation of Church and State in the US but in the context of a vibrant associational life where religion, with its various expressions in civil society, continues to play an important role in the lives of many people (Davis 1990; Freedland 1998; Carnes and Fenggang eds. 2004). One might speak of religion as a way of life in the US. In spite of formal and constitutional church-state separation, the church – and religion more generally – has long played a crucial institutional role in the social welfare systems in both the US and The Netherlands.

The chapter begins with a historical overview of the main lines of development in the American welfare system and shows that the US case presents a typical example of liberal welfare provision, highly residualized and closely linked to the labour market. The second section summarises three trends that constitute new expressions of chronic deprivation, particularly in US cities, presents data on the extent of the problems and pays attention to the underclass discourse that underpins these developments. Churches' and religious thinking in general, I argue, play a central role in legitimising this discourse. The third section addresses the revival of arguments on both the Left and Right that characterizes American politics and society as "associationist", where organizations that mediate between the individual and state, particularly churches and other FBOs, are commonplace and provide the bedrock of local community social, economic and political life. The fourth examines in detail two forms of faith action on new expressions of poverty: one, as part of the current faith-based agenda under the Bush II administration; the other, as participants in progressive multi-agency responses to urban poverty and injustice. The conclusion alludes to issues for further investigation with respect to progressive coalitions involving faith actors and other governance agents for the eradication of poverty and the achievement of social justice in cities in the US, The Netherlands and beyond.

Liberal and residual welfare

The welfare system in the US never developed in the universalist and social democratic way typically associated with regimes in Scandinavia and The Netherlands. Following welfare regime theorists like Esping-Andersen, the US embodies key features of what he calls a *liberal* regime (Esping-Andersen 1990; ed. 1996). Under this regime, poverty is often seen, certainly by those on the right, as the result of state intervention that serves to foster and uphold a culture of dependency among a pathological and morally deficient underclass (Beaumont 2004). Highly residualised state provision remains strictly at a minimum for the minority of people that are unable to work. Antipoverty efforts are therefore typically associated with the free market and the reduction and withdrawal of state support, alongside an adherence to means-tested benefits, punitive welfare-to-work programmes and reliance on self-help and entrepreneurial initiative. The resulting meagre state provision and commodification of welfare leads to the stigmatisation of benefit recipients and high numbers of people constituting a severely deprived underclass marginalised from the social and economic mainstream. Poverty, moreover, is closely connected with racial inequality, discrimination and racism, particularly among African Americans, Latinos and Chicanos etc. (Tillman and Tillman 1969; Massey and Denton 1993). Liberal and residual patterns are deeply rooted in history.

While various welfare state arrangements had their roots in the interwar years and were consolidated in the immediate post war period, particularly in the UK, comparable social legislation was not enacted in the US until the "New Deal" agreements of 1935 during the Roosevelt administration. While the New Deal displayed and advanced a strongly social democratic and universalist tone, the programmes and initiatives that developed were limited and partial in comparison with the UK and elsewhere (Janoski and Hicks 1994). Memories of economic and social strife in the aftermath of the Great Depression in the late 1920s arguably influenced the universal rhetoric of the New Deal in the context of a more fragmented, liberal and particularist reality. Right from the start employment schemes were linked to the labour market, offering jobs in the public sector when the private sector was unable to soak up unemployment itself. Although these schemes were phased out during World War II, they left a legacy of large-scale transfer payments according to social insurance principles via large bureaucracies (Leiby 1978) and in continuation of long-standing individualistic and liberal characteristics (Handler and Hasenfeld 1991; King 1995; Myles 1996).

During the post war Keynensian/ Fordist boom in the US, unprecedented levels of economic prosperity were coupled with widespread sense of social well-being and quality of life. Two critical social investigations at the time therefore came as quite a surprise for many people. Kenneth Galbraith's indictment of "private affluence, public squalor" in *The Affluent Society* in 1958 and Michael Harrington's *The Other America* published in 1962 (Galbraith 1977; Harrington 1962), led to the rediscovery of poverty in the US which greatly influenced the Economic Opportunity Act that created the "War on Poverty" in 1964 as an integral element of Lyndon Johnson's Great Society programmes. The War on Poverty aimed to ensure every citizen shared in all opportunities of society. Federal spending (albeit limited) went to community action against deprivation, channelled to the local level via the Office of Economic Opportunity (Clarke and Hopkins 1969; Higgins 1978; Marmor et al. 1990). Notions of self-help were a central feature within the Model Cities Program and the Community Action Program that drew upon central funds for experimental community development as a remedy against poverty. Generous income maintenance was characteristically absent from these initiatives. The Vietnam War largely put paid to the War on Poverty as the "war effort" diverted to the international arena. The "Skirmish on Poverty" as Hilfiker (2002) prefers was rather short lived and limited in scope.

As Manuel Castells shows in *The City and the Grassroots*, certain urban protests and community based actions in US inner cities in the 1960s emerged in the context of the War on Poverty, the Civil Rights Movement and the church-based and multicultural "Alinsky model of community organization" (Castells 1983: 60-5; see also Alinsky 1969; 1971; Connolly 1976; Lancourt 1979). Basing his insights largely on the experience of multiethnic neighbourhood mobilization in San Francisco's Latino Mission District (Castells 1983: 106-37), Castells sees the Saul Alinsky myth – the idealised blueprint for grassroots community organization – in some ways more significant than the reality. The principles that underlined his vision, however, exerted an important effect in numerous examples of local antipoverty efforts from the mid to late 1960s and beyond.

In principle Alinsky aimed to increase the capacity and voice of powerless and poor people in decision-making, through mobilization, confrontation and negotiation with government, for more equitable and just distribution of wealth. As self-reliance and self-help would be maintained through community-based organization against political centralisation, the Alinsky model stressed pluralism, government accountability, local autonomy and concerted resident participation to those ends. The model relies on the presence of a professional outsider committed, but also to a degree distant from the community itself and importantly paid by funds generated within and by the community. In the Alinsky vision these funds would flow from a progressive network of FBOs of various types and denominations as the basic and fundamental ally of the people from diverse ethnic, cultural and religious backgrounds. The model emphasises that antipoverty action should be initiated among the people themselves. Castells cites the example of the Northwest Community Organization established in 1961 in Chicago through support from the Catholic Church. The organization aimed to help preserve the physical attributes of a working class neighbourhood, improve local services and expose the corruption of local government officials (1983: 63). The growing influence of a local Hispanic community throughout the 1960s and early 1970s in the area galvanised the activities of the alliance in the later years.

As the Keynesian/ Fordist period of prosperity came under duress in the late 1960s and early 1970s, as well as the taming and quieting of Alinsky-ite neighbourhood struggles from the 1970s onwards, the gradual moves towards a post-Fordist economy and society has meant the continuation and deepening of the liberal and residual tendencies in the US welfare system. The most significant development in this respect is *workfare*, a punitive system of work incentives to encourage the transition from welfare to work, certainly from the early 1980s onwards (Walker 1991; Hill 1992; Peck 2001). Writing from a regulationist perspective, Jamie Peck discerns two sets of contested meanings of workfare that developed in the US at this time (Peck 2001). First, there is a "hard" conception referring to the New Right era under Reagan, illustrated by the "Work First" model in Riverside, California, as well as other examples in Massachusetts, New York and Wisconsin. Under this model benefit entitlement is subject to a compulsory work requirement – a process whereby potential welfare beneficiaries have to prove they have actively sought work (any job regardless of security, wage levels and wider social utility) through "job clubs", "job search" and other mechanisms in the transition from welfare to work. Second, he indicates a "soft" conception referring to the increasingly technical language of welfare reform under successive Republican administrations as well as the Clinton administration in the 1990s. Both meanings of workfare represent a deepening of liberal and residual principles in welfare, away from universal provision towards a punitive, moral and work imperative conception of benefit entitlement. If people experiencing poverty "choose" to avoid work (regardless of job availability), their poverty, according to advocates of workfare, is voluntary and as a consequence they do not deserve state handouts. Central to Peck's thesis is that these workfare initiatives amount to the beginnings of new labour market regulation under neoliberal conditions, as a putative successor to whatever form of welfare (state) arrangements ostensibly existed before.

The new system of labour market regulation serves to punish and coerce the "workshy" through the flexibilisation of labour markets where low wages, job insecurity, temporary and part-time contracts and dead-end jobs are the norm and the route out of poverty. As a result of the individualist, non-structural and moral underpinnings of workfare, where issues of personal responsibility (or its alleged absence) lie at the heart of the so-called welfare crisis, I argue that the church and the Christian community at large in the US played an important role in the discussion over its design, conceptualisation and implementation (see Goudzwaard 1993; CPJ 1994; Carlson-Thies and Skillen eds. 1996). The Center for Public Justice in Washington D.C., for example, an independent civil education and policy research foundation, is grounded in a comprehensive Christian political perspective. The Executive Director James W. Skillen has played a key role in debates over the US public realm in general and the reform of welfare in particular (Skillen 1990; 1994; Skillen and McCarthy eds. 1991). Thinkers in this mould argue that welfare in the US fails because it rests on an untenable conception of human nature that leads to a responsibility crisis external to the problems associated with poverty and low income. Part of their solution lays in the strengthening fundamental accountability structures, such as churches and other FBOs like religious-oriented private schools, as organic components of interaction and the institutional cornerstone of a morally superior and responsible social fabric. Implicit in the argument is that poverty will be substantially reduced under these arrangements. It remains unclear for Peck and other critical observers how a punitive and repressive policy development as workfare can reverse deep-seated structural inequalities, widespread poverty and deprivation across the country. The persistence of chronic poverty in US inner cities (Sawhill 1988) despite the alleged successes of various workfare schemes is testimony to that uncertainty.

New expressions of poverty in cities

David Hilfiker (2002) provides an accessible account of the processes that produced the abysmal conditions experienced by many African Americans in US inner cities. Drawing on this account and other key works (Katz 1986; 1989; ed. 1993; Wilson 1990; 1996) three main trends are identified: (1) the urbanization of poverty; (2) ghetto impoverishment and persistent deprivation and (3) poverty wages and the plight of the working poor.

The abolition of slavery in the south and rapid industrialization in northern cities in the late 19th and early 20th centuries facilitated the first major urbanization of poverty in the US. During "The Great Migration" in the run up to the First World War, many Blacks left the rural south in search of work in the burgeoning and thriving factories in the north. In the 1920s between 1.5 and 2 million largely unskilled African-Americans moved north and settled in cities. While work was abundant, blacks faced persistent racial discrimination in terms of access to essential public services, like housing, as well as workplace insecurity and victimisation. The Great Depression brought misery to groups across the country but was felt in a particularly acute way by African-Americans. Between 1945 and 1960 as many as 4.5 million blacks came to reside in the urban north.

In the post-war period black ghettos were more or less consolidated and subsequently worsened by zoning policies that earmarked certain neighbourhoods as "industrial" thus limiting prospects for residential development and improvement. Two events considerably aggravated the problems in these areas. Federal Urban Renewal programmes for the most part selected black areas for demolition and upgrading. The Loop in Chicago presents a case in point, as does the Gateway Arch in St. Louis. Those people displaced were squeezed into already overcrowded and inadequate public housing elsewhere, deepening the extent of problems of the pejoratively but aptly named "slum renewal" areas. Political bargaining and power plays between urban elites, including Church authorities, were typical in this process (see Caro 1975: 740-1 for New York City and the Catholic Archdiocese in the 1950s). The other major factor was Eisenhower's Interstate Highway programme in 1956. The construction of superhighways meant the destruction of "undesirable" areas, usually black ghettos, or their physical isolation and separation from other parts of the city. The superhighways led to further deterioration by encouraging the flight of affluent whites from the city centres to reside and work outside the city limits. With the decentralization of employment to the suburbs and the wider deindustrialization of urban areas, increasing numbers of people from working class, black families lost their jobs and entered a spiral of decline related to unemployment, family breakdown, single parenthood, child poverty, drugs and crime – aspects typically associated with the modern day ghetto.

The third trend is the emergence of poverty wages and the working poor. By the middle of the 20th century, the US was unquestionably the world leader in manufacturing production. Since the 1960s and through the 1970s until today, restructuring of the global economy, including deindustrialization, growth in services and the post-industrial economy and the regulatory shifts to post-Fordism (Bell 1973; Storper and Walker 1989; Amin ed. 1994), has meant that many people formally working in factories lost their jobs (see Sugrue 1996 for the Detroit story). Some of the resulting unemployment for poorly trained people was taken up by low-wage service jobs such as domestic services, janitors, clerks, salespeople, nursing aides and cashiers, where wages are historically low and benefits limited or non-existent (Sassen 1991). The garment sweatshops employing immigrants for poverty wages in central Los Angeles remains a key example. Wage levels, moreover, have systematically declined in these sectors, both in real terms and relative to other sectors. Even full-time workers in these services increasingly find it difficult to avoid poverty, as well as the growing number of people who, for a whole host of reasons, cannot find work and are often trapped in a benefit-dependent and sometimes illicit sub-culture as their only means for survival.

As Hilfiker (2002) shows by 2000 it was estimated that 11.3% of all Americans, more than one in nine people, lived below the official poverty line that by most accounts grossly underestimates acceptable standards of living and quality of life. Alarmingly, over 16% of American children under 18 and almost a third of all African American children under that same age were officially considered poor (see: www.census.gov/prod/2001pubs/p60-214.pdf). The wealthiest country in the world continues to be home for a vast number of deeply deprived, impoverished and marginalized people.

Taken together, these people have been subject to discursive treatment in the US as the urban *underclass* (for a review see Beaumont 2004; see also Katz 1986; 1989; ed. 1993; Jencks and Peterson eds. 1991; Peterson 1991; Massey and Denton 1993). The "poverty paradox", as Paul Peterson (1991) explains, refers to the situation where growing affluence in American society, particularly in the post war years, is coupled with worsening poverty in American inner cities. He suggests four distinct explanations. The first holds that inner city poverty is attributable to an inadequate welfare state rather than to wider social changes or the cultural and behavioural characteristics of the poor. Secondly, the idea of the "culture of the poor" follows the work by Oscar Lewis that the style of life to which the poor have become attached is attractive and exhilarating and therefore self-perpetuating (Lewis 1961; 1966; 1969). The third follows Charles Murray and Lawrence Mead and refers to perverse government incentives arising from the Great Society reforms in the 1960s that encouraged a culture of dependency and disincentives to work. A final explanation following William Julius Wilson holds that poverty and the "underclass" reflect the inner city in a changing economy, in other words the social by-product of economic restructuring in areas where unemployment is a particularly acute problem.

The debate about the underclass was provided with ideological impetus with the rise of the New Right in the early 1980s, and indeed it is difficult to separate behavioural, moral and pathological explanations associated with writers like Charles Murray and Lawrence Mead from this ideological imperative. The original notion of an "underclass" is generally attributed to observations by the journalist Ken Auletta on four distinct categories of poor Americans:

> (a) the *passive poor*, usually long-term welfare recipients; (b) the *hostile* street criminals who terrorize most cities, and who are often school drop-outs and drug addicts; (c) the *hustlers*, who, like street criminals, may not be poor and who earn their livelihood in an underground economy, but rarely commit violent crimes; [and] (d) the *traumatized* drunks, drifters, homeless, shopping-bag ladies and released mental patients who frequently roam or collapse on city streets (Quoted in Katz 1986: 277 – *original emphasis*).

With the rise of Reaganism in the early 1980s perspectives seeking ideological justification and legitimization for New Right welfare reform appropriated the notion of the "underclass". While Christian political commentators span the ideological divide, it is not difficult to make connections between Right-wing debates on social policy and the notion of a morally degenerate "underclass" with discussions about the alleged responsibility crisis in US welfare. Hutton argues that conservative philosophers like Leo Strauss built on John Locke's conservatism to justify the legitimacy of property as the proper "desert[s] for working on nature's endowment from God' and the proper deserts for 'simply working'" (2002: 56). The most notorious voice was Charles Murray from the Manhattan Institute for Policy Research. In *Losing Ground* he argued that the Great Society Reforms and the growth in US welfare expenditure caused the large-scale increase in levels of inner city poverty since the 1960s (Murray 1984). By encouraging a culture of dependency and providing disincentives to work, he claimed that welfare creates rather than relieves poverty, contributing to the material and moral degeneration of the working aged poor. Murray was immensely critical of those he saw as "apostles of structural poverty" who claim it is not the fault of the poor that they are poor. Explaining poverty in terms of innate moral and behavioural deviance from conservative middle class "norms", he argues for a substantial withdrawal of state provision to the barest minimum, leaving life chances of poor people to the job market, their families and other informal support networks and survival strategies.

The "underclass" debate has quite understandably attracted a great deal of critical attention. Michael Katz and other critics on the Left challenge the stereotypical social categories offered by the proponents of the thesis and call for a longer-term perspective in the analysis of poverty (Katz 1986; 1989; ed. 1993; Handler and Hasenfeld 1991). Alluding to the ideological dimensions of the discourse, Katz argues that since the late 1970s social commentators use the notion as a convenient metaphor to evoke the novelty, danger and complexity of contemporary urban crises. Furthermore, the discourse suggests a rise in poverty and social problems of unprecedented proportions in recent history, a rise unsubstantiated with sufficient evidence (Jencks and Peterson eds. 1991; Peterson 1991). Critics also claim that the discourse is conveniently mobilised to uphold individualist, cultural and pathological explanations of poverty, distinguishing in classic liberal fashion between the "deserving" and "undeserving" poor and also to justify the elimination of state action by placing the blame on the poor themselves. As historically important actors in American associational civil society, churches and other FBOs occupy a certain position among local antipoverty efforts in the absence of generous state redistributive mechanisms, as well contributing to the moralist interpretation of poverty in the inner city.

Renewed interest in associations

Vibrant associational civil society through community and neighbourhoods organizations, clubs, schools, churches and other FBOs, are often claimed to represent the institutional backbone of local community life in the US (cf. Putnam 2000). Political scientists typically refer to the US as a pluralist model of liberal democracy (Nicholls 1974; 1994; Hirst 1994). Largely influenced de Tocqueville's *Democracy in America* (de Tocqueville 1945), the American pluralists claim that democratic politics are sustained by a wider society where plural forms of representation and influence are institutionalised and maintained. Less concerned with formal representative mechanisms of participation, this approach stresses the importance of numerous autonomous associations in civil society that mediate between the individual and the state. Aiming to counter the tyranny of majoritarian democracy, these intermediary organizations are said to disperse opinion and influence more or less equally throughout society in the context of a relative egalitarian distribution of power. A polity is "democratic" when composed of many competing minority factions, none able to exert inordinate influence at any one time. Developed formally in US political science since the 1940s (Truman 1951; Parsons 1969), one of the most important voices was Robert A. Dahl who constructed a theoretical model of the conditions a polity must satisfy to ensure "polyarchy", the plural and successive influence of interest groups (Dahl 1961; 1966; see also Polsby 1980). Depicted as "pork-barrel politics" by the journalist Jonathan Freedland, the channelling of federal funds to local causes remains a characteristic feature of the US political system and depends to a large extent on the influence of local organizational lobby tactics and the personal ambitions of influential politicians (Freedland 1998).

Joshua Cohen and Joel Rogers revisit and radicalize the associationist realm in the US and beyond (Cohen and Rogers 1992; 1995). By strengthening the role of secondary associations, a plethora of civil society organisations that intermediate between the individual and the state – such as FBOs, trade unions, work councils, neighbourhood and community groups, and minority ethnic organisations – can engender, for Cohen and Rogers, a process of democratisation by encouraging active participation of people from the grassroots in politics. Paul Hirst (1994) elaborates and calls for empowerment of poor and excluded people at the grassroots of society for reversal of their deprived situation and maintenance of social cohesion at the local level. Archon Fung and Erik Olin Wright (2003) go further and argue for "empowered participatory governance" where ordinary people make sensible decisions through rational deliberation among participants. Neighbourhood governance councils for public schools and policing in Chicago are important examples (Fung and Wright 2003; Fung 2003). Given the ideological diversity (and complexity) of civil society, the more explicitly Biblical arguments of Skillen at the Center of Public Justice also tally with the associationist conception. Along with his followers he advocates the revitalization of social and economic well-being among the poor through restoration of families, friends, churches and service organizations to: (1) advance personal responsibility and avoid government dependency; (2) promote full religious freedom in public life; (3) the flourishing of coexisting public and private education through genuine educational pluralism; and (4) the achievement of a truly representative electoral system.

Picking up the pieces? Faith-based action on new poverty

The contemporary picture regarding faith-based action on poverty, I argue, reflects the ideological diversity of associational civil society in the United States. This diversity means that it is possible for innovative but conservative church based antipoverty action in the context of the Bush II faith-based agenda for the delivery of social services to run parallel with the tentative emergence of more progressive, multi-agency coalitions contesting urban poverty regimes that strive for social justice in cities. While the former development is more pronounced than the latter, both are important policy and political advances in the faith-based antipoverty arena in the US.

Bush II Faith-Based Agenda

Largely drawing on extensive and ongoing research by Greg Smith (Smith 2003), current policy developments in the US increasingly look to faith communities as potential partners for consultation, local governance and service delivery for tackling poverty in cities. The Republican and fervently religious president George W. Bush makes no apologies for pronouncing an avowedly Christian crusade against the forces of evil that he claims afflict the world. The "gun-ho" aftermath of the September 11 attacks on the World Trade Center and the Pentagon in 2001, and the subsequent military trouncing of Afghanistan and Iraq on dubious neoconservative "axis of evil" grounds, diverts attention from the moral underpinnings of the faith-based agenda for welfare reform on the domestic scene. It would seem that poverty is included in the list of evils requiring the intervention of FBOs to save the American ideal.

The development of the current faith-based agenda needs placing in its proper context. The underclass debate and arguments for wholesale welfare reform during the 1980s was, I argue, legitimized with explicit reference to religious arguments that, in turn, provided the moral framework for the extension of a faith-based agenda under Clinton and subsequently Bush. In the shadow of 1980s New Right theorists like Murray and Mead, the leading contemporary ideologue of the Christian support for faith-based welfare is Marvin Olasky. Three important texts, *The Tragedy of American Compassion* (1992; 1995), *Renewing American Compassion* (1996) and *Compassionate Conservatism* (2000) advance the notion of "compassionate conservatism" that has proved particularly influential on Republican politicians, most notably George W. Bush. Under the Clinton presidency, but with a Congress dominated by Republicans, the "Charitable Choice" legislation was implemented in 1996 (Carlson-Thies 1997) facilitating funding programmes for a variety of FBOs in welfare activities. The main thrust of the policy was to offer State and Federal government funds to FBOs in the form of contracts to deliver welfare services such as food and housing aid, drugs and prisoner rehabilitation services and educational mentoring. Urban redevelopment is another important area. The Antioch Missionary Baptist Church in Chicago, for instance, has rehabilitated many apartments and townhouses in the city with Federal government assistance and is heralded as an important inner city success (Cisneros 1996; Kramnick and Moore 1997).

So, when George W. Bush was elected to the presidency at the end of 2000 the implementation of his faith-based agenda for welfare provision extended an ongoing commitment to involving FBOs in public policy. During his governorship of Texas in the late 1990s, the State had pioneered faith-based welfare as part of a programme of Olasky inspired "compassionate conservatism", which, incidentally, also imposed record levels of the death penalty. After inauguration one of President Bush's first acts was the creation of a new executive agency to promote the faith-based agenda. The agency's first director was John Dilulio, a leading academic in the field and a Democrat. Dilulio advanced a clear vision of the revival of poor and declining neighbourhoods and rural enclaves through the approach (Dilulio 2001). A broad political consensus combined with substantial public confidence in the policy was enjoyed by the Bush administration for a short while. Towards the end of 2001 debates about national identity and the relation between religion and politics was rocked asunder and transformed by the September 11 attacks. Waves of patriotic and, let it be said, unconstitutional Christian religious fervour against the evils of fundamentalist Islam came to dominate political discussions about foreign policy intervention and the "war on terrorism". The domestic faith-based agenda was largely eclipsed by events on the international stage and it was not until January 2002 that funding arrangements for religious organizations became law with the operation of the $30 million Compassion Capital fund.

Evidence from research on FBOs in the US is extensive. I allude to some of the main findings. The edited volume by Dionne and Dilulio (2000) summarises a number of studies that include congregational studies, policy issues and evaluations and provides a useful overall assessment. Sherman (2000) presents an optimistic view on the Charitable Choice programme based on a review of 84 new government/ faith-based partnerships focused on workfare style initiatives for tackling poverty at the local level. Other commentators, such as Cnaan (1999), consider the activities of FBOs as indicative of the hidden safety net in the US welfare system, picking up the pieces where other organizations, agencies and initiatives fail to meet the needs of chronically deprived people. Following a survey of three low income wards in Washington, D.C., De Vita and Palmer (2003) reveal that FBO dealings with government can be complicated and smaller congregations in poverty areas are limited in their ability to take advantage of possible funds. On the basis of their findings De Vita and Palmer call for the earmarking of new money to small congregations in poverty areas, improve the coordination and reduce the duplication of effort among government agencies and create incentive to stimulate volunteering among a wider diversity of individuals and social groups. Similarly, Chaves (1999) claims that large congregations, namely African American, are most likely to apply for government grants and enter into Charitable Choice partnerships, as are Catholic and theologically liberal or moderate Protestant congregations. Theologically conservative and orthodox groups are far less likely to approach government for support.

A recent survey of almost 400 leaders from FBOs in possession of government social service contracts indicates that almost all (92%) are content with their relations with government (Green and Sherman 2002). Over half of these groups were new to contracting-out from government, only entering the fray since the implementation of Charitable Choice in 1996. A staggering 42 per cent of contractors were Evangelical and minority ethnic churches, were more active than white churches in securing contracts. Overall, American research emphasizes the importance of the religious dimension for motivating errant youth and other groups towards the "right path" away from drugs, gangs and crime. Constitutional dilemmas remain, particularly when faith groups are required to do away with "pervasive sectarianism" to maintain eligibility for government money. As Kramnick and Moore (1997) show, the training programme provided by the Joy for Jesus Church in Detroit experienced a drop in its success rate when it dispensed with Bible instruction to secure funding. It would seem that spiritual renewal, however implicit, covert and informal, lies at the heart of the faith-based agenda for tackling poverty and related social problems in the US.

Progressive coalition formation in Los Angeles

Drawing upon recent work on the urbanization of justice movements (Nicholls 2003; Nicholls and Beaumont 2004), I present evidence for the reformulation of religious-based agents in progressive network formation in the US, outside the official faith-based Charitable Choice partnerships and involving diverse contestatory organizations committed to the eradication of poverty and the achievement of social justice in cities. While turning to the case of the contemporary justice movement in Los Angeles, I do not claim that progressive urban networks are a new phenomenon (see Fainstein and Hirst 1995; Mayer 2000; Pickvance 2003), nor do I maintain that such networks involving FBOs are particular to that city (see, for example, Goetz 2002 for progressive church involvement in justice issues in Minneapolis). It is also not the intention to deny the mainstream role of churches in the social sphere in Los Angeles. The importance of corporate patrons, like the Walt Disney Company and Atlantic Richfield that gave $800.000 and $500.000 respectively to a project of the First African Episcopal Church of Los Angeles, cannot be overlooked. The findings of Orr (2000), however, suggest that numerous constraints and obstacles have in many instances prevented both statutory agencies and FBOs from successfully engaging with the Charitable Choice legislation and workfare contracts in the State of California. The Los Angeles case presents a vivid case study that provides insights into similar developments in other urban contexts.

Within recent years Los Angeles has witnessed a number of labour and community struggles contesting the entrepreneurial policies that have come to dominate political and economic life in the city (see Davis 1990; Keil 1998). These struggles have involved many different organizations including to a certain degree churches, for instance the St. Philip's Episcopal Church, forming a broader alliance known as the Progressive LA Network (PLAN) in 1999 (Pastor 2001; Nicholls 2003; Nicholls and Beaumont 2004). PLAN is structured around a series of anchor organizations composed mainly of members of labour unions, community-based organizations and universities. The formation of the network was the result of a conference held in 1998 that brought together a number of institutions including Occidental College, The Nation Institute, Liberty Hill Foundation, LA

Weekly and the Los Angeles County Federation of Labor, all committed to the plight of the urban poor through public policies and progressive, community based mobilization efforts to challenge the persistence of poverty in the inner cities.

The galvanizing of these organizations including the role of faith-based actors should be placed in a historical perspective on progressive politics in Los Angeles. Mike Davis in *City of Quartz* provides a detailed account (Davis 1990: 323-72). He identifies three essential themes in the role of religion, namely the Catholic Church, and politics in LA: first, since the mid 1980s the aggressive leadership of Archbishop Mahony at the Cathedral of St. Vibiana, located on "Skid Row", has oscillated between openness to socially progressive forces – through early sympathy with the labour movement and the implementation of the Latino Aid Plan (1987) – to a reversal of position vis-à-vis organized labour and a crackdown on "safe sex"; second, the Catholic power structure and the seamless interweaving of spiritual authority and the economic influence of significant laymen that comprise the "invisible government" of the Catholic hierarchy, real estate developers and investment bankers; and third, the tension between the conservative restorationists from the Catholic hierarchy, on the one hand, and the mounting importance of Father Luis Olivares and his fellow radical Claretian and Jesuit priests representing Downtown LA's version of liberation theology and the "preferential option for the poor" involving direct action in favour of the vulnerable and marginalized. The conflict between the gradualist and legalistic Latino Aid Plan and the confrontational and radical stance of Olivares and his followers at the La Reina de Los Angeles church (or La Placita as it was popularly known) provides the context for subsequent progressive movement development in the 1990s and beyond.

The long tradition of Irish-American archbishop appointments in LA was a growing issue of concern among a large and ever-expanding (and for a large part undocumented and deprived) Latino population. Mahony attempted to deal with Latino grievances with the imposition of the Latino Aid Plan that aimed to combine evangelization with social activism. The foundations were laid in the previous years with experiments within Eastside parishes via the introduction of (1) the Charismatic Renewal in the

1970s to placate the needs of the Latino faithful and to stave off drift to new Pentecostal churches, and (2) the acceptance of community organizing and self-help initiatives within parishes that built upon Alinsky-ite experiences of the 1950s and 60s (such as the Community Services Organization), leading to the creation of the United Neighbourhood Organization (UNO) in late 1970s. The UNO combined, paradoxically, radical grassroots mobilization with the maintenance of certain conservative principles derived from traditional Catholic family values and adherence to hierarchical organizational forms. It successfully mobilized around local transport issues, as well as concerns over housing rehabilitation, new supermarkets and Eastside school improvements. With these experiences in mind and the institutionalisation of local assemblies in these parishes, Mahony's Latino Aid Plan aimed to bring into the mainstream initiatives to deal with gang violence, to address housing problems of undocumented migrants, to provide day care centres for children and to bring more Latino youth ministers to Eastside parishes, as well as a to initiate a broad evangelization strategy among all Latino households. The Plan gave the archdiocese the appearance of adopting a preferential option for the Hispanic urban poor.

It was soon apparent for Father Luis Olivares and his liberationist followers at La Placita that the Plan was little more than a smoke-screen for Catholic hierarchy "business as usual", with little or no real decentralisation of power to base communities. Since 1981 Olivares, with experience with Alinsky-ite UNO actions, had advanced liberationist principles at La Placita and provided a welcome community resource for refugee Central Americans. The congregation was comprised almost entirely of poor and desperately deprived people. In a sense radicalising Alinsky, Olivares of his own volition made the church a safe haven for the poor, opening the doors to undocumented and illegal migrants, political refugees, homeless people and street vendors and other oppressed people in society. Deriving inspiration from revolutionary fervour in Central America, as well as liberationist struggles as mythologized by Archbishop Romero in El Salvador, Olivares provided an important link between Catholic radicalism in Latin America and Latinos in LA. Later declaring the church an official sanctuary (joined soon after by Mission Delores, led by Father Gregory Boyle in

Boyle Heights), La Placita extended open acts of defiance against US foreign policy in Central America and increasingly hostile and punitive immigration laws after 1987. Despite treading a dangerous line between secular legality and illegality, undeniable was the consistency of Olivares and his followers in maintaining their preference for the poor and dispossessed and offering an organizational space for radical community resistance and solidarity.

Much to the dismay of his supporters Olivares left La Placita in the early part of 1990, ostensibly the result of official archdiocesan rotation. Despite the legacy, radical para-church action on poverty in LA has not matched the heady days of Olivares and his fellow liberationists in the 1980s. While the UNO continued its activities for a while, far less parishes were involved and a degree of grassroots mobilization was muted by bureaucratic incorporation. Spin-off organizations, like the South Central Organizing Committee (SCOC) in South Central Los Angeles, that had engaged in a successful minimum wage campaign in 1987, continued in a similar vein but increasingly focused on moral and law enforcement issues at the expense of justice demands for minimum wages, insurance, healthcare and other welfare services. Their impact on antipoverty and justice efforts, particularly among the more deprived, new immigrant communities was diminished. It would seem that the conservative Catholic hierarchy held sway in the end.

With the declining radicalism of Catholic liberationists and the increasing entrepreneurial direction of LA's politics, the inequalities between rich and poor, exacerbated by racial and ethnic discrimination, played a key role in sparking the uprisings that shook the city in April 1992, bringing into sharp relief the deteriorating conditions of the poor in the inner cities. Mayor Bradley initiated Rebuild LA to try and turn around the fortunes of the city, including the improvement of the worst neighbourhoods via "trickle down" through private sector led investment strategies. Progressive grassroots activities and organizations throughout the 1990s increasingly came together to contest LA's brand of entrepreneurialism, forging new alliances between progressive leaders from Black, Asian, Hispanic, Jewish communities to form the MultiCultural Collaborative and address racial tensions and difficulties. Churches and other FBOs remain important institutional support mechanisms as part of a wider community infrastructure for people from these ethnic communities, including new arrivals from Central America (Hamilton and Chinchilla 2001). Campaigning for the equal rights of immigrants remains an important element of PLAN's activities.

When these organizations began to establish closer links with certain city politicians and elements of the labour movement (e.g. the Service Employees International Union and the Hotel Employees and Restaurant Employees Union), a more concerted, politically viable and "bottom-up" alternative to Rebuild LA was born. Sherman and Voss (2000) call this new model "social movement unionism", contrasting it with the model of "service unionism" that characterized the corporatist era. Other commentators refer to "community unionism" to capture new multi-agency responses (Waterman and Wills eds. 2001). While the workplace has become increasingly fragmented, households and their immediate socio-institutional environment anchored in community and religious organizations have achieved a certain level of stability that makes them important arenas to organize people, particularly in non-Anglo, immigrant-rich communities. FBOs and community groups have become opporture gateways into the daily lives of potential members, in ways tamer than the radical liberationist activism of the 1980s but no less important in the current mobilization form. In the context of the Federal government's workfare programmes, participant organizations have mobilized to address inner-city deprivation in riot-torn neighbourhoods, demanding decent wages through welfare-to-work contracts, food security, community economic development initiatives in place of liquor stores and childcare available on demand.

In the context of the inauguration of James K. Hahn as Mayor in June 2001, recent PLAN achievements include: a contract to raise the wages and benefits of janitors in the city following a three-week Services Employment International Union strike (2000); progress towards a $100,000 million Housing Trust Fund to support housing development for low income groups by a coalition of housing advocates, religious leaders, unions and community organizations (2001); and the creation of the Garment Worker Center to bring garment workers together to improve working conditions and to help workers realise their rights (2001) (see www.progressivela.org/

resources/victories_00.pdf). PLAN remains an important alliance of progressive organizations, including enlightened clergy and their institutional bases, for tackling poverty and seeking social justice in Los Angeles.

Progressive antipoverty and social justice coalitions?

This chapter shows that FBOs in the United States are reaching out into the secular world and "de-privatising" (Haynes 1998) in new and sometimes contrasting ways. These organizations are exploring possibilities for mainstream social service provision as well as participating in progressive alliances to contest entrepreneurial politics and for the achievement of social justice in cities. The observed double dynamic simultaneously reflects new urban political opportunities wrought by deepening processes of ("roll-out") neoliberalisation and the historical specificities of associationist civil society in the US. The two sides of the faith-based action on poverty "coin" reflect the enduring ideological variety of associational life in the country.

It would, however, be misleading to overplay the simple distinction between the two sides of the equation. As Greg Smith (2003) reminds us, religion thrives in the US in the context of a strict constitutional demarcation between Church and State, rigorously upheld by many militant anti-Catholic Protestant leaders since the 1950s, where Congress is forbidden from establishing a State religion and ostensibly protects and upholds the right of freedom of religious expression and toleration of all forms of faith. The advance of the faith-based agenda on the domestic social welfare scene wreaks havoc among secular groups and devout believers over the increasingly indeterminate line between religion and the delivery of public services. Whether the issue concerns social service contracts, local antipoverty efforts or parochial schooling, the degree of indoctrination and proselytising continues to plague the minds of many liberal observers. As Kramnick and Moore (1997) note, the problem of conversion would seem contradictory among liberals who seldom question the previous role of Christianity in bolstering a self-help ethic among slaves in the South, while denouncing religious implications of workfare initiatives for the contemporary urban poor. Those in favour of an explicit religious dimension tend to come from the more conservative strands within Christianity that form the so-called Christian Coalition. The growing corpus of born-again, conservative Christian evangelicals that comprise the New Christian Right, exerts an enormous influence on politics particularly around election time (Haynes 1998). While the caricatured polarisation between conservative, Republican voting, fundamentalist churches and liberal, internationalist Democrat voting, progressive churches holds some connection with reality, one should remember the presence of dissenting voices and elements in all faiths. The peculiar blend of radical grassroots activism and organizational hierarchy in the evolution of social action in LA's Catholic community is a potent reminder of the importance of dissension in addressing poverty in US cities. Whether we like it or not, religion continues to play an important role in social welfare in general and antipoverty efforts in particular.

The chapter concludes with some thoughts for further investigation. First, the role of FBOs in tackling poverty and achieving social justice in the US might help illuminate current developments in the social welfare realm in European countries like The Netherlands that profess a similar constitutional separation between Church and State. Removing the official shroud of constitutional separation in the US unveils complex and unofficial relations at the interface between religion and the state in the realm of social welfare. Similar research in The Netherlands suggests that many so-called civil associations, including faith-based actors, are at the sharp end in dealing with the most vulnerable, marginalized and deprived people in urban society. These people are often, but not exclusively, immigrants, asylum-seekers and undocumented and illegal people, moving through intricate transnational networks in an increasingly globalized world. Further research in The Netherlands should prioritize the extent of "externalization" and "de-privatization" of FBOs in the antipoverty and social justice arena. Second, internationally comparative work on the changing faith-based relations with secular institutions like government, trade unions and community associations, in the field of antipoverty action and social justice politics, would help deepen our understanding of possibilities and constraints for radicalization of existing multi-agency approaches in cities in the US, The Netherlands and beyond. Urban progressives inside and outside the academy, irrespective of context and united in their efforts to eradicate poverty and bring about a more just society, have a key role to play in such a process.

Acknowledgements

My thanks to the editors as well as Bob Goudzwaard, Ronald van Kempen and Walter Nicholls who provided very useful comments on an earlier draft of this chapter. The final responsibility, of course, remains my own.

Annotations

1 The term "faith-based organization" – FBO for short – is used throughout the chapter and relates to all para-religious action on poverty including those predating the current legislative context.
2 Neoliberalisation across Europe rarely matches the wholesale state withdrawal as experienced in the US. But the tendency remains. The "Wet Werk en Bijstand" (law on work and assistance) that was enacted 1 January 2004 under the Balkende 2. Christian Democratic coalition in The Netherlands aims to decentralize responsibility for welfare provision to municipalities, reduce social expenditure in absolute terms and make eligibility criteria for benefits stricter including a more concerted enforcement of a work requirement.

References

Alinsky, S. D. (1969) *Reveille for Radicals*, New York: Basic Books.
- (1971) *Rules for Radicals: a practical primer for realistic radicals*, New York: Basic Books.
Amin, A. (ed.) (1994) *Post-Fordism: a reader*, Oxford: Blackwell.
Beaumont, J. (2004) *Governance and Democracy: popular involvement against poverty*, Aldershot: Ashgate, forthcoming.
Bell, D. (1973) *The Coming of Postindustrial Society: a venture in social forecasting*, New York: Basic Books.

Brenner, N. and N. Theodore (2002) "Cities and the geographies of 'actually existing neoliberalism'", *Antipode*, 34(3): 349-79.

Carlson-Thies, S. W. (1997) *A Guide to Charitable Choice: the rules of section 104 of the 1996 Federal Welfare Law governing state cooperation with faith-based social service providers,* Washington DC: Center for Public Justice and Christian Legal Society.

Carlson-Thies, S. W. and J. W. Skillen (eds.) (1996) *Welfare in America: Christian perspectives on a policy in crisis*, Grand Rapids, Michigan: Wm. B. Eerdmans Publishing Co.

Carnes, T. and Y. Fenggang (eds.) (2004) *Asian American Religions: the making and unmaking of borders and boundaries*, New York: New York University Press.

Caro, R. A. (1975) *The Power Broker: Robert Moses and the fall of New York*, New York: Vintage Books.

Castells, M. (1983) *The City and the Grassroots: a cross-cultural theory of urban social movements*, London: Edward Arnold.

CPJ (1994) *A New Vision for Welfare Reform*, from the project "Welfare Responsibility: an inquiry into the roots of America's welfare policy crisis", Washington D.C: The Center for Public Justice.

Chaves, M. (1999) "Religious congregations and welfare reform: who will take advantage of 'charitable choice'?", *American Sociological Review*, 64(6): 836-46.

Cisneros, N. (1996) "Higher ground: faith communities and community building". See www.huduser.org/Periodicals/CITYSCPE/SPISSUE/ch5.pdf (accessed 13 January 2004).

Clarke, K. B. and J. Hopkins (1969) *A Relevant War Against Poverty: a study of community action programs and observable social change*, New York: Harper Torchbooks.

Cnaan, R. (1999) "Our hidden safety net: social and community work by urban American religious congregations", *Journal of Brookings Institution*, 17(2).

Cohen, J. and J. Rogers (1992) "Secondary associations and democratic governance", *Politics and Society*, 20(4): 393-472.

- (1995) "Secondary associations and democratic governance". In Wright, E. O. (ed.) *Associations and Democracy*, the real utopias project volume 1, London: Verso, pp. 7-98.

Connolly, M. P. (1976) *A Historical Study of Change in Saul D. Alinsky's Community Organization: practice and theory, 1939-1972*, PhD dissertation, Minneapolis: University of Minnesota.

Dahl, R. (1961) *Who Governs? democracy and power in an American city*, New Haven: Yale University Press.

- (1966) *A Preface to Democratic Theory*, New Haven CT: Yale University Press.
Davis, M. (1990) *City of Quartz: excavating the future in Los Angeles*, New York: Vintage Books.
De Vita, C. J. and P. Palmer (2003) "Church-state partnerships: some reflections from Washington, D.C.", Charting Civil Society No. 14, September, Washington, D.C: The Urban Institute. See www.urban.org/UploadedPDF/310865_cnp_14.pdf (accessed 13 January 2004).
Dilulio J. (2001) *Rallying the Armies of Compassion*. See www.whitehouse.gov/news/reports/faithbased.html, now attributed to George W. Bush (accessed 20 October 2003).
Dionne E. J. and J. J. Dilulio Jr. (eds.) (2000) *What's God got to do with the American experiment? essays on religion and politics*, Washington: The Brookings Institution.
Esping-Andersen, G. (1990) *The Three Worlds of Welfare Capitalism*, Cambridge: Polity Press.
- (ed.) (1996) *Welfare States in Transition: national adaptation in global economies*, London: Sage.
Fainstein, S. and C. Hirst (1995) "Urban social movements". In Judge, D., Stoker, G. and H. Wolman (eds.) *Theories of Urban Politics*, London: Sage.
Freedland, J. (1998) *Bring Home the Revolution: the case for a British republic*, London: Fourth Estate.
Fung, A. (2003) "Deliberative democracy, Chicago-style: grass-roots governance in policing and public education". In Wright, E. O. (ed.) *Deepening Democracy: institutional innovations in empowered participatory governance*, the real utopias project volume 4, London: Verso, pp. 111-43.
Fung, A. and E. O. Wright (2003) "Thinking about empowered participatory governance". In Wright, E. O. (ed.) *Deepening Democracy: institutional innovations in empowered participatory governance*, the real utopias project volume 4, London: Verso, pp. 3-42.
Galbraith, J. K. (1977) *The Affluent Society*, 3rd revised edition, London: Andre Deutsch.
Goetz, E. G. (2002) *Hollman v. Cisneros: deconcentrating poverty in Minneapolis*, Report No. 2: Planning for North Side Redevelopment, Minneapolis: Center for Urban and Regional Affairs, University of Minnesota. See www.cura.umn.edu/publications/Hollman/Hollman-2.pdf (accessed 13 January 2004).
Goudzwaard, B. (1994) "Who cares? poverty and the dynamics of responsibility: an outsider's contribution to the American debate on

poverty and welfare", paper presented at the Public Justice & Welfare Reform national conference, May 19-20, Washington D.C: The Center for Public Justice.

Green, J. C. and A. L. Sherman (2002) *Fruitful Collaborations: a survey of government funded faith-based programs in 15 states*, Hudson Institute, Inc.

Hamilton, N. and N. Chinchilla (2001) *Seeking Community in a Global City: Guatemalans and Salvadorans in Los Angeles*, Philadelphia: Temple University Press.

Handler, J. F. and Hasenfeld, Y. (1991) *The Moral Construction of Poverty: welfare reform in America*, Newbury Park: Sage.

Harrington, M. (1962) *The Other America*, New York: The Macmillan Company.

Haynes, J. (1998) *Religion in Global Politics*, London and New York: Longman.

Higgins, J. (1978) *The Poverty Business: Britain and America*, Oxford: Basil Blackwell.

Hilfiker, D. (2002) *Urban Injustice: how ghettos happen*, New York: Seven Stories Press.

Hill, D. (1992) "The American philosophy of welfare: citizenship and the politics of conduct", *Social Policy & Administration*, 26(2): 117-28.

Hirst, P. (1994) *Associative Democracy*, Cambridge: Polity Press.

Hutton, W. (2002) *The World We're In*, London: Little, Brown.

Janoski, T. and A. M. Hicks (1994) *The Comparative Political Economy of the Welfare State*, Cambridge: Cambridge University Press.

Jencks, C. and P. E. Peterson (eds.) (1991) *The Urban Underclass*, Washington D.C: The Brookings Institute.

Katz, M. B. (1986) *In the Shadow of the Poorhouse: a social history of welfare in America*, New York: Basic Books.

- (1989) *The Undeserving Poor: from the war on poverty to the war on welfare*, New York: Pantheon.

- (ed.) (1993) *The "Underclass" Debate: views from history*, Princeton: Princeton University Press.

Keil, R. (1998) *Los Angeles: globalization, urbanization, and social struggles*, Chichester, U.K: John Wiley & Sons Ltd.

King, D. (1995) *Actively Seeking Work? the politics of unemployment and welfare policy in the United States and Great Britain*, Chicago: University of Chicago Press.

Kramnick, I. and R. L. Moore (1997) "Can the churches save the cities? faith-based services and the constitution", *American Prospect*, Issue 35, Nov – Dec 1997.

Lancourt, J. E. (1979) *Confront or Concede: the Alinsky citizen-action organizations*, Lexington, MA: Lexington Books.

Leiby, J. (1978) *A History of Social Welfare and Social Work in the United States*, New York: Columbia University Press.

Lewis, O. (1961) *The Children of Sanchez: autobiography of a Mexican family*, New York: Random House.

- (1966) *La Vida: a Puerto Rican family in the culture of poverty*, London: Secker and Warburg.

- (1969) "The possessions of the poor", *Scientific American*, 221: 144-24.

Lister, R. (1996) "Introduction: in search of the 'underclass'". In *Charles Murray and the Underclass: the developing debate*, London: IEA Health and Welfare Unit in association with The Sunday Times.

Marcuse, P. (1997) "The enclave, the citadel, and the ghetto: what has changed in the post-Fordist U.S. city", *Urban Affairs Review*, 33(2): 228-64.

Marcuse, P. and R. van Kempen (eds.) (2002) *Of States and Cities: the partitioning of urban space*, Oxford: Oxford University Press.

Marmor, T. R., Mashaw, J. L. and P. L. Harvey (1990) *America's Misunderstood Welfare State: persistent myths, enduring realities*, New York: Basic Books.

Massey, D. S. and N. A. Denton (1993) *American Apartheid: segregation and the making of the underclass*, Cambridge, MA: Harvard University Press.

Mayer, M. (2000) "Social movements in European cities: transitions from the 1970s to the 1990s". In A. Bagnasco and P. Le Galès (eds.) *Cities in Contemporary Europe*, Cambridge: Cambridge University Press.

Murray, C. (1984) *Losing Ground: American social policy, 1950 – 1980*, New York: Basic Books.

Musterd, S. and W. Ostendorf (eds.) (1998) *Urban Segregation and the Welfare State: inequality and exclusion in western cities*, London: Routledge.

Myles, J. (1996) "When markets fail: social welfare in Canada and the United States". In Esping-Andersen, G. (ed.) *Welfare States in Transition: national adaptation in global economies*, London: Sage.

Nicholls, D. (1974) *Three Varieties of Pluralism*, London: The Macmillan Press Ltd.

- (1994) *The Pluralist State: the political ideas of J. N. Figgis and his contemporaries*, second edition, London: Macmillan in association with St. Anthony's College Oxford.

Nicholls, W. (2003) "Forging a 'new' organizational infrastructure for Los Angeles' progressive community," *International Journal of Urban and Regional Research*, 27(4): 881-96.

Nicholls, W. J. and J. R. Beaumont (2004) "The urbanization of justice movements? possibilities and constraints for the city as a space of contentious struggle", forthcoming special issue *Space & Polity*, 8(2).

Olasky, M. (1992) *The Tragedy of American Compassion*, Washington: Regnery Gateway (reprint edition 1995).

- (1996) *Renewing American Compassion*, New York: Free Press.

- (2000) *Compassionate Conservatism: what it is, what it does, and how it can transform America*, New York: Free Press.

Orr, J. (2000) *Faith Based Organisations and Welfare Reform: California religious community capacity study: qualitative findings and conclusions*, Los Angeles: Centre for Religion and Civic Culture, University of Southern California.

Parsons, T. (1969) *Politics and Social Structure*, New York: Free Press.

Pastor, M. (2001) "Common ground at ground zero? the new economy and the new organizing in Los Angeles," *Antipode*, 33(2): 260-89.

Peck, J. (2001) *Workfare States*, New York: Guilford Press.

Peck, J. and A. Tickell (2002) "Neoliberalizing space", *Antipode*, 34(3): 380-404.

Peterson, P. E. (1991) "The urban underclass and the poverty paradox". In Jencks, C. and P. E. Peterson (eds.) *The Urban Underclass*, Washington DC: The Brookings Institute.

Pickvance, C. (2003) "From urban social movements to urban movements: a review and introduction to a symposium on urban movements", *International Journal of Urban and Regional Research*, 27(1): 102-9.

Polsby, N. (1980) *Community Power and Political Theory*, second edition, New Haven: Yale University Press.

Putnam, R. D. (2000) *Bowling Alone: the collapse and revival of American community*, New York: Simon & Schuster, Inc.

Rex, J. (1988) *The Ghetto and the Underclass: essays on race and social policy*, Aldershot: Avebury.

Sassen, S. (1991) *The Global City: New York, London and Tokyo*, Princeton: Princeton University Press (second edition 2001).

Sawhill, I.V. (1988) "Poverty in the US: why is it so persistent?", *Journal of Economic Literature*, 26(3): 1073-1119.

Sherman, A. (2000) "A survey of church-government anti-poverty partnerships", *American Enterprise Online*. See www.taemag.com/issues/articleid.17219/article_detail.asp (accessed 20 October 2003).

Sherman, R. and K. Voss (2000) "Organize or die: labor's new tactics". In Milkman, R. (ed.) *Organizing Immigrants: the challenge for unions in contemporary California*, Ithaca, NY: Cornell University Press.

Skillen, J. W. (1990) *The Scattered Voice: Christians at odds in the public square*, Grand Rapids, Michigan: Zondervan Books.

- (1994) *Recharging the American Experiment: principled pluralism for genuine civic community*, Grand Rapids, Michigan: Baker Books.

Skillen, J. W. and R. M. McCarthy (eds.) (1991) *Political Order and the Plural Structure of Society*, Atlanta: Scholar's Press.

Smith, G. (2003) "Faith in the voluntary sector: a common or distinctive experience of religious organisations?", Working Papers in Applied Social Research, Department of Sociology, Manchester: University of Manchester.

Storper, M. and R. A. Walker (1989) *The Capitalist Imperative*, Oxford: Blackwell.

Sugrue, T. J. (1996) *The Origins of the Urban Crisis: race and inequality in postwar Detroit*, Princeton, NJ: Princeton University Press.

Tillman, J. A. and M. N. Tillman (1969) *Why America Needs Racism and Poverty: an examination of the exclusivity compulsion in American race and poverty relations*, Four Winds.

Tocqueville, A. de (1945) *Democracy in America*, 2 vols., New York: Vintage.

Truman, D. B. (1951) *The Governmental Process*, New York: Alfred Knopf.

Wacquant, L.J.D. (1993) "Urban outcasts: stigma and division in the black American ghetto and the French urban periphery", *International Journal of Urban and Regional Research*, 17: 366-83.

- (1996) "The rise of advanced marginality: notes on its nature and implications", *Acta Sociologica*, 39: 121-39.

Walker, R. (1991) *Thinking About Workfare: evidence from the USA*, London: HMSO.

Waterman, P. and J. Wills (eds.) (2001) *Place, Space and the New Labour Internationalisms*, Oxford: Blackwell.

Wilson, W. J. (1990) *The Truly Disadvantaged: the inner city, the underclass, and public policy*, Chicago: University of Chicago Press.

- (1996) *When Work Disappears*, Boston: Harvard University Press.

V. Epilogue

Herman Noordegraaf and Rainer Volz

Concluding remarks

The following remarks are an attempt at a synthesis of the insights gained from the articles and to give some preliminary indications that we feel to be relevant.

Religion and welfare states
The role of religion and churches regarding the implementation of social security and welfare has only been a small part of the comparative research on the welfare state and of the input from churches in post-communist societies. Esping Andersen's typology, the result of pioneering work, only examines the influence of religion and churches in a selective way (Esping Andersen 1990, 1999).[1] However, the way economy, politics and culture are related, especially the interconnectedness between economic-technological development and the normative discourses has been of influence on how social and welfare politics have taken shape: how social questions were raised, how the most important problem was formulated, have had a great influence on the national development of welfare and social security (Kaufmann 2003, pp. 32/33).

Of course, power relationships between social classes with their different interests play a big role, but, as Max Weber stated, worldviews have often determined the ways in which the dynamics of interests go forward (Weber 1963, p. 252). For instance, to provide some very rough guidelines and hypotheses, the Lutheran folk church in Germany and Nordic countries with the doctrine of the "two kingdoms" ascribes a particular role to the state in the organization of social welfare. This made it easier in modern industrial capitalist societies to give central responsibility for social matters to the state.[2] In Southern Europe and partly also in Germany, Belgium and the Netherlands, Catholic social teaching has been influential with its so-called concept of subsidiarity (which also plays a role as one of the principles of the European Union) and the emphasis which is laid on the role of the family. The influence of Protestant social thought is less obvious than that of Roman-Catholic thought, because it was more fragmented and to some extent "negative", that is to say that reformed and denominational Protestantism denied the adequacy or even legitimacy of state intervention in social problems. The Anglican Church has a tradition as a provider of social welfare and of participating in the public debate. This contributed to the consensus reached on the welfare state, as was formulated by archbishop William Temple in his *Christianity and Social Order*, which he summed up in the sentence: "The aim of a Christian social order is the fullest possible development of individual personality in the widest and deepest possible fellowship." (Temple 1976, p. 97). The Orthodox viewpoint is not easy to formulate, because these churches were in "captivity" during the Ottoman period and later on during the communist regime. We can see a sometimes impressive whole of diaconal work, but participation in the public debate has been somewhat lacking. That is also applicable to the Greek Church, which in the past did not take any significant part in public socio-political debates, but is an important provider of services, especially in the field of care (Belopopsky 2003; Diakonivetenskapliga Institutet 2003, p. 81). In general, it can be stated that the churches in Central and Eastern Europe have to take up their role in society again after the communist period in which it was forbidden to develop activities in the diaconal field or at least only allowed within narrow limits. They have to revitalize their traditions but in a new situation (see contribution Pavlovic).

The need for new guiding views

What we need, is the formulation of a fundamental guiding church view on the changes which are taking place now and which we can find in all the contributions: the influence of globalization and technological developments, privatization, the introduction of market principles in the care sector, the rising cleft between rich and poor and the way people and even entire regions that are not of "economic use" are made superfluous, as paid labour (because they are unskilled or low skilled) and as consumers (because they do not have spending power), demographic developments (the growing amount of elder people), cultural changes as individualization, the coming of migrants and refugees. A lot of contributions have been made in statements, declarations, reports and other church publications. Examples of these are given in the articles. But we can also find implicit views in the concrete work carried out with regard to poverty. In all countries, we can observe that churches are involved in activities connected with poverty. And that is seen as an integral part of their being churches (compare Pavlovic's remark regarding the churches in Eastern Europe). It means that churches are going through a learning process, adjusting their traditional background to the new situation, they are learning how to become churches in society as seen from the viewpoint of the poor. The Church of Finland, for instance, published its message *Towards the Common Good* in 1999. This implied a changing of the old role to a new, more critical one: not only to be a loyal partner of the state, but also to be much more conscious of their own essence (see article Malkavaara). The Church of Denmark has recognized the importance of diaconia besides liturgy, education and mission (see article Iversen). Churches' involvement in the struggle against poverty leads to reflection on how to be a church. This is of ecclesiological relevance. The ecumenical dialogue about these issues strengthens this learning process.

Types and aims of church activities

We get more understanding of what this fundamental view can be, if we look at the types and aims of church activities. In what follows, we use a schematic approach to make things clear. We can distinguish between the following church responses to poverty and unemployment: The relief type, the reformist type and the transformation type.[3]

The Relief Type aims at direct help for the casualties of poverty and social exclusion and at the relief of misery inflicted on them by poverty and social exclusion. There is little analysis of the problems, maybe a short description of the situation and no criticism of government, business or other powerful policy makers. The approach is one of charity with the traditional work ethic as a background. Church action consists of individual care and help.

The Reformist Type aims at reintegration of unemployed people in the employment system and at a reform of the existing socio-economic system and policies. There is a start towards more structural analysis, an extended description of the situation and its consequences and a criticism of policy makers. The approach is led by concepts of justice and solidarity, there is a reflection on the work ethic (attention is also paid to the value of non-paid labour and criticism of the over-valuing of paid labour being necessary for personal identity). There is a plea for reform in existing socio-economic policies or criticism of mainstream politics that adjust the existing system in a way that strikes at the poor. Poor people are assisted in the struggle to improve their position.

The Transformative Type aims at a structural and radical transformation of the present socio-economic and cultural system towards a just, participatory and sustainable society. There is an extensive analysis of structural and cultural backgrounds, discerning the long-term and complex character of poverty and social exclusion and criticizing the social and economic order. There is a plea for justice, participation and sustainability and structural changes in that direction. The church should plead for that and develop alternative activities as structural and radical changes.

It is our impression that the church agents and organizations which are described in the articles have left the relief type well behind them, which of course does not mean that this is the case in the whole church. We see an acknowledgment of analyses of structural and cultural backgrounds, which implies that poverty is recognized not as a personal failing, but as a situation that has to do with supra-personal developments. We also find recognition that churches should participate in the public debate and have an advocacy role on behalf of the poor. Moreover, churches should not act for the poor, that is to say, not primarily, but work with the poor and take the poor themselves as their starting point.

The choice between a reformist or transformative approach has much to do with the context. For instance: if you are pleading for a welfare state in a society which does not have one, then you can speak about a transformative approach. That is the case in Eastern Europe and in the United

States.[4] If you want to take part in the debate about the restructuring of the existing welfare state in northern and western Europe to be an extensive welfare state on the principle that everyone should contribute from his or her earnings, then you are more of the reformist type.

It is important to realize that with respect to the transformative type, our typology is concerned with a specific direction that is determined by the ecumenical perspective of a just, participatory and sustainable society.

It is our impression, from the church activities which are described, that the churches are pleading for a strong(er) welfare state that guarantees social security and access to essential provisions in the field of care, welfare, housing, education etc. Special attention is paid to the position of the poor in the sense that their position should not be worsened, rather just the opposite: it should be improved. The context in which churches find themselves in Western and Northern Europe make this position somewhat defensive, but there are good reasons for this: the welfare state was and is very important for social security. There should be debates about paternalism and bureaucracy of welfare provisions and the extending of claims, but the hard core of the welfare state – social security and access – should be upheld. We should combine this position with a reflection on further-reaching questions, for instance about the relationship between economic growth and environmental problems, the sharing of paid and unpaid labour especially between men and women, a critical look at the relationship between income, time and paid labour[5], the orientation in the middle classes and rich parts of society on growing material welfare. This more "holistic" approach seems to have fallen into the background in society and also in debates in the churches.

Theological points of view
Regarding the theological method of reflection on the developments, we can see that no one has the pretension to formulate a blueprint for solutions. We see a mix of theological criteria, analyses, narratives by particularly poor people and, based on all this, recommendations. A fundamental consensus has grown on the criterion "option for the poor": Every policy and every decision has to be judged on the question of what they

have as consequences for the poor. There should be guarantees that everyone has access to the requirements for life. That means that everyone can fulfil his/her material needs (food, clothing etc.), can participate in society (integration instead of exclusion) and is treated with respect. More and more, attention is paid to the growing gap between poor and rich and the point of wealthiness. This last point has explicitly been made a theme in the campaigns against poverty in Austria and the Netherlands (see the articles of Schenk and Noordegraaf). We think that this point should be worked on further: how is the relationship between growing "private wealth" and "public poverty", what are the consequences of a growing gap between rich and poor for the quality of a society, what is a just distribution of income and property?[6]

We think that the concept of "oikos", as developed by the American theologian Douglas Meeks is of relevance here. The words economy, ecology and oekoumene (= the whole inhabited world) have the same Greek words as origins: oikos (house) and nomos (rules, law): the rules for the house, we find in the Torah and the Gospel (Meeks 1989). The rules of the house are connected with the story of the redemption of God, and with His/Her promises and commandments. It is the opposite of the "oikos douleias" (this means: house of slavery; the Greek word for slave is "oiketes") (cf. Exodus 20:2; Deuteronomy 5: 6, 7-21). The rules of the house have to do with liberating and sustainability: the rules of the Torah, which are based on God's promises of liberation and justice, intend to protect the poor and to give them a place of full value in society; the sabbath and the commandments for giving rest to the land (sabbatical year, compare Leviticus 25: 4) to put limits on exploitation, also of the land. Limits are also put on great discrepancies in wealth through the sabbath years and the Jubilee Year. Again, this gives no blueprint for an economy of justice and sustainability, but, we repeat, it gives a fundamental perspective that is of relevance for the direction we have to work towards.

Activities

If we look at the activities of churches, a certain pattern can be discerned. This does not mean that every church is doing all these activities. That depends on views on their task in society, the resources which churches have and the position of churches in society. For instance, it makes a big difference if the church is a folk church or a minority church. An important criterion for all work is, we repeat, recognition of the subject of being poor. The implication of this view is that churches should work with the poor, that they should learn from them and that they should try to get to know their life-world as well as possible. Making room for the life stories of poor people and really listening to them is very important. This point must be kept in mind when we sum up the activities in a rather schematic way.

- Giving direct aid to people, material and immaterial, and be involved in care activities and institutions.
- Supporting the networks and organizations of the poor.
- Empowerment of individuals and at the community level.
- Raising awareness in the churches and in society at large. Many churches are middle class churches. It is very important in societies in which the poor are minorities, as is the case in Western societies, that other groups in society are prepared to support measures on behalf of the poor. In this way, the churches can make use of the fact that they have a middle class background!
- Advocacy, that is to say working to promote the interests of the poor. That can be on an individual level (for instance, assisting a person to get his rights), but also on a more collective level (pleading for measures for low paid people).
- Participating in the public debate, for instance by publishing reports, messages, national campaigns etc. In most articles from the different countries, we can find examples of these activities. Some have been realized by the way of consultations, hearings and discussions, which already are of value, because of the questions which are put in the debate. See for instance the reports of the churches in Great Britain, the *Gemeinsames Wort* (Joint Memorandum) of the Protestant Church of Germany (EKD) and the Roman Catholic Bishops (DBK) in Germany and the *Sozialwort* of the Council of Churches in Austria.

- We underline that for church activities to have influence in politics and society, it is important to create a profile for a movement. To realize that, it is necessary to have an organization on a national level that connects the different groups on a local and regional level. It is also encouraging for these, often small, groups to know that they are part of a larger network which has a face in society. In Finland, Great Britain, the Netherlands, Belgium and Austria, we can find examples of these networks connecting the different groups.
- It is very important that the different levels of work (local, regional, national, European) and the different types of activities are connected with each other. For instance, the strength of input of churches can be found, among other things, in the bringing of poor people's concrete experiences (their stories) into the public eye and reflecting on what these tell us about the developments in society and politics.[7] This is also necessary to prevent churches helping people without working on measures that can solve problems on a more structural level. For instance, churches can give financial assistance, and make it clear to politics and society, that they have helped, but that they have the opinion that this should not have been necessary. This formula *helping under protest* is explicitly used in the contributions about Austria and the Netherlands. We find a similar discussion about the food banks in Finland. In a different context, we find this point in the United States: churches are engaged in activities regarding poverty and are encouraged by the government to do this, but this happens without the background of a well developed welfare state (see article Justin Beaumont).

So, the formula "Helping under protest" means: seen from a Christian perspective, you should help people when they are in need. However, you should combine this with working towards political and structural changes. Churches and diaconal institutions should make it clear to politicians and society as a whole that they have helped people, but that we need political measures and social changes that make this type of help superfluous or, at least, less necessary.

European Union

It seems very important to us to view things on the European Union level. As we can read in the article by Scheer, there is a considerable number of churches' institutions and diaconia on the European level. With the exception of the Roman Catholic Church, most churches are nationally oriented. This is even more so when a church was involved in the process of nation building after the reformation as most protestant churches were. Of course, there is the influence of the international oecumene, but it is only during the last decade that Europe has become a theme in the ecumenical discussion. Only from that time on, did it get more attention.

Although legislation in the social field is, for the greater part, the responsibility of the national governments, all kinds of measures on the level of the EU have a great influence on the member countries. Step by step, European legislation and European decision-making and, above all, European economic policy influences politics on a national level. A very important question is whether the decision-making in the EU solves problems or produces problems itself! The European Council in Lisbon in March 2000 set out a ten year strategy "to become the most competitive and dynamic, knowledge-based economy in the world, capable of sustainable economic growth and more and better jobs and greater social cohesion." Economic, environmental and social aims can be found in one formula. But there is an internal contradiction in this formula, because to be competitive, you have to strive for more productivity, less costs of production etc. What happens with people who are, seen from the dominating economic paradigm, less productive and low- or unskilled in the so called knowledge society? Also on the EU level, the question of what norms guide views is a very important one (see the articles by Benz and Boeckh). Roughly speaking, will there be a shift to the American, residual type of welfare state or will it be possible to keep our own type of welfare state? Already at the beginning of the nineties in the last century, the French employer Michel Albert put this question: which model of capitalism – the neo-American, based on individual achievements and profit in the short term, or the "Rhinelandmodel", which stresses collective responsibility, consensus and long term approach? (Albert 1991). The question concerning the future of the welfare state in Europe is also connected with the question of whether changes at work now are only incremental changes within the paradigm of the welfare state. Or are they leading, in their cumulative effects, to a silent, but nevertheless fundamental and radical change (cf. Schmidt 1990) towards a neo-liberal concept of welfare that means a merely residual state with the emphasis on workfare instead of welfare, with emphasis on self-responsibility and the accumulation of life-risks for the individual? This also makes it clear that employment as such is not always the solution to poverty: the increasing number of "working poor" in the United States, but also in Europe shows this. We have to ask what type of work under what conditions do we want to see in our societies?

"Social exclusion" is a core concept in the anti-poverty programs of the EU (see the article by Benz). This concept refers to the "dialectic" of being in society, but at the same time being outside, which is so characteristic of poor people in wealthy societies.[8] But the concept can be used in a way that implies a mere continuation of the traditional poverty research and policies that tend to reify "the poor" to a static and unchangeable group that is combined with an individual approach negating structural tendencies (Steinert 2003). In our opinion, it is much more fruitful to see the dynamic dimension of social exclusion, as a process that is produced by societal developments, political decisions and dominating social policies. This process is not a natural one but a social one that can be revised and changed by political decisions. If there are social movements and political pressures in the direction of more social justice, human dignity and basic standards of welfare for all people, then it will be possible to realise the humanising potentials of the concept of social exclusion, namely to turn social policy into a general policy of social *in*clusion.

The debate about the welfare state is also of relevance for the countries in Eastern Europe: Which guiding visions are there concerning the countries which have become members of the EU (and the countries which will become members in the future)? As Boeckh stresses in his contribution, the realization of a welfare state is a precondition for democratic development. It is necessary to see the extension of the EU not only as an economic project, but also as a social project. How can the fact be dealt with that the social and material differences between member states and regions within the EU are bigger than ever? There is a real danger of continuing deterioration. The EU at present offers no real concept for a solution to this situation.

To conclude, we think that it is important that churches change gear up from the local to the European level (and of course with regard to the problems of poverty in the world on a still more international level) to struggle against poverty. We repeat: This goes from providing individual assistance right up to taking political action. Now the welfare states are under pressure and in Central and Eastern Europe there is a gap between the communist society and a new type of society with democracy and social justice, we need a new "social contract" connected with the social idea of solidarity and justice (Gabriel 2003). Together with other groups and movements, churches and diaconal institutions should assist and promote this idea.

Annotations

1 Since Esping Andersen's publication, some studies have been published which pay attention to the religious factor, for instance: Van Kersbergen 1995, Manow 2002, Kaufmann 2003.
2 See: Manow 2002, p. 211; Diakonivetenskapliga Institutet 2003, pp. 60/61. This institute, with other instituës in a number of European countries with different religions, is to carry out extensive research on the function of majority churches as providers of social welfare in a comparative European perspective. cf. Kaufmann on Sweden: "... hat das lutherische Landeskirchentum wesentlich zur selbstverständlichen Aktzeptanz einer extensiven Staatstätigkeit beigetragen, die für ganz Skandinavien charakteristisch ist." ("... the lutheran folk-church had contributed in an essential way to the acceptance as a

matter of course of an extensive role of the state, which is characteristic for the whole of Scandinavia."), pp. 163/164.
3   We are using the typology which was developed by Koelega (1986, p. 23), who developed this typology regarding the problem of unemployment. We adjusted this for our aims.
4   The pastoral letter from the Roman Catholic Bishops' Conference in the United States about the economy of the United States *Economic Justice for All* (1986) contains among other things a plead for measures which have to do with building up a more universal type of welfare state. In the American context this is transformative, in the Scandinavian context that is not the case.
5   See for instance about the plead for this: Addy (2003).
6   See for instance: Goudzwaard/De Lange (1995);Douglas A. Hicks (2000); Volz (2001), Forrester (2001); Huster/Volz (2002); Goldstein (2002); Taylor (2003); Atherton (2003).
7   An example of this combination of stories and the development of recommendations for politics and society is the report of Caritas Europe (2004).
8   This view was already developed by the German sociologist Georg Simmel in a classical essay (Simmel 1971).

References

Addy, Tony, "The Value(s) of Work and Employment", in: Eva-Sibylle Vogel-Mfato/Jürgen Klute (ed.), *Working Together for Sustainable Life. Experiences from Diaconia in Europe.Texts from the First European Diaconal Forum in Järvänpää/Finland September 2001*, Conference of European Churches, Geneva 2003, 9-14.

Albert, Michel, *Capitalisme contre Capitalisme*, Paris 1991.

Atherton, John, *Marginalization*, London 2003.

Belopopsky, Alexander, *Orthodoxy & Social Witness. Presentation at the Institute for Orthodox Christian Studies, Cambridge 9 July 2003* (World Council of Churches; www.wcc-coe.org/wcc/europe).

Caritas Europe, *Povery has faces in Europe. The need for family-oriented policies, 2nd Report on Poverty in Europe*, Brussels, February 2004.

Diakonivetenskapliga Institutet (Uppsala Institute for Diaconal and Social Studies, *Welfare and Religion in a European Perspective. Project description*, Uppsala 2003.

Esping-Andersen, Gosta, *The Three Worlds of Welfare Capitalism*, Cambridge 1995 (1990).
Esping-Andersen, Gosta, *Social Foundations of Postindustrial Economies*, Oxford 1999.
Forrester, Duncan B., *On Human Worth. A Christian Vindication of Equality*, London 2001.
Gabriel, Karl, *The Transformation of the Welfare State as a Challenge for the "Caritas" as an church' welfare organization*, Ms., 5 April 2003.
Goldstein, Horst, *"Genieß das Leben alle Tage". Eine befreiende Theologie des Wohlstandes* ("Enjoy life every day". A liberating theology of prosperity), Mainz 2002.
Goudzwaard, B./H.M. de Lange, *Beyond Poverty and Affluence: Toward An Economy of Care*, Grand Rapids/Geneva 1995.
Hicks, Douglas A., *Inequality and Christian Ethics*, Cambridge 2000.
Huster, Ernst-Ulrich; Volz, Fritz-Rüdiger (eds.), *Theorien des Reichtums* (Theories of Wealthiness), Münster 2002.
Kaufmann, Franz-Xaver, *Varianten des Wohlfahrtsstaats. Der deutsche Sozialstaat im internationalen Vergleich* (Varieties in welfarestates. The German Socialstate in international comparison), Frankfurt am Main 2003.
Kersbergen, Kees van, *Social Capitalism. A Study of Christian Democracy and the Welfare State*, London 1995.
Koelega, D.G.A., *Unemployment: work for the churches. A survey of church resolutions, publications, projects and initiatives in the United Kingdom, Western Germany and the Netherlands. Final Report*, Driebergen 1986.
Manow, Philip, "'The Good, the Bad, and the Ugly'. Espings-Andersens Sozialstaats-Typology und die konfessionellen Wurzeln des westlichen Wohlfahrtsstaats" ("'The Good, the Bad and the Ugly'. Esping-Andersens Typology and the confessional roots of western welfare states"), in: *Kölner Zeitschrift für Soziologie und Sozialpsychologie*, Jg. 54, Heft 2, 2002, pp. 203-225.
Meeks, Douglas, *God the Economist. The Doctrine of God and Political Economy*, Minneapolis 1989.
Ostner, Ilona, et al., *Sozialpolitische Herausforderungen. Zukunft und Perspektiven des Wohlfahrtsstaats in der Bundesrepublik Deutschland* (Challenges in Social Policy. The Future and the Perspectives of the Welfare State in Germany), Working Paper No. 49 of the Foundation "Hans Böckler", Düsseldorf 2001.

Schmidt, Manfred G., Die Politik des mittleren Wegs. Besonderheiten der Staatstätigkeit in der Bundesrepublik Deutschland (The Policy of the Way in-between. Particular characteristics of the state action in Germany), in: APUZ, No. B 9-10/1990, 23 - 31.

Simmel, Georg, "The poor", in: *On individuality and social forms*, Chicago 1971, 150-178 (originally "Der Arme", in: *Soziologie* 1908).

Steinert, Heinz, "Die kurze Geschichte und offene Zukunft eines Begriffs: Soziale Ausschliessung", in: *Berliner Journal für Soziologie*, 2/2003, 275-285.

Taylor, Michael, *Christianity, Poverty and Wealth*, London/Geneva 2003.

Temple, William, *Christianity and Social Order*, London 1976 (1942).

Volz, Rainer, Armut an Nahe und Glan. Ein Bericht zur sozialen Lage im Landkreis Bad Kreuznach (A Report on Poverty and Wealthiness in in the Bad Kreuznach district [Germany], Bochum 2001.

Weber, Max, *Gesammelte Aufsätze zur Religionssoziologie I*, Tübingen 1963 (1920).

Personalia

Bartmann, Peter, dr. theol., is working at the Social Services Agency (Diakonisches Werk) of the Protestant Church of Germany;
email: bartmann@diakonie.de

Beaumont, Justin, dr., urban geographer, coming from the United Kingdom he currently holds a post-doctoral research fellow position at the Urban and Regional research centre (URU) at Utrecht University in the Netherlands;
email: J.Beaumont@geog.uu.nl

Benz, Benjamin, dr. sc. pol., executive at the German "Zukunftsforum Familie" in Bonn and Berlin
email: ben@awobu.awo.org

Boeckh, Jürgen, dr. sc. pol., executive at the Protestant University of Applied Sciences at Bochum (Germany);
email: boeckh@efh-bochum.de

Cooper, Niall, National Coordinator of Church Action on Poverty in Great Britain;
email: niallc@church-poverty.org.uk

de Clermont, Jean-Arnold, rev., President of the Conference of European Churches (CEC/KEK), Brussels
email: fpf@protestants.org

Gohde, Jürgen, dr. theol., rev., President of the Social Services Agency (Diakonisches Werk) of the Protestant Church in Germany, Stuttgart
email: gohde@diakonie.de

Hermans, Herwig, studies religion sciences, Director of Welzijnszorg (an anti-poverty NGO with activities in Flanders and Brussels), Belgium;
email: herwighermans@welzijnszorg.be

Iversen, Hans Raun, dr. theol., Associate Professor in Practical Theology, Department of Systematic Theology, University of Copenhagen;
email: hri@teol.ku.dk

Jung (former: Richter), Saskia, dr. sc. pol, MA (Public Policy), is working at the Social Services Agency (Diakonisches Werk) of the Protestant Church in Germany.
email: jung@diakonie.de

Malkavaara, Mikko, dr. theol., Docent of Church History at the University of Helsinki, permanent occupation as Director of Diaconia Polytechnic, Järvenpää Unit;
email: mikko.malkavaara@diak.fi

Noordegraaf, Herman, dr. theol., is lecturing in the field of diaconia at the Theological Faculty of Leiden (The Netherlands);
email: H.Noordegraaf@let.leidenuniv.nl

Pavlovic, Peter, dr. theol, rev., ordained minister of the Evangelical Church of the Augsburg Confession in Slovakia; currently working as the Study Secretary in the Church and Society Commission of the Conference of European Churches (CEC) in Brussels;
email: ppt@cec-kek.be

Scheer, Doris, diploma in Social Work, executive for European questions at Social Services Agency (Diakonisches Werk) of the Evangelical-Lutheran Church of Slesvig-Holstein (Northern Germany) at Rendsburg;
email: scheer@diakonie-sh.de

Schenk, Martin, is expert for social questions of the Diaconia of Austria and collaborator at the Protestant Academy of Austria at Vienna. Speaker of the "Austrian Conference on Poverty";
email: schenk-mair@utanet.at

Smedberg, Ninni, Theologian and ordained deacon, Strategist of Diaconal Work in the Church of Sweden;
email: ninni.smedberg@svenskakyrkan.se

Volz, Rainer, Sociologist, has been resarcher at the Institute for Social Sciences and Social Ethics of the Protestant Church of Germany at Bochum for over than thirteen years. Since May 2004, working for the Men's Services Department of the Protestant Church of the Rhineland at Düsseldorf;
email: r.volz@maennerwerk.ekir.de

**SozialWissenschaftliches Institut
der Evangelischen Kirche in Deutschland**

lieferbare Veröffentlichungen

Wolfgang Belitz
Arbeit unser täglich Brot
Sozialethische Texte zu Arbeit und Wirtschaft
SWI Verlag Bochum 2003
340 Seiten, ISBN 3-925895-84-1   29,90 Euro

Jürgen P. Rinderspacher (Hg.)
Zeit für alles – Zeit für nichts?
Die Bürgergesellschaft und ihr Zeitverbrauch
SWI Verlag Bochum 2003
276 Seiten, ISBN 3-925895-83-3   22,00 Euro

Lutz Finkeldey
Jugend im Hexenkessel.
Zwischen Anpassung und Ausgrenzung
SWI Verlag Bochum 2002
168 Seiten, ISBN 3-925895-77-9   15,50 Euro

Heiko Kastner
Mythos Marktwirtschaft
Die irrationale Herrschaft des Geldes über Arbeit, Mensch und Natur
SWI Verlag Bochum 2002
520 Seiten, ISBN 3-925895-81-7   32,00 Euro

Hartmut Przybylski
Wir könnten auch anders ...
Sozialethische Notizen
SWI Verlag Bochum 2002
216 Seiten, ISBN 3-925895-80-9   16,00 Euro

Zu beziehen über den Buchhandel

**SOZIALWISSENSCHAFTLICHES INSTITUT
DER EVANGELISCHEN KIRCHE IN DEUTSCHLAND**

lieferbare Veröffentlichungen

Günter Brakelmann
Für eine menschlichere Gesellschaft
Band II: Historische und sozialethische Vorträge
SWI Verlag Bochum 2001
348 Seiten, ISBN 3-925895-72-8   25,00 Euro

Joachim Weber
Diakonie in Freiheit?
Eine Kritik diakonischen Selbstverständnisses
SWI Verlag Bochum 2001
160 Seiten, ISBN 3925895-70-1   20,00 Euro

Klaus Heienbrok, Harry W. Jablonowski (Hg.)
Blick zurück nach vorn!
Standpunkte, Analysen, Konzepte zur Zukunftsgestaltung
des Ruhrgebiets
SWI Verlag Bochum 2000
139 Seiten, ISBN 3-925895-66-3   12,78 Euro

Elisabeth Conradi, Sabine Plonz (Hg.)
Tätiges Leben
Pluralität und Arbeit im politischen Denken Hannah Arendts
SWI Verlag Bochum 2000
185 Seiten, ISBN 3-925895-69-8   14,21 Euro

Lutz Finkeldey (Hg)
Tausch statt Kaufrausch
SWI Verlag Bochum 1999
281 Seiten, ISBN 3-925895-64-7   19,68 Euro

Zu beziehen über den Buchhandel

www.ingramcontent.com/pod-product-compliance
Lightning Source LLC
Chambersburg PA
CBHW030130240426
43672CB00005B/92